;ICS

Now in a second edition, *Theatre Studies: The Basics* is an incisive guide to contemporary theatre studies. The practical and theoretical dimensions of theatre – from acting to audience – are woven together throughout to provide an integrated introduction to the study of drama, theatre and performance. Topics covered include:

- dramatic genres, from tragedy to political documentary
- theories of performance
- the history of the theatre in the West
- acting, directing and scenography.

With a glossary, chapter summaries and suggestions for further reading throughout, *Theatre Studies: The Basics* remains the ideal starting point for anyone new to the subject.

Robert Leach is a writer and theatre director who has taught drama at the Universities of Birmingham and Edinburgh. His books include *Makers of Modern Theatre* (Routledge, 2004) and *Theatre Workshop: Joan Littlewood and The Making of Modern British Theatre* (University of Exeter Press, 2006).

The Basics

THEATRE STUDIES

THE BASICS

Second edition

Robert Leach

Routledge
Taylor & Francis Group

LONDON AND NEW YORK

First edition published 2008, this edition published 2013
by Routledge
2 Park Square, Milton Park, Abingdon, Oxon OX14 4RN

Simultaneously published in the USA and Canada
by Routledge
711 Third Avenue, New York, NY 10017

Routledge is an imprint of the Taylor & Francis Group, an informa business

British Library Cataloguing in Publication Data
A catalogue record for this book is available from the British Library

Library of Congress Cataloging in Publication Data
Leach, Robert, 1942-
Theatre studies : the basics / Robert Leach. -- Second edition.
pages cm
Includes bibliographical references and index.
1. Drama. 2. Theater. I. Title.
PN1655.L35 2013
792--dc23
2012051056

ISBN: 978-0-415-81167-5 (hbk)
ISBN: 978-0-415-81168-2 (pbk)
ISBN: 978-0-203-76667-5 (ebk)

Typeset in Bembo and Scala Sans
by Taylor & Francis Books

Printed in Great Britain
by Bell & Bain Ltd, Glasgow

CONTENTS

BOXES

PREFACE

In the age of iPods and mobile phone cameras, downloads and broadband, when certainly cinema and perhaps even television are beginning to seem passé, what business has that old impostor, live theatre, got clamouring for our attention? It's alive, that's what! Perhaps the theatre has never been more necessary than today, when it stands so firmly against the rush into recorded media. It is true that more and more students want to study it, to do it, to present it. An informal festival like the Edinburgh Fringe exhibits many hundreds, perhaps thousands, of groups of people wanting to make live theatre. Which is justification enough for a book like this.

This book tries to treat the basics of modern theatre, to raise at least some contemporary ideas, problems, concerns, but the subject is so colossal it cannot claim the last word even on the basics. Some of its limitations are obvious. It only attempts to address issues in the theatre of the West. There is a vast theatre culture beyond the West, in India, China, Indonesia, all over Africa and among all sorts of people, which is not even mentioned in this book. A line had to be drawn somewhere.

The book aims to air ideas about Western modern theatre, to explain, to illustrate, to stimulate. Its basic premise is that theatre and drama offer a unique combination of thinking and doing, and that anybody who tries to practise it, at however simple a level, will gain by it. This book tries to suggest the links between theory and practice (which explains why some chapters move from the very theoretical suddenly into the absolutely hands-on practical). There is an implicit belief in the integration of theory and practice which underlies everything that is written here. Perhaps the link is in the explorations and references to theatre practitioners – actors, play-wrights, stage designers, directors – from the past and the present, whose thoughts and achievements this book so frequently draws on.

It is the author's hope that the book may open a few doors, perhaps suggest ways to think about its subject, and stir the reader to go out and get involved. That would be a mark of its success.

Finally, I would like to thank my editors for the first edition of this book, Rosie Waters, David Avital and Aimee Foy. For this second edition, Siobhan Poole has been supportive and constructive at all times, and to her I offer my sincere thanks. I would also like to thank Iram Satti and Abigail Humphries Robertson for brilliant editorial support. Thanks also go to John Topping, a challenging and supportive colleague; all my students, past and present, who have endlessly challenged and supported me; and Joy Parker, whose steadfastness and friendliness has kept me going through it all.

R. L.

PERFORMANCE

PLAYING

Peter Brook (b. 1925) ends his well-known book, *The Empty Space*, with the enigmatic sentence: 'A play is play.' And 'play' is a good place to begin (as well as end) any consideration of performance, for play is something we have all experienced, and it has surprising affinities with drama and theatre.

Perhaps the first thing to say about play is that it is the opposite of work. Whereas work takes place at specified times, in a particular place, and the worker's identity is fixed – she or he is a plumber, a librarian, a politician – play takes place at any time, anywhere, and enables the person playing to be whoever they want to be – a fireman, a footballer, a beggar or a queen. Their identity is not fixed. Moreover, at work, one has tools – a computer, a screwdriver, a notebook and pencil – whereas one can play with anything – mud, a saucepan lid, mummy's shoes. Indeed, one may ask: are toys really necessary?

Play has been divided into three 'types' – active play (running about, tumbling over, etc.), playing with things (mud, saucepan lids, etc.), and playing with others (chasing, playing schools or hospitals, etc.). Each of these is a kind of performance because each involves a measure of pretending, a 'magic if' which enables the player to enter a world of make-believe. And though she is only 'play-acting' here, the play-acting is still absorbing enough to arouse genuine emotions. Children playing in a playground may be seen laughing 'for real', crying 'for real', really losing their tempers – in play.

Play opens up possibilities, and enables us to explore situations of difficulty, without any 'real life' consequences. It is perhaps a training for the imagination. When we have to cope with cops and robbers, or mummies and daddies, in play, we are practising life, learning how to survive. We experience deep emotions and the reality of relationships in play, but at the back of our minds, we know we are safe. We can escape – stop the game – when we want to.

We don't play 'in order to' do anything, such as increase our productivity, impress our bank manager, placate our parent. We play 'for fun'. And therein lies the problem of play, for many in authority see playing as frivolous, a waste of time and energy, even wicked. 'The devil makes work for idle hands,' says the old saw. Plato (427–347 BCE) wanted to ban play – and the theatre – from his ideal Republic. The seventeenth-century Puritans cancelled Christmas and closed the theatres. But people – of all ages, and through all times – have wanted to play, so that authorities have been forced to set aside times when play is 'licensed' – bank holidays, festivals, Carnival – and places to play – fairgrounds, football pitches, nurseries, and so on. Those who have persisted in playing at the 'wrong' time and in the 'wrong' place have often been cast outside the law, as actors were for centuries castigated as 'rogues and vagabonds'. They played; play-acted; performed.

PERFORMANCE, PERFORMATIVE, PERFORMATIVITY

It is clear even from the foregoing that any definition of performance cannot confine it to theatres, or similar places of licensed entertainment. Children playing mummies and daddies 'perform'; lecturers on their podiums 'perform'; hip-hop dancers perform in nightclubs; clergymen or registrars perform marriage ceremonies.

Perhaps we might go so far as to propose that any piece of behaviour/doing/action which is in some way marked off, or framed, is a performance. The framing enables us to comprehend it as an entity, and we can think about it in clear terms, such as where it happens, who is present, how the performance unfolds, and perhaps what is its purpose, or indeed whether it has any purpose. If we examine segments of life as discrete performances, we can extend the notion of performance to include virtually any social interaction – buying a meal in a restaurant, walking to your room with a friend, catching the bus – and even to 'solo' events, such as eating an ice cream or surfing the internet.

If we see pieces of behaviour as performances, we can analyse them particularly interestingly. It is soon apparent that we 'perform' different roles in different situations. Thus, we perform the role of interviewee when going for an interview – respectful, inquiring, eager to learn; but we perform the 'cool dude' in the nightclub – laid back, all-knowing, chilled out. We even dress up for these roles, but the costume for each is very different because they are different 'parts'. We can take this further, and consider many different roles which we play: for our parents, we play the child, even when we are long past childhood; for the bank manager, we play the innocent; for our beloved, we play the saucy, the sensitive or the seductive. In fact, given that we perform so many identities, we may ask: Is there a real me?

We shall return to the conundrum of identity. First we need to notice that the problem of performance is further complicated by the fact that to 'perform' means not only to do something, to act, to achieve or produce ('The factory performed well'); it also means to pretend to do something. 'What a performance!' we say, when a footballer lies on the ground writhing in fake agony. 'It's not real, it's only a performance.' Where does doing something for real end, and pretending begin? Or, is there indeed, as we may suspect, no real difference between them?

To consider this problem, we must first consider how we understand things which happen, that is, how we construct meaning. 'Construct' is perhaps the key word here. Nothing has any meaning until we give it one. We see something, but it has no intrinsic meaning until we make one for it. We construct the meaning.

The French linguist Ferdinand de Saussure (1857–1913), first showed how meaning is made. He examined how language uses sounds, or written marks, to convey ideas. Language, de Saussure showed, consists of two parts, first, the signifier (the sound or mark, the word) and, second, the signified (the idea, image or meaning). These two separate entities comprise the sign, and are as tightly bonded together as the two sides of a piece of paper. It is also clear, however, that the relationship between sound (or mark) and idea is arbitrary, that is, though they are indivisible, there is no reason why one relates to the other. If the signified is a slippery silvery thing with fins swimming through water, we tend to call it a fish; but there is no reason why it should not be called a *poisson*, as people in France do; or a *ryba*, as people in Russia do. It is therefore clear that people who agree to call the slippery silvery swimming thing by the same name form a sort of community – one based in language. The word in the language is itself purely arbitrary.

Language, then, is a kind of social contract between members of a defined community. But it is not a neutral entity which exists simply in the form of sounds (or marks). It is a vital tool in our living social experience. It is in fact the prime means whereby we construct our reality. And, since it is a social contract, it is clear that it can only do this when there exists a society, that is, not only a speaker (or writer), but also a listener (or reader).

How can the listener (or reader) construct the meaning? By using her pre-existing experience of manipulating language. The words and phrases of the speaker (or writer) must each be within the experience of the listener (or reader), and so must the manner in which these are linked together by the speaker. The listener's experience can only come from what she has heard, and said, herself before this interchange. This is what the French philosopher Jacques Derrida (1930–2004) meant when he said that all language is citational – any speech act only succeeds in conveying meaning by the way it 'cites' previous usages of the terms it employs.

This concept of 'citation' may be applied to performance as we have observed it in social life: when children play 'mummies and daddies' they are citing their own parents, or other parents they have observed. A wedding achieves meaning precisely because it has been performed a million times before; and its performance 'cites' those million other weddings. The bride, the priest, the member of the congregation all really only know how to play their part in this performance because they have been to weddings before. They 'cite' earlier behaviour. Someone who has never been to a wedding before is likely to be somewhat puzzled by the proceedings, and, having nothing themselves to cite, may only manage to behave appropriately by observing others who have that experience.

So performance, like language, only acquires meaning through the earlier experience of the participants, and because of their ability to cite other similar performances.

We can now access a keener understanding of the two kinds of performance – the genuine and the fake, reality and fiction. We can see that they are not so different after all. When an actor plays a role in a drama, we can all agree that she is creating a fiction. But what about when a child plays a doctor in a game of hospitals? What about the lecturer giving a lecture?

The question was posed urgently by the film *Zidane*, in which more than twenty cameras were placed all round a football arena, and all were trained on one player, Zinedine Zidane (b. 1972), who was playing in a real match for Real Madrid. The film lasted for the ninety minutes of the match. In it, Zidane sweated profusely. The sweat was surely real. The pass with which he made the goal was also real, was it not? But these things happened – were performed – before a huge, roaring crowd. Did this make them part of a performance? And the ending, when Zidane became embroiled in a mêlée, and was sent off by the referee, highlighted the problem. He had to leave the field, that was clearly real, yet as he trudged lonely away, and the camera drew back and away from him, he seemed to be lonelier and lonelier till he finally disappeared into the dressing room – an ending which almost uncannily echoed (or cited, perhaps) a thousand old Hollywood movies. So was it fiction? Or reality?

And we may pose the same question about many other features of contemporary life: is 'reality' TV really reality? What about the news – or sporting events – on television? In what sense do surveillance cameras in city centres turn anyone who hurries past them into a performer? Is Disneyland real or fake? This leads to a reconsideration of the Romantic concept of 'originality'. How do we explain a photocopy which is 'better' than the original? Is Dolly the sheep's clone really Dolly, or is it an individual sheep in its own right? The questions could be multiplied. They indicate how art and life seem to have collapsed into each other, and reality and fiction have become one. This is the postmodern condition.

Moreover, it has been noticed that, in some senses, words and actions are also one. This notion is behind the concept of the performative. In the 1950s an Oxford philosopher, J. L. Austin (1911–60), noticed that certain kinds of speech formulations were in fact acts in themselves. 'I take thee for my lawful wedded wife' is spoken and the act is done. 'This country hereby declares war on Germany.' Once the words are out, the new situation prevails. Such utterances are what Austin called 'performatives'.

The performative seems to elide what is, with what appears, fact and fiction. It is also a performance in its own right. The relationship between a performative and a performance is, therefore, particularly hard to disentangle. For instance, it might be said that a performative is an act; in which case a performance might be considered as a showing of an act. I get married: this is a performative; when, later, I show a video of myself getting married, that may be regarded as a performance. But the marriage itself, as we have already seen, is a performance. The performative is also a performance. Perhaps it may be opined that to view an act as a performative emphasises the significance of the engagement between the parties involved, whereas to view it as a performance emphasises the act as one between performers and spectators. Such distinctions may not always hold, however.

The whole is further complicated when we add the term 'performativity' to the mix. Though the meaning of this, too, is contested, it may be suggested that it refers to something which has the potential to be a performative, or perhaps a performance, or even both.

Performance, the performative and performativity have probably been most convincingly theorised by the German scholar, Erika Fischer-Lichte (b. 1943). She argues that performance, and the performative, are able to effect a 're-enchantment of the world'. She proposes an 'aesthetic of performance' which will cover not only conventional performance but equally non-theatrical art forms which have often tended to find their most urgent expression in the performance mode. So she includes fashion, design, cosmetics and advertising which, because they require some form of staging, are inherently performative. Street festivals, carnivals, sports events and political gatherings are other examples of performatives, and these transform public spaces and, for a time at least, create their own communities. Artistic and non-artistic performances thus become difficult to tell apart: both are performative, both offer liminal experiences, and both encourage people to enter into new relationships with themselves and beyond themselves. The living performance is thereby made an inclusive rather than exclusive experience, which implicitly nudges everyone to act in life as in performance. And this is the re-enchantment of the world.

Box 1.1: Performance studies

Performance studies is a new academic discipline, developed largely out of university departments of drama or of theatre studies, and driven mostly in USA, especially by Richard Schechner (b. 1934). Schechner was something of a polymath: theatre director with his own Performance Group in New York, editor of the influential Drama Review, professor at the Tisch School of the Arts at New York University, writer and theorist. But his energetic championing of this new way of looking at a traditional area of the academic curriculum was also fuelled by a dissatisfaction with the practice of theatre in the West, at a time when other cultures seemed to many Western practitioners to offer new and greater potential for the performing arts. In the 1970s and 1980s, many began to see the theatre as a privileged space for privileged people: 'performance' seemed to offer something more democratic, more egalitarian. Traditional models of theatre seemed to regard the spectator merely as a customer, the traditional arrangement of the space for theatre seemed incorrigibly hierarchic, and above all it seemed to exclude local communities, black people, the avant-garde, and indeed virtually anyone who might make it exciting.

Performance was – or seemed to be – opposed to traditional text-based drama. It offered ways to mediate between performance practice and performance theory. It focused on process, suggesting that the conclusion was perhaps less important than the creative process. Moreover, it expanded beyond the walls of the traditional theatre and concerned itself with anything that was, or could be, framed or presented or highlighted or displayed. These categories were Schechner's touchstones for defining performance. Following Erving Goffman (1922–82) and others, he also saw performance as a way of understanding behaviour. He argued that the new discipline should therefore cover performance in its broadest sense, and should be potentially a tool of cultural intervention. He also believed that it was a crucial site for the collision of cultures, able to broaden academic and aesthetic concerns from the stultifying white, Western tradition. Least important for Schechner was the investigation of theatrical performance. Others saw performance studies as a way of foregrounding theories of the performative so that they would acquire a central place in the ongoing movement of theory. At the same time, it was acknowledged that performativity was (and is) an elusive, unstable and fragmented concept.

University departments, especially in the USA, changed their names to include performance studies, and broadened their curricula into some of the areas mentioned above. Performance studies now often includes at least some of the elements of sociology, fine art, psychology, anthropology and more. Where it will go from here is a matter of speculation.

PERFORMING IDENTITY

Erving Goffman was a Canadian social anthropologist who examined how we present ourselves in everyday life. He theorised that essentially each person's social life was a series of performances.

Goffman argued that in each social situation we present an appropriate 'front', a 'mask' or 'persona'. We perform this during the encounter. And we expect the other person to be similarly presenting a 'front'. We – or they – think: 'That's how doctors/ businessmen/window cleaners or twenty-five-year-olds/pensioners or people on holiday or people short of money or whatever, behave', and so we – or they – behave accordingly during the encounter. And during the encounter, each participant 'reads' the other's performance and responds as appropriately as they can. It is a little like a drama improvisation.

The encounter is further encoded in its 'frame', that is, effectively, the context of the encounter, or performance. This will include the setting – the time, the place, and so on – and the way we present ourselves – what we wear, our demeanour and so on. Thus, one might meet one's tutor in the sauna in the evening, but the encounter would be fraught and difficult for both participants. More likely would be a meeting in the seminar room, when the frame would help to make the encounter fruitful.

Goffman's conclusion from this was that there is effectively no difference between 'appearance' and 'reality'. The 'performance' we give in any encounter is, in one sense, simply skin-deep, an 'appearance'. But it is also the reality of how we behave. The performance, in other words, is the reality. This is a highly resonant conception, and has a direct bearing on how we perceive performance.

Goffman's ideas, together with those of Derrida concerning 'citation', may be applied to the problem of identity. This has been pursued most persuasively and most powerfully by Judith Butler (b.1956), an American philosopher and scholar, whose work in the area of gender identity has made her into something of a cult figure. Butler argued that our gendered identity – for many people their deepest identity – is not a biological phenomenon, but is actually produced socially through the repetition of ordinary day-to-day activities. Such activities 'cite' learned, gender-specific actions. Thus: this is what a girl – or a boy – does, so therefore if I do it, I too must be a girl (or boy). Boys learn not to cry; girls learn not to be aggressive. By behaving in line with convention, we seem to be discovering a vital part of who we are.

Yet, Butler argues, this is a trap. It fixes us in a rigid 'this, not that' state from which our true identity is excluded. Actually, she goes on, our identity is more fluid, more diffuse and more changeable than any such inflexible formulation allows. Such thinking leads, in her words, to 'gender trouble'. Her ideas have spawned a whole new way of looking at, and experiencing, identity. This has become known as 'queer theory', whose central tenet concerns the elusiveness of identity, especially gendered identity. It bears directly on how we 'perform' our lives, and therefore must influence sharply such theatrical matters as how we understand 'character', and indeed on the process of acting itself.

Equally significant for the actor, perhaps, is the contention of Susan Bordo (b. 1947) that the body itself, particularly perhaps the female body, is a social construct. Gender differences are among the first to be inscribed on the body, as the young girl strives to meet the expectations society places on her. The ideal she seeks is slim, long-legged, blonde ... But the body is at all times in life, by natural forces, subject to change: in the light of contemporary illnesses such as anorexia or bulimia, the question is, what changes result from what social demands?

Besides the ideas of Butler and Bordo, we need to note those of the French writer, Monique Wittig (b. 1935) who, as a lesbian, refuses gender classification altogether. To oversimplify her argument, perhaps, she suggests that 'man' and 'woman' are simply political labels designed to further the interests of an oppressive heterosexual dominance: a lesbian is not dependant on men, therefore she is not a 'proper' woman; but she does not have the economic or political clout of a man, therefore she cannot be a man.

Once one notices how gender is socially constructed, it is a short step to noticing that the same is true, though perhaps differently forged, of race and class. This was most forcefully articulated, perhaps, by Edward Said (1935–2003) in his famous *Orientalism*. This book examined the ways in which 'the orient' is a construction of western imperialism, made with the unspoken aim of continuing to subjugate southern hemisphere or eastern people, who are 'other' or 'not one of us'. 'They' are exotic and fascinating, but *different*. This makes them inferior, and inescapably affects the performance of 'oriental' identity.

Gayatri Chakravorty Spivak (b. 1942) has further explored this problem, and especially in relation to the difficulties the 'other' may encounter when trying to escape from her own objectification. Here the question 'who am I?' becomes particularly acute. And Homi K. Bhabha (b. 1949), perhaps partially in answer to it, developed his theory of 'hybridity', by which he meant that in the post-colonial world, the former colonial subject became a kind of hybrid, neither belonging to the imperialist master nation, nor to the new nation, the former colony – an indeterminate identity which paradoxically may have some strength.

We need to take note of such ideas, because they have fed into modern notions of performance, and have indeed extended the concept of performativity in significant directions.

ALL THE WORLD'S A STAGE

Contemporary ideas about performance, performatives and performativity have complicated our approach to specifically theatrical performance. As John Cage (1912–92), a controversial American performance artist remarked, 'Theatre is in the mind of the beholder.' And, as suggested, it can be helpful to see social interactions as performances.

One significant means of bridging the gap between performance and reality, or perhaps of pointing it up, which was developed in the second half of the twentieth century, was 'performance art', or 'live art', that is, art in which the artist (or her surrogate(s)) 'perform', not a play, but the artwork itself. Sometimes known as 'happenings', these works may take place in a pub, on a street corner, in a gallery, or anywhere where the artist may attract attention, or an audience. In live art there is no story line, and no 'character' in the traditional theatrical sense. Rather, something 'real' is performed. Live art banishes pretence, in order to perform.

For example, *Moments of Decision/Indecision*, made in 1975 by Stuart Brisley (b.1933), was a 'performance' lasting six days. The artist appeared naked and constantly poured black or white paint over himself, and tried – and failed – to climb the walls of the room he was in. *Dinner Dress, Tales About Dora* by Tamar Raban (b. 1955) was presented in a flat in Vienna in 1997. Raban provided a five course dinner for her 'audience' who sat round a huge circular table. The tablecloth was her dress, and she waited on the table – that is, she sat, stood, moved physically on the table itself – so that there was a sense that the 'guests' were eating her. Meanwhile the transparent banqueting dishes acted as screens, through which could be seen moving images. It is worth noting, by the way, that both these performing artists trained in fine art, not theatre.

Live art certainly reinvigorated theatre in the 1970s and 1980s. It forced theatre specialists to consider their specialism in new ways. Ideas about performance per se, its meaning and its significance, gradually moved to the forefront of debates about theatre, and these were conducted in a new kind of language – at least for discussions about theatre – a language which could be called 'postmodernist'. Many of the matters on which these debates focused will be discussed later in this book.

Here it is worth briefly considering ways in which contemporary ideas about the nature of performance may be applied to what happens in a theatre. It is possible to distinguish several layers of simultaneous performance interactions, or to use Goffman's word, encounters, in the theatre. First, the characters on the stage interact in a fiction presented as a 'play'. The characters also interact with the spectators, who follow their fictitious adventures at a highly conscious level of their attention. These interactions are mirrored by the interactions between the actors themselves on the stage, and by those between the actors and the spectators (at a simple level, between a spectator who is in the audience because she wants to 'see' a particular actor). (See also Chapter 8 for further discussion of this issue.)

These – and other – interactions are governed by a series of conventions to which this book will pay particular attention. Thus, the audience in the theatre agrees to 'believe' in the characters and their world; the actors agree to 'present' the characters in that world, their intentions, emotions, reactions and all; but the characters are of course also pawns in the grand narrative conceived by the author, and set on stage by the director. The interrelationships between these various persons – spectator, actor, author, director – provides the site for theatre's special kind of creativity, and are perhaps what makes theatre uniquely complicated as well as exciting.

What happens during a theatrical performance is therefore highly complex. We can detect the psychological melding with the perceptual, what is abstract becoming concrete, thought directly relating to action. And it is important to note that without an audience – unlike many social performances – the theatrical performance cannot happen. And it is in the audience's living response, what might be called the audience's performance, that the theatrical performance is completed.

Performance, therefore, may be seen as a kind of gangplank between life and theatre. It exists in both, and helps us to understand both. We can travel from the theatre to life through our understanding of performance, just as we can go from life to theatre across the same gangplank of performance. In *As You Like It*, William Shakespeare (1564–1616) expresses something of this idea in a particularly famous speech:

> All the world's a stage,
> And all the men and women merely players.
> They have their exits and their entrances,
> And one man in his time plays many parts,
> His acts being seven ages. At first the infant,
> Mewling and puking in the nurse's arms.
> Then the whining schoolboy with his satchel

And shining morning face, creeping like snail
Unwillingly to school. And then the lover,
Sighing like furnace, with a woeful ballad
Made to his mistress' eyebrow. Then, a soldier,
Full of strange oaths and bearded like the pard,
Jealous in honour, sudden, and quick in quarrel,
Seeking the bubble reputation
Even in the cannon's mouth. And then the justice,
In fair round belly with good capon lined,
With eyes severe and beard of formal cut,
Full of wise saws and modern instances,
And so he plays his part. The sixth age shifts
Into the lean and slippered pantaloon,
With spectacles on nose and pouch on side,
His youthful hose, well saved, a world too wide
For his shrunk shank, and his big manly voice
Turning again towards childish treble, pipes
And whistles in his sound. Last scene of all,
That ends this strange eventful history,
Is second childishness and mere oblivion,
Sans teeth, sans eyes, sans taste, sans everything.

(As You Like It, Act 2, Scene 7)

READING PERFORMANCE

Shakespeare's Jacques read life as performance in his 'All the world's a stage' speech – or performance as life. We all read performances all the time, and so expertly that we hardly notice we are doing it.

The stage gives the performance a peculiar power, but essentially the semiotics of stage performance are similar to those of life, though the reading may be more self-conscious and therefore probably more sophisticated. We comment on the vicar's performance as performance; some lecturers are clapped at the end of their hour; and we replay in our memories those romantic moments we wish always to remember. By marking off the performance, we agree to invest each action with a specially-charged meaning, one which may perhaps carry symbolic overtones. (As the music-hall star Marie Lloyd (1870–1922) sang: 'Every little movement has a meaning of its own.')

But 'signs' (as the structuralists called them), such as these, are often ambiguous. For instance, dragging one's feet may imply dejection, but may be an act of defiance against an authoritarian parent or teacher who has ordered that feet be 'picked up'. Similarly, what someone is wearing may suggest that person's socio-economic status (starched shirt front or out-at-elbows jacket), but may also suggest psychological clues to the person's ambitions, mood or predilections, or may even reflect on their morality. It may do any or all of these simultaneously. Similarly, an actor may signify little more than a prop (a passive sign), as the 'spear carrier', whose most important function as he stands at the back of the stage is to indicate the power of the generalissimo he serves; whereas a prop may become an active sign, as when Macbeth's dagger appears covered in blood. The signs which performance generates are always dynamic and evolving, and constantly produce new possibilities. The way we read signs like this is called 'semiotics'. (See also Chapter 8 for further discussion of this.)

The complexities of theatre semiotics, the interpreting of the signs of performance, are of course increased by the sheer number of them which are generated in a theatre, and which have to be processed and ordered by any spectator. The director tries to foreground what she considers to be significant, but naturally the spectator may misread this. It is, however, possible to classify signs into three types. First, there is what is known as the 'icon', a sign which is what it is: that is, a hat is a hat, or the words spoken mean what they say. Second is the type of sign known as an 'index', a name deriving from the index finger which points at something else. A simple index sign might be a knock at the door which points to the fact that someone is outside; a motley costume points to the fact that the character is a clown. Finally there is the 'symbol', when the sign bears no obvious relationship to what is signified. A good example of a symbol is the word – 'mountain' has no logical or obvious relationship to the thrust-up land with heather and rocks. We simply accept the connection. Almost all theatre conventions work symbolically, as a painted flat which becomes the symbol for a castle, though there is no direct relationship, and a stage arrangement with one character on a level higher than another which may symbolise the former's power.

The theatre performance gives out a multitude of messages of these different types simultaneously. They are further complicated by the fact, already noted, that there are so many different kinds of communication (actor–actor, character–character, character–spectator, etc.) operating in the theatre. The spectator is asked primarily to unravel the dynamics of on-stage relationships in order to be able to understand the messages which are being sent out. Because of this, and despite the fact that plays almost always include a good deal of dialogue, it is the ability to 'read space' which is perhaps the spectator's most valuable skill. A speaker may speak with varying degrees of sincerity, but movement in space usually points towards the truth.

The spectator therefore has to understand the different kinds of space which can communicate in the theatre, and how they do so. First, there are certain fixed kinds of space, often to do with the architecture of the building. The proscenium arch in traditional theatres is fixed, the audience's seats are fixed, and so on, so that certain spatial relationships are clearly marked and unchangeable. But second, some spatial features are only partially fixed, such as the on-stage furniture which may be moved occasionally, and may be entirely changed during any interval. Similarly, the lighting may vary, and this also alters the spectator's relationship with other objects and actors. Third, some spatial relationships are completely unfixed, most notably in the actor–actor relationship, but also in the actor–furniture and actor–spectator relationships. The actor, even when standing still, is in a sense in constant motion.

Space may also be categorised as 'pictorial', that is, when the theatre is attempting to create the illusion of real life with perspective settings for the spectator to look at from the outside; or 'three-dimensional', when the apparently false relationship between the three-dimensional actor and the two-dimensional painted backdrop is done away with. It was Adolph Appia (1862–1928) who first attempted to place the actor in architectural and volumetric 'real' settings, and he more than anyone is responsible for the gradual demise of that important worthy of the Victorian theatre, the scene-painter.

Finally, as hinted above, the most telling use of space lies in the actor's physicality. Movements, gestures, poses, facial expressions – all are non-fixed features of spatial communication which the spectator rightly reads more carefully than anything else. Western directors have often in the last hundred or more years sought to codify gesture, to make a grammar of movement, by means of which the audience would not be led astray. But this is impossible to achieve in a fundamentally realistic theatre, which is what the West has. In other cultures this is not necessarily the case: the highly stylised *Kathakali* theatre of south India, for example, relies on a limited number (eighty or a few more) *mudras*, which are symbolic hand and finger movements which signify specified objects, emotions or actions. In other words, they really do operate like a sign language. In the West, this cannot be made to work, partly because of the dynamic and changing relationship between movement, gesture, and facial expression on the one hand and what is spoken on the other. In fact it is often in the movement which may contradict the spoken words that intentions, attitudes and relationships are clarified.

The special potency of the theatrical performance lies precisely in the fact that it is watched, or overlooked. In other words, it is designed to be read. This is the reason, by the way, that no matter how 'naturalistic' any performance may be it can never be a true replication of life, for life is not designed to be overlooked. But some of the most effective drama exhibits precisely that: characters watching – and reading – other characters' performances. In Shakespeare's *Troilus and Cressida*, the faithless Cressida is wooed by Diomedes, watched by Troilus and Ulysses, and all four are watched in turn by Thersites. As Cressida flirts with Diomedes, Troilus voices his despairing anger at her faithlessness, and Thersites pours scornful mockery on *all* love, faithful as much as faithless. In *The Caucasian Chalk Circle* by Bertolt Brecht (1898–1956), Simon the soldier returns home to find his beloved Grusha with a child. He is certainly not the father. The two are reduced to inarticulate staring at one another, and the anonymous Narrator, who is watching the scene, intervenes between them and the audience: 'Hear now what the angry girl thought but did not say,' he says, before telling us the unspoken thoughts of the character.

In *The Real Inspector Hound* by Tom Stoppard (b. 1937), the watching is set up from the beginning as two critics, Birdboot and Moon, discuss the play we are about to see. The characters in the 'real' play are little more than stereotypes – Mrs Drudge, the charlady, and Simon, the errant lover, for instance, and their roles are dissected by Birdboot and Moon, the watchers. Finally the telephone rings when the stage is empty, and Birdboot is constrained to get up and answer it: speaking at the other end is his 'real' wife. The watching becomes acting, and the acting is mere performance. An actress 'performs' Mrs Drudge, Mrs Drudge 'performs' the charlady. An actor performs Birdboot, who performs a spectator who 'performs' his fantasy of leaving his wife for one of the characters on the stage – or is it the actress playing that part? The play reverberates beyond asking merely, What is performance and what is reality? and, How do we read performance? and engages with the very essence of individual and communal identity. What has watching, and watching performance, to do with these? (The specialised concentration of this kind of stage watching is further explored in the section, 'The play within the play' in Chapter 2, p. 32.)

THEATRE AND PERFORMANCE

Performance images the world. From the images we can find explanations of the world, and how we participate in its ongoingness. In other words, performance is a particular way of reflecting on our identity, perhaps especially our communal identity, and communicating about it.

Performance can affirm or question identity. It can seem to confirm power structures (the dominance of the male, the white, the heterosexual, and the 'eternal' values of society); or, it can question these.

Performance is therefore a battleground on which is continually fought a fierce struggle about community, and our place in the human community. Whose community is it? How can community find itself, affirm its values, interrogate its purposes, express its hopes and aspirations? In the past, theatre has often suppressed minority voices, and reaffirmed the status quo, even perhaps without meaning to. I have seen a very conservative former chancellor of the exchequer at a performance of *Don Carlos* by Friedrich Schiller (1759–1805), a revolutionary play explicitly directed against all the values this man had spent his life upholding. Yet he was thoroughly enjoying the evening, and felt in no way threatened by what he was watching. The signs and messages are always multifarious, and we may see most easily only those which chime with our own experiences or outlook.

But for that very reason theatre is able to open up or subvert the status quo. It can offer alternatives. If that were not the case, Britain and her governments would not have supported theatre censorship laws for at least 500 of the last 600 years. The lord chamberlain rigorously used his powers before 1968 (when Parliament abolished them) to censor plays without any form of democratic control whatsoever. Only the communist and Nazi states have introduced more draconian censorship laws than Britain's were; and it is perhaps worth noting that it was under the tyranny in Russia that the significance of the 'subtext', the unspoken meaning below the spoken text, was first properly understood and valued.

For theatrical performance, like playing, can offer up alternative realities, and different possible identities. It is especially dangerous when these alternative identities are elusive, shifting, uncontrollable. In a play such as *Cloud Nine* by Caryl Churchill (b. 1938), problems of identity, and the performance of identity, are explored subtly and often uncomfortably. In this play, we are initially presented with a happy family of imperialistic Britons, singing loyally around the Union Jack. But it soon becomes obvious that they are only performing. Disconcertingly, Betty, the wife and mother, is played by a man. Joshua, the black servant, is played by a white actor. And so on. The roles are being performed perfectly, but they cannot represent a 'true' identity because they are of the 'wrong' sex or the 'wrong' colour. But what is a 'true' identity? The second act takes place 100 years later, but the characters are only twenty-five years older. Their identities – our identities – and the performance of these identities must be constantly rethought, reconfigured, for nothing is as it seems. The theatrical performance is able to point to continual change in ourselves, in our lives and in our relationship with our communities.

In this sense, theatre performance presents an ongoing metaphor for life, neither real nor unreal, neither precise nor too blurred. It is a flow of images which we should go along with as they clash, fade into one another, exist in parallel, complement and contradict each other. Just as a metaphor is powerful because of the unarticulated reference to worlds beyond itself, so is theatre.

At the same time, the performance of the play is play. It provides experiences, emotions, ideas to extend us. We know we can walk away, but if we remain and watch, our imaginations will be richer.

Summary

- Playing as children do is (a) a kind of performing, and (b) a way of exploring situations and emotions without serious consequences.
- It is possible to see adult social behaviour as a series of performances. This seems to confound distinctions between pretence and reality.
- Performance may be understood by analogy with language. Language is 'citational': it makes meanings by citing earlier usages.
- A 'performative' is a pronouncement which enacts something, as 'I do' enacts marriage.
- 'Performativity' refers to anything which is potentially a performative.
- Erving Goffman explored how social encounters involve people adopting roles. The consequent role-playing conflates appearance and reality.
- Judith Butler and other theorists have suggested that identity is not a biological 'given' but is socially constructed.
- Performance art, also known as live art, involves artists performing 'real' actions in front of audiences.
- Many different forms of encounter take place on stage simultaneously: actor–actor, actor–spectator, character–character, character–spectator, etc.
- Stage encounters and other visual and aural stimuli are decoded through semiotics, the science of signs.
- Because performance images the world, it enables us to explore our identities without serious consequences.

FURTHER READING

Peter Brook's short *The Empty Space* (Harmondsworth: Penguin, 1972) is one of those rare books, endlessly provocative and stimulating, of which there are far too few: it is strongly recommended. On performance, performativity and more, Erika Fischer-Lichte,

The Transformative Power of Performance (London: Routledge, 2008) is an outstanding work. The most straightforward account of the theory of performance, and the place of performance studies within it, is Richard Schechner's *Performance Studies: An Introduction* (London: Routledge, 2002).

Erving Goffman's *The Presentation of Self in Everyday Life* (Harmondsworth: Penguin, 1959) was a ground-breaking book, and is still influential. Judith Butler, *Gender Trouble* (London: Routledge, 1999) is brilliant and persuasive, but it is not always an easy read! *The Semiotics of Theatre and Drama* by Keir Elam (London: Methuen, 1980) is eye-opening and detailed. RoseLee Goldberg, *Performance: Live Art since the 60s* (London: Thames and Hudson, 1998) is the best examination of this significant form.

Plays which are worth reading in connection with this area of the subject include: Caryl Churchill, *Cloud Nine*, in Caryl Churchill, *Plays: 1* (London: Methuen, 1985); and Tom Stoppard, *The Real Inspector Hound*, in Tom Stoppard, *Plays: 1*, (London: Faber & Faber, 1996).

2

THE TEXT

TEXT AND TEXTS

Drama was once studied simply as a branch of literature. Mary and Charles Lamb (1764–1847 and 1775–1834) even suggested that plays were preferable when thought of as stories, and published their *Tales from Shakespeare* to illustrate their opinion. George Bernard Shaw (1856–1950) argued that the reading of a play should be as rewarding as seeing it in the theatre. Chapter 1 of this book has perhaps shown something of how this attitude has been dispelled. Rightly or wrongly, the traditional play text is no longer seen as the primary carrier of meaning in the theatre. But the primacy of the text was not easily destroyed, and the battle in the 1960s and 1970s to 'save' the theatre from irrelevance by downgrading the script as such, also led some members of the self-proclaimed avant-garde to suggest that a text was not needed at all.

Nevertheless it is still true that the vast majority of play productions begin with the text. It is also true that after the performance is over, all that is left is the text. The text is often a spur to production, and always a record of words spoken on the stage.

However, we should enquire what we mean by 'text' in the context of performance. It is no longer enough to suggest that 'word' refers simply to 'words on the page'. A structuralist or semiotic definition might urge that we should refer to a distinct theatre text that is the articulation in time and space of the multiplicity of signs produced. There are of course a huge number and variety of these, and they give theatre performance its unique density, not simplified by unexpected but typical discontinuities within it. Not all the sign systems operate all the time, and during any performance they are likely to start and stop, restart, slow down and so on without warning. The theatre text is therefore notably unstable.

This chimes with the post-Derrida argument that the 'uncertainty principle' of Werner Heisenberg (1901–76) may also be applied to text, that there is no stable centre when a text flows, that there is only discourse. Derrida argued that the 'centre' is a function, not a 'place'. This is a profoundly subversive idea, because power and authority can only be exercised from some sort of centre, and it legitimises chance, uncertainty and fluidity in performance. In turn, such factors – or, better, practices – destabilise notions of text as a fixed entity, as is demonstrated in the work of, for example, John Cage, the Fluxus Group or most manifestations of live art. Thus, meaning is 'played', or 'performed', and is different at each playing. Each performance – each text – offers new meanings. 'Text' in this sense is a word for anything which is 'inscribed': an 'inscription' being a way of ordering or packaging pieces of experience. It covers ritual, tradition, the law, the military hierarchy, the political process and much more. It connotes the urge to authority, and substitutes for the 'centre', the focus of authority. We note that the word 'author' is included in 'authority'. Creating text is in this argument a bid for power.

However, Roland Barthes (1915–80) showed that the text was 'a multi-dimensional space'. Creating text may be a bid for authority, but meaning only happens in the process of communicating, the series of images produced by the text only acquire significance when the spectator reacts to them. This process is at its most complicated in the theatre, because there the communication is not simply between a writer and a reader, the performer intervenes between these two. That is why it is legitimate to talk of the performance as the text. Or rather, to say that the dramatic text exists in two forms – the written text and the performance – whose relationship is unpredictable, unstable and subject to the processes of production. The playwright then is perhaps the provider of starting-points. Her initial text is what makes the actor get up and begin work; what the actor does is to create a second text, related to the first, but different in kind. T. S. Eliot (1888–1965) described how beyond the words of the most moving Greek drama, was also the tone of voice, 'the uplifted hand or tense muscle' of the actor, and so on.

This and the following chapter of this book concentrate on the first kind of text, the written text, the playwright's text; Chapters 5, 6 and 7 on the creation of the second, performance text.

PLAYWRIGHTS AND WRITERS OF PLAYS

The play text is a spur to production. Most managers, directors, producers or committees who wish to mount drama begin by looking at a playwright's written script. In other words, in the huge majority of cases, the source of the final production's primary ideas is the playwright.

Some contemporary playwrights have found different ways to make play texts, and some of their ideas are discussed towards the end of Chapter 3. But generally speaking the playwright, unlike other writers, casts her work entirely in dialogue. Of course she may also describe the scenery, indicate the music, add stage directions to the script, and so on. But initially, and unlike the novelist, say, she has only spoken words with which to work.

This is more problematic than might be imagined, because people use words as much to conceal as to communicate. We all know how some people chatter continually in order to avoid having to bring up a painful subject. Similarly, a simple spoken word like 'Goodbye' may equally conceal heartbreak or delight that the other person is leaving. Rarely does a phrase or sentence mean no more than it says. 'Have a cup of coffee,' might be a phrase used to stall another person; it might be genuine hospitality; or it might be the first move in a seduction scene. The playwright Heiner Müller (1929–95) remarked that when the eastern part of Germany was ruled by a communist dictatorship, even 'Guten Tag' ('good morning') sounded like a lie! The playwright's text, therefore, carries a 'subtext' which is where the 'real' drama happens.

A second problem arises from the fact that drama does not *relate* its story, it *presents* it. This means that it – like real life – operates in time and space. These need some elucidation. First, the action of the play moves through time: one thing happens after another. Love is consummated, and then decays. Achievement is nullified by death. In this sense the playwright resembles a composer, whose works also move through time, from the opening bars to the dying fall. Time is therefore a vital tool in the playwright's bag. She can create urgency, or suspense, by drawing attention to it. The action is regulated by varying tempos, and the playwright manipulates time, for instance, by setting up a climax in advance, or hinting at what is to come. But, second, the playwright's action also moves through space: one person encounters another. The chase moves from one place to another, and on to a third. The playwright is in this sense like an architect, concerned with the way spaces are arranged, vistas perceived, and how people can negotiate these. In the drama, it is the playwright who decides the setting for the scene, and which characters will be present – and therefore those who will be absent. She can make one character overhear another, speak to an absent friend on the telephone (or by a letter brought by a messenger), or pretend to exit. The time–space nexus provides an unspoken but ever-present tension between what a character does and what she says, or between what we as an audience see and what we hear. The playwright's ability to manipulate this time–space nexus is perhaps her single most telling skill.

Heiner Müller also asserted that the playwright creates 'a world of images' which does not 'lend itself to conceptual formulation'. These images amplify and modify the basic verbal imagery: for instance, the open grave, the skull and the coffin of Ophelia in *Hamlet* all affect our apprehension of the references to death and decay – and in turn they modify the pictures of the grave and the skull which the stage presents. Music can also function as dramatic imagery, as when Hamlet commissions 'hautboys' to play before 'The Mousetrap' and afterwards calls for 'the recorders', whereas Claudius always insists on trumpets and drums. Hanns Eisler (1898–1962) was perhaps the first composer to call for music to be considered as part of the dramatic text, but his work has been followed by numerous others, including Philip Glass (b. 1937), Gavin Bryars (b. 1943) and John Adams (b. 1947), all of whom have enriched the specifically dramatic tradition.

The playwright also suggests action through the stage directions. Usually printed in italics, they serve the function of filling in minimally necessary facts which the reader (or, more likely, the director or actor) will need to know to understand the dialogue. Though sometimes, especially in the case of some naturalist dramatists, rather florid and detailed, most stage directions simply and concisely inform the reader where and when the action is supposed to be taking place. They indicate who is present ('Enter X', 'Exit Y') and suggest possibilities to the actors, such as moves on the stage, ways of speaking particular lines ('tearfully', 'angrily', etc.) and perhaps emotional states. Often, too, stage directions contain something of the playwright's ideas for staging the scene. Actors often wonder how scrupulously these should be followed. It must be remembered that the playwright conceives the stage directions in terms applicable to the stage she imagines the play will be presented on. Consequently, it may be that the further away in time – and perhaps place – that the play was conceived, the less appropriate may be the stage directions. Shakespeare's plays contain hardly any stage directions, probably because he oversaw the staging of his plays himself. In *The Tempest*, when Ferdinand and Miranda are 'discovered' playing chess, this would be easily presented on the Elizabethan stage: they wait behind the arras, which is then drawn to reveal ('discover') them. But what if today it were to be staged in a theatre in the round? The original stage directions would be thoroughly unhelpful.

But before all an author's stage directions are jettisoned, it should be remembered that the playwright is – or should be – a poet and a craftsman, not a mere writer of plays, that she understands the 'world of images' being created in this script, and that this should be respected or the play might as well not be presented. As John Arden (1930–2012) has pointed out, the playwright is a 'wright', a maker, like a wheelwright, or a shipwright. If the sailors don't trust the shipwright, they are likely to sink. Henrik Ibsen (1828–1906) was one playwright who was a 'maker', able to use words and silence, movement and stillness, furniture, sound effects and more to create his 'truth'. Here is the end of *A Doll's House*:

(*Nora goes out through the hall.*)
HELMER (*sinks down on the chair by the door, burying his face in his hands*):
   Nora! Nora!

> (*He stands up, looks round.*)
> Empty! She's gone, gone!
> (*Then a glimmer of hope.*)
> 'The greatest miracle of all … '
> (*From below the noise of a door slamming is heard.*)
>
> (Henrik Ibsen, *A Doll's House*, Act 2)

And at the end of Ibsen's *Ghosts*, as Oswald succumbs to perhaps his last and fatal attack, slumped and twitching in his chair, while his anguished mother looks on horror-struck, the sun slowly rises. Light floods the room. It is dawn. These are poetic dramatic images, fashioned by a poet-dramatist.

Harold Pinter (1930–2008) writing a century after Ibsen, demonstrates the same poetic-dramatic skills. At the beginning of Act 2 of his play *The Caretaker*, Pinter creates a taut image visually, which is then manipulated through language, sound and rhythm in a uniquely dramatic way:

> (*Mick is seated, Davies on the floor, half seated, crouched. Silence.*)
> MICK: Well?
> DAVIES: Nothing, nothing. Nothing.
> (*A drip sounds in the bucket overhead. They look up. Mick looks back to Davies.*)
> MICK: What's your name?
>
> (Harold Pinter, *The Caretaker*, Act 2)

And so on. Pinter's mastery is of time and space, visual and aural.

But what happens when the play director does not have respect for the playwright's craft? In the USA, Richard Schechner's production for the Performance Group of *The Tooth of Crime* by Sam Shepard (b. 1943) certainly excited its audiences, but the author felt betrayed. In 1972 the Royal Shakespeare Company staged *The Island of the Mighty* by John Arden and Margaretta D'Arcy (b. 1934), a deft reordering of certain myths about the legendary King Arthur and his court. The company decided to present the play as a sort of Dark Ages Shakespearean history play, complete with heavy leather overcoats and slow, weighty pauses. The authors objected at the first run-through that 'among other things, the meaning of the play had been crucially shifted out of balance', and they requested a meeting of the company to discuss the problem. It is worth noting that the actors still spoke the authors' words: it was in the creation of the succession of stage images that the playwrights felt betrayed. The directorate of the Royal Shakespeare Company refused the authors a company meeting, and in the ructions which followed, at least one governor of the RSC resigned, and the playwrights went on strike, supported by the Society of Irish Playwrights. The dispute was never properly resolved: the RSC's reputation was badly bruised, and Arden and D'Arcy never wrote again for a major British theatre company. It was a significant loss, and illustrates perfectly the nature of the playwright's problem in a system where she works, as it were, independently of the producing company.

However, in more cases than not, the dramatist is able to learn, in the words of Thornton Wilder (1897–1975)

> to take account of the presence of the collaborators [and] to derive advantage from them; and he learns, above all, to organize the play in such a way that its strength lies not in appearances beyond his control, but in the succession of events and in the unfolding of an idea.

Wilder adds:

> Theatre is unfolding action and in the disposition of events the authors may exercise a governance so complete that the distortions effected by the physical appearance of the actors, by the fancies of scene painters and the misunderstandings of directors, fall into relative insignificance. It is just because the theatre is an art of many collaborators, with the constant danger of grave misinterpretation, that the dramatist learns to turn his attention to the laws of narration, its logic and its deep necessity of presenting a unifying idea stronger than its mere collection of happenings.
>
> (Thornton Wilder, in Toby Cole, *Playwrights on Playwriting*, p. 108.)

The dramatist who learns this is a playwright; she who does not is a mere writer of plays!

THE PLAY TEXT

Conventionally, the play text is set out on the page in a way which may not be particularly accessible to the general reader. Perhaps it is aimed in the first instance at directors or actors who might wish to make a production from it. The average reader who obtains a printed play script must herself, when reading, stage the drama in her own imagination. This is a special kind of reading. Because the play is intended to be acted, it shares features with ritual or festivals, and therefore needs a crowd, an audience, in order to 'work'. The reader must imagine herself into the crowd.

The drama happens in the present, and therefore it heightens life, and intensifies the experience of life. Because it is taking place here and now it is fundamentally different from the novel or the film, which are reports on events which have happened in the past. In drama, we can see for ourselves what is happening among living, breathing people (the actors) in front of us. A novelist tells us what did happen, a film records something which is past and gone. This gives theatre its special vitality, and perhaps explains why it remains viable and in demand, even in the days of multi-channel television.

In most play scripts, what first confronts the reader is the list of characters, or *dramatis personae*. Sometimes the list explains who the characters are, perhaps their social position ('King of Denmark'), perhaps their relationships ('uncle to Hamlet'). Readers sometimes want to keep a finger in the page which lists the characters so that when a new character appears they can check who she is. Most plays have a protagonist (sometimes a hero) and an antagonist (sometimes a villain); sometimes the characters are 'stock types', but more often now they are conceived as individuals, and are more or less quirky, distinctive or memorable. The playwright in naturalistic plays tries to create characters who convince the audience that they are 'real': whether this means that they behave consistently, or that they seem to adapt to situations (that is, they adopt different masks according to who they are with and in what circumstances) is a matter for the dramatist to consider. It is worth saying, however, that character is properly shown, in life as well as in drama, through action. It is how you behave, especially in fraught situations, which reveals what you are like. The playwright usually attempts to make each character's utterances appropriate to her or him, and may consider the character's idiolect, or personal way of speaking, and sociolect, the way the social group to which the character belongs, typically speaks. However, the playwright on the whole is at least as concerned with the story, plot or narrative as with the character, and is often content to let that be developed by the actor. Thus, in *Waiting for Godot*, Estragon is the more earthy character, and is often to be found fiddling with his boot, whereas Vladimir is more intellectual, and often plays with his hat. But neither is given a detailed character by the author, Samuel Beckett (1906–89): different actors make very different characters out of them.

The reader will also quickly discover that the play is divided into acts and scenes. The act is the major division made in most plays, and may initially be thought of as the equivalent of a chapter in a novel – though there are rarely more than five acts in a play. It is a division of the play into digestible slices. One act traditionally lasts as long as it takes a candle to burn down: after an act, in the days before electricity or gas lighting, it was time to replace the candles. In ancient Greece the tragedies were usually divided into five segments, each marked off by an interlude by the chorus, and this may be where the traditional five act structure of later drama, especially Renaissance drama, derives from. It is worth pointing out, however, that it is unlikely that Shakespeare, for instance, thought of his plays as being in five parts. Their structure is less uniform, and subtler, than this implies, and the act divisions were usually made by later editors of his work. The nineteenth-century 'well-made play' also divides into five parts (see Chapter 3). It is perhaps most useful to think that an act ending marks a shift in the pace, or focus, or rhythm of the play, and the act itself works a little like a movement in a symphony. Many plays, especially in the last century and a half, have used fewer than five acts: Ibsen typically used four or sometimes only three; Beckett used only two in *Waiting for Godot*. Directors appreciate an even number of acts since it makes a decision about where to incorporate an interval simpler.

Some plays, of course, have only one act. They are usually over considerably more quickly than plays with several acts, and some of Beckett's plays, for instance, are very short indeed. A single unbroken act allows for strong concentration and focus, or the development of a single idea, perhaps even a dramatic joke.

In many plays the acts are further subdivided into scenes, smaller units of action, usually self-contained and perhaps set in a different place or among different characters. In classical French drama, a new scene was marked each time a character entered or left the stage, but this convention is now obsolete. A scene change (or an act change) used to be marked by a lowering of the front curtain, but this practice too has now been largely abandoned, and scenes in plays like Shakespeare's are usually made to flow into one another almost without pause. The medieval mystery plays comprise twenty or more self-contained episodes, or pageants, which may be thought of as scenes in the overall single mystery play. Each is self-contained, and was even performed originally by its own cast. *Peer Gynt* by Henrik Ibsen consists of three acts set in Norway, a fourth act in Africa, and a fifth act back in Norway. The first scene shows Peer and his mother; the next shows Peer meeting guests on their way to a wedding; the next is the wedding itself, when Peer steals the bride. Each scene is clearly self-contained, but then so is the whole act, showing the daring ne'er-do-well that is Peer up to his mischief. The next act has more scenes, each showing Peer in relation to one or more women, which again gives the whole act its unity. And so on.

What is often considered the most typical aspect of the written play script is dialogue. A character's name appears in the left margin; she speaks. On the next line, another character's name appears in the left margin; he speaks. There is a pause. This seems to be the essence of the play.

Dialogue may derive originally from the dialectic of philosophical disputations. In Greek drama, rapid one-line exchanges between characters was known as stichomythia, and it can still be found in modern drama, as in *Waiting for Godot*:

VLADIMIR: You must be happy, too, deep down, if you only knew it.
ESTRAGON: Happy about what?
VLADIMIR: To be back with me again.
ESTRAGON: Would you say so?
VLADIMIR: Say you are, even if it's not true.
ESTRAGON: What am I to say?
VLADIMIR: Say, I am happy.
ESTRAGON: I am happy.
VLADIMIR: So am I.
ESTRAGON: So am I.
VLADIMIR: We are happy.
ESTRAGON: We are happy.

(Samuel Beckett, *Waiting for Godot*, Act 1)

However amusing or slangy, this is highly artificial writing: actually most drama has used artificial or stylised language throughout most of history. For centuries, dramatic dialogue was couched in verse, and it was perhaps only after Ibsen decided to try to make dialogue from contemporary speech in his series of modern dramas that dialogue began to resemble the way people speak. In 1888 August Strindberg (1849–1912) claimed to have avoided one character catechising another in order to elicit a 'smart reply', and to have rejected symmetrical, mathematically constructed dialogue. He was seeking a dialogue which meandered almost aimlessly, apparently, like real dialogue in life, with thoughts picked up, dropped, reworked, and so on, in what he tellingly compares to 'the theme in a musical composition'. In other words, Strindberg found that wholly natural dialogue was almost impossible. Even today, some of the most seemingly natural dialogue, such as Harold Pinter's, is actually very finely constructed, like composed music. This is a major paradox at the heart of dramatic dialogue.

Part of the reason for this has already been mentioned. Unlike in real life, for a line of dramatic dialogue to be convincing in the heightened reality of the stage, it must have a purpose: in other words, the character must have a good reason for saying it, and it is the actor's business to unearth this reason. This reason provides the subtext, and it is almost a condition of dramatic dialogue that it have a subtext. For dialogue, finally, is itself a kind of action, which counterpoints the other kinds of action on the stage.

Dialogue is complemented by monologue (a long speech by a single character) or soliloquy (when a character speaks, but not to another character), as in the following:

VLADIMIR: Was I sleeping while the others suffered? Am I sleeping now? Tomorrow, when I wake, or think I do, what shall I say of today? That with Estragon my friend, at this place until the fall of night, I waited for Godot? That Pozzo passed, with his carrier, and that he spoke to us? Probably. But in all that what truth will there be? (*ESTRAGON, having struggled with his boots in vain, is dozing off again. VLADIMIR stares at him.*) He'll know nothing. He'll tell me about the blows he received and I'll give him a carrot. (*Pause.*) Astride of a grave and a difficult

> birth. Down in the hole, lingeringly, the gravedigger puts on the
> forceps. We have time to grow old. The air is full of our cries.
>
> (Samuel Beckett, *Waiting for Godot*, Act 2)

It is worth noting that most stage soliloquies, like this, are actually 'dialogic'. This word, coined probably by the Russian critic Mikhail Bakhtin (1895–1975), does not mean 'relating to dialogue', it means 'double-voicedness', and connotes the intense 'interanimation' between 'voices' in any discourse. Vladimir is not simply speaking to himself, he is asking questions, arguing two (or more) possibilities, restlessly exclaiming and observing. He is also, of course, communicating with the audience. Indeed, such is the intensity of 'dialogic' monologue in the theatre that whole plays have been built with it, including *The Stranger* by August Strindberg, *Smoking Is Bad for You* by Anton Chekhov (1860–1904), *Talking Heads* by Alan Bennett (b. 1934) and *The Vagina Monologues* by Eve Ensler (b. 1953).

Box 2.1: The play within the play

Theatre is a voyeur's medium. We watch people exhibiting themselves in public. (See the section, 'The gaze' in Chapter 8, p. 192.) Theatre, perhaps uneasily aware of this, surprisingly often draws attention to this propensity for voyeurism with plays staged within plays. We watch others (characters in the 'real' play) watching a play.

In the Elizabethan theatre, revengers and others often present allegorical dramas to other characters, and we watch them watching them. *The Spanish Tragedy* by Thomas Kyd (1558–94) and *Women Beware Women* by Thomas Middleton (c.1580–1627) contain excellent examples. Shakespeare, too, seems to have been fascinated by a play within a play, and created several such – *Love's Labours Lost, A Midsummer Night's Dream* and *Hamlet* are justly famous for their plays of *The Seven Worthies, Pyramus and Thisbe* and *The Mousetrap*.

Pedro Calderón de la Barca (1600–81), in *The Great Theatre of the World*, created a whole drama out of such an idea. Here, God (the Author), summons his characters onto the stage of the world, and watches as the characters – from king to beggar – play out their parts. At first they object to the roles they have been assigned, and to the fact that they do not know when they will be called on stage. But eventually the play begins, and each in turn is summoned towards the door of death. The World takes from them before they go whatever props they had been lent, and so in the end death levels them all, to the greater glory of the Author.

More recently, Anton Chekhov's *The Seagull* contains a significant play within it. All Konstantin's dreams are bound up in his drama, set in the future and performed by his adored Nina. He seeks, as perhaps Chekhov also sought, 'new forms' of drama, and it seems almost as if Chekhov is testing the limits of the fashionable symbolist style of the contemporary stage in this creation, which however brings neither happiness nor success to Konstantin. Yet Chekhov's own symbolism, especially of the seagull itself, remains to tease the real spectators.

A contemporary example appears in *The America Play* by Suzan-Lori Parks (b. 1963). Here, a black Abraham Lincoln lookalike sets up in a kind of fairground booth, dressed as the president, with stovepipe hat and round black beard. He invites the public to enter, choose a pistol and shoot him, thereby re-enacting the assassination of President Lincoln (1809–65), with themselves as John Wilkes Booth (1838–65). Several punters play out the murder, and the repetition, like a kind of ghastly rehearsal, emphasises the theatricality of the scene. In the second act, when this character has apparently died, his wife and son search for him, while *Our American Cousin* by Tom Taylor (1817–80) is performed in the background.

Historically, of course, the assassination took place in a theatre while the president was watching this play. Parks' drama, play within a play, within plays, has a kind of mesmeric, farcical horror, and our voyeurism suddenly connotes our complicity in the assassination of black history and culture.

DRAMATIC STRUCTURES

Plays tell stories. They move through time – this happened, then this happened, then this happened, and so on. They are rooted in narrative, or plot (see Chapter 3, p. 47–48 for a definition of 'plot'). Critics have tried to suggest that plots must conform to certain rules, or types, to be effective. Such is the old nostrum for drama, the 'three unities', which argued that plays must be set in a single place, must be no more than a day in duration and must contain a single focused plot. Experience has undermined this argument. The Russian formalists suggested that there were only seven basic plots for stories, though the variations allowed are extremely diverse. The American critic Northrop Frye (1912–91) suggested four kinds of plot which he identified, perhaps wilfully, with the seasons. One useful distinction which may be made to indicate how plot affects structure is to consider the end of the play. Thus, Shakespeare's *Richard III* has a 'closed ending':

> Now civil wounds are stopp'd; peace lives again.
> That she may long live here, God say Amen.
>
> (William Shakespeare, *Richard III*, Act 5)

The Good Person of Szechuan by Bertolt Brecht (1898–1956), on the other hand, has an 'open ending':

> There's only one solution that we know:
> That you should now consider as you go
> What sort of measures you would recommend
> To help good people to a happy end.
> Ladies and gentlemen, in you we trust:
> There must be happy endings, must, must, must!
>
> (Bertolt Brecht, *The Good Person of Szechuan*, Epilogue)

Embedded in the plot of the play is the theme, or themes, the subjects the author wants the audience to consider, the bees in her bonnet. The playwright does not have the luxury of the novelist, who can, like Leo Tolstoy (1828–1910) in *War and Peace*, expand at will on his theories of history, heroism and the like. The playwright must select events, construct dialogue and so on in order to allow the theme, or themes, to emerge. The themes in *Hamlet* might be revenge, or justice perhaps; in *Waiting for Godot*, they might be boredom, or friendship, or time, or all of these, and more. Thornton Wilder wrote of

> a succession of events illustrating a general idea – the stirring of the idea;
> the gradual feeding out of information; the shock and counter-shock of

circumstances; the flow of action; the interruption of action; the moments of allusion to earlier events; the preparation of surprise, dread, or delight – all that is the author's.

(Thornton Wilder, in Toby Cole, *Playwrights on Playwriting*, p. 108)

It is not, incidentally, the director's or actor's.

One way of highlighting the theme may be to introduce a second story, or subplot, which may evoke parallels, develop the themes in unexpected ways, or offer alternative perspectives. In Thomas Middleton's *The Changeling*, the tragedy is echoed by a comic subplot set in a madhouse, so that the mix is a potent one of absurdity and terror. In *King Lear* the subplot about Gloucester is so interwoven with the main plot that each intensifies the compassion and fear which Shakespeare creates in the other. In Brecht's *The Caucasian Chalk Circle*, the second plot does not even begin until the play is half complete, and then it becomes the central focus of the story. In other words, Brecht separates the two plots, and plays them one after the other, even though they are supposed to happen simultaneously, thereby dissipating any sense of dramatic urgency and re-angling the expected climax.

Dramatic plot almost always involves exposition, that is, a laying out of information the audience will need to understand the story, or the author's treatment of the material. Again, the playwright does not have the luxury of the novelist, who can recapitulate what has happened in the past before the main action begins in many novelistic ways. The playwright's way must be different. In *Hamlet*, the return of the old king, or rather the appearance of his ghost, enables the exposition to occur remarkably easily. In *The Tempest*, Shakespeare had much more trouble, and the second scene in this play has Prospero relating to his daughter – in perhaps too much detail – what is sometimes today called the 'back story'. In Tom Stoppard's *The Real Inspector Hound*, the author parodies crude play writing by having the radio announce that a 'man has been seen' in the vicinity of the action, and a few moments later the charlady speaks into the telephone: 'Hello, the drawing room of Lady Muldoon's country residence one morning in early spring.' Ideally the dialogue will contain the information the spectators need in an interesting way: who are these characters? What is their relationship? How is the situation significant? How has it become so?

Finally, the dramatic plot usually involves a climax and a denouement. The climax is the highest point of tension in the play, and usually occurs late in the plot. But 'all is revealed' in the denouement, when everything is untied, or wound up, the problem is solved, or what was unknown becomes known. The climax may be unwound catastrophically, as in, say, *Hamlet*, when the stage is strewn with corpses, including that of the hero. Alternatively, the denouement may show that in this story 'all's well that ends well'. This is usually more problematic than it may seem, however, as for example at the end of *Twelfth Night*, when the 'happy ending' is marred by the curse of Malvolio.

All these are matters for the playwright.

DEVISING

One way to produce a play text is for the theatre company to dispense with the playwright and create a script specially tailored to its own concerns and personnel. This process is usually known as 'devising', and it is precisely its collaborative nature which distinguishes it from play writing. Indeed, when first practised to any great extent in Britain in the 1960s, devising was seen as a way of subverting the 'great tradition' of literary drama, though this attitude is now considered unnecessarily oppositional, and perhaps discounts the sheer variety of devising practices.

The basic tool in the devising of any show is improvisation. The creators, whether an egalitarian group or under less democratic circumstances, always develop their ideas through improvisation, which means that thinking and experimenting is theatrical and physical, not intellectual. This may not always be regarded as a strength, but it does mean that improvisation-based devising tends to be well grounded in the inherently dramatic. It also means that each member of the group has some input, however slight, into the work. Moreover, it seems that improvisation as a process resists institutionalisation as well as the tyranny of tradition.

The particular 1960s mix in radical and artistic circles of libertarianism, progressive politics and a desire to break free from the social and cultural constrictions and repressions of the stagnant affluence of post-war capitalism directed new attention to processes of creation rather than final production. One result of this was the development of performance studies in universities (see Chapter 1). Another was the increasing attraction of anti-establishment ideals of collectivism and participatory democracy, which had long sustained the lonely radical Theatre Workshop in Britain, where Joan Littlewood (1914–2002) led the most artistically challenging and politically progressive company of the time. But she dominated the group, so that when they researched in libraries and through improvisation material about the First World War, for instance, it was she who controlled the creative work, and she who shaped it into *Oh What a Lovely War*. At the same time, similar artistic and political drives were being articulated in the USA, where first the Living Theater and then also its offshoot, the Open Theater, were formed on deliberately progressive principles. Both produced striking work, such as the Living Theater's *Paradise Now* and the Open Theater's *The Serpent*, but it was notable that though collective creative practices were advocated and explored – all the actors researched material, read and discussed it – in the end, as with Theatre Workshop, both groups depended to a large extent on the strong personalities of their leaders – Julian Beck (1925–85) and Judith Malina (b. 1926) of the Living Theater; Joseph Chaikin (1935–2003) of the Open Theater.

Later in the 1960s a number of politically-motivated British groups dedicated more or less wholly to devising were established. The best known of these was probably the Agitprop Players, who became Red Ladder, and who operated as a collective, by which they meant that all members took equal responsibility for all aspects of the productions. The group would choose a subject, research it in whatever ways seemed appropriate, and share the fruits of their researches. From this, further research was likely to be called for. The first ideas were meanwhile being explored dramatically through improvisation, and a synopsis, perhaps a scenario, was worked out. Again this skeleton was subject to criticism and discussion, and was modified, and further developed. By now a 'proper' script was emerging, and the embryonic play could be cast, rehearsed and presented. It sounds idyllic, and the group lasted – with changes in personnel – for two decades, but it was not all always as easy as this description may make it seem. The collective principle can turn to mere anarchy, though Red Ladder members had regular political meetings to question their own working and guard against such a development. It can also conceal anti-democratic hierarchies based on personality. In other words, the political ideals of such a group may collide with their aesthetic ideals.

Red Ladder were one of the best known among a throng of ardent left-wing theatre groups, most of them devising their own scripts as a matter of principle, who were active in the 1970s. Interestingly, though they repudiated the capitalist state in which they lived and worked, most of them were funded by the government's Arts Council. It was probably predominantly their influence which led to the introduction of devising processes in the work of many of the much less politically-driven community groups and theatre-in-education companies of the time. When the Thatcher government came to power in 1979, state funding of these groups stalled, and by 1990 hardly any of the political agitprop devising companies remained.

Their place was taken on the fringes of mainstream theatre by companies whose work was based in physical performance, and who often survived into the twenty-first century. Frequently a-political, at least in any overt sense, these groups used much more sophisticated theatre skills to develop their own pieces, including dance, mime, traditional Asian forms, circus skills and masks. Among the most prominent of these groups were Theatre de Complicité, Forced Entertainment and DV8, all founded in the 1980s, and all using ensemble improvisation techniques to create their productions. The companies usually researched their subject matter, and discussed its implications together, but when they came to dramatise the material, they often sought extreme theatrical forms, bizarre physical images or unexpected movement sequences. Their props were often culled from the circus – stilts, ladders, ropes from the flies above the stage, they were not afraid of using digital technology, they often worked closely with fine artists, and their work often appeared dream-like or elusive to more conventional spectators.

Forced Entertainment's first show, *Jessica in the Room of Lights*, for example, used a soundtrack by the bassist of a local industrial noise band, a deliberately blurred story line about a cinema usherette whose real life became entangled with films she had half seen, and it was presented in the upstairs gallery of an artist-run space. If they seemed to be on the margin, they were not upset by that: they were trying to discuss 'the concerns of the times in a language born out of them'. Forced Entertainment's material was designed to be provocative, to ask questions about collaboration, documentation, stories ('Are they a means of escaping? Or of learning? Or of organizing the world?'). In *Certain Fragments*, Tim Etchells provides texts ('ghosts') of work done, suggesting something of the disturbing power and elusiveness of the group's performances.

A very different kind of devising was developed by playwright and theatre practitioner, Tara Goldstein (b. 1957). Her Gailey Road Company was founded in 2008 and is based in Toronto, Canada. Goldstein and her company created 'performed ethnographies', which aimed to work ethnographical data into performance 'text', with the aim of specifically challenging the racism and colonialism that ethnography too easily allows. The process had three stages – first, the research from which the play is created, then the performance of the play, and finally the follow-up discussions and analysis which are central to the whole project. Thus, *Staging Harriet's House* was presented at Toronto's 2010 Pride Festival: it told the story of a mother and her three daughters in order to address problems of national identity and same-sex families. It had a specifically Canadian dimension, and some of the research involved interviewing local Toronto families.

In Britain before 1968, no company which devised most of its work received any formal subsidy. In the early twenty-first century, approximately thirty did. Whereas in the middle of the twentieth century only a tiny handful of people understood anything of devising processes, now devising is taught regularly in higher and further education, at drama schools and even at GCSE and 'A' level. 'A' level also provides examinations in circus skills, physical theatre, and more.

Devising always takes longer than rehearsing a scripted play, for obvious reasons. Indeed, for some of the companies mentioned above, a new show can take as long as two years from initial conception to final production, but that is partly because time is allowed for the ideas to mature on the brain's back burner, while other projects continue. Nevertheless, the emphasis is often much more firmly on the process of creation than is the case in the mainstream theatre, and it is argued with some force that group creation allows for multiple perspectives, for a de-centred and non-dogmatic approach, and for chance discoveries in rehearsal to be brought forward. It is, however, noticeable that all three British devising companies mentioned here are led by dominant male directors – Simon McBurney (b. 1957) for Theatre de Complicité, Tim Etchells (b. 1962) for Forced Entertainment and Lloyd Newson (b. 1957) for DV8.

For all that these groups exist mostly outside the conventional theatre sector, it may be that they offer more to the speculative audience than most traditional theatre companies.

Summary

- The 'text' of a play may refer to its written script; or it may refer to what is performed.
- Play texts are written in dialogue; dialogue contains a subtext, which is often regarded as the 'real' drama.
- The playwright contrives a text which operates in time and space, and creates dynamic stage images.
- Play scripts are set out conventionally, with a list of characters, and divisions into acts and scenes. Dialogue is set out conventionally, too.
- Dramatic plots are so developed that the playwright's themes emerge.
- Dramatic structure includes exposition, climax and denouement.
- Devising is an alternative way of making a play without a playwright. It is notable, however, that most successful devising is achieved under strong leadership.

FURTHER READING

Theoretically, probably the most useful book on the subject of text is Roland Barthes' *Image Music Text* (London: HarperCollins, 1977). Toby Cole, *Playwrights on Playwriting* (London: MacGibbon and Kee, 1960) is an invaluable work, and may be complemented by Alan Ayckbourn's *The Crafty Art of Playmaking* (London: Faber and Faber, 2002). The most accessible work on devising is probably *Devising Performance* by Deirdre Heddon and Jane Milling (Basingstoke: Palgrave Macmillan, 2006); but see also Tim Etchells,

Certain Fragments (London: Routledge, 1999). You might also care to find a copy of Charles and Mary Lamb's *Tales from Shakespeare* (many editions).

Plays to read include: William Shakespeare, *Hamlet*, Pedro Calderón de la Barca, *The Great Theatre of the World*, and Henrik Ibsen, *A Doll's House*. More modern plays include: Samuel Beckett, *Waiting for Godot* (Faber and Faber, 1955 and later editions), Harold Pinter, *The Caretaker* (in *Harold Pinter, Plays: 2*, London: Faber & Faber, 1991, and later editions), and Suzan-Lori Parks, *The America Play* (New York: Theater Communications Group, 1995).

3

DRAMATIC FORM

The consideration of dramatic form has become rather unfashionable. Yet it was through discussion of form that the earliest attempts at analysing drama were conducted, notably by Aristotle (384–22 BCE), and theatre practitioners who ignore form do so at their peril.

The justly renowned German director, Peter Stein (b. 1937), directed a production of Shakespeare's *Troilus and Cressida* at the Edinburgh Festival in 2006. He clearly knew that the story as it is usually told has a tragic ending – Troilus is betrayed by Cressida, his faith is shattered – and so he altered the play to fit his preconception. He created an episode in which Troilus died. But Shakespeare's Troilus does not die. He is still alive at the end of the play. Shakespeare's play is – unexpectedly – not a tragedy, it is a tragicomedy. And by thus attempting to alter the dramatic form, Stein made nonsense of the whole work. It simply didn't make sense as presented.

The conscientious practitioner will therefore spend time thinking about dramatic form.

TRAGEDY

The word 'tragedy' in common usage today means little more than a sad or unnecessarily unpleasant event: a motorway crash in which several people died is described as a 'tragedy' in the newspapers; a promising career cut short by cheating is described as 'tragic'. But in drama, the term 'tragedy' is specific, even technical, and refers to a particular type of play.

Discussion of tragedy as a dramatic form must begin with the Greek scholar and philosopher, Aristotle. In his small book – perhaps it is no more than lecture notes – known as *Poetics*, he attempts a dispassionate, intellectual examination of poetry, focusing especially on drama, and within drama on tragedy. He never saw the plays of Aeschylus (c.525–456 BCE), Sophocles (c.496–06 BCE) and Euripides (c.485–07 BCE) – but he read them closely and tried to draw conclusions about what typifies their works.

Aristotle begins his examination with the assertion that poetry, like the other arts, is an 'imitation' of life. By this, he does not mean that poetry, or the arts in general, merely imitate the surface experience of living day-to-day; he means that art reproduces the rhythms of life, it creates experiences which, if we enter into them, are like the experiences of life. The sensitive spectator at a good performance of Shakespeare's *As You Like It* has an experience something like 'falling in love': the play *imitates* falling in love. The appreciative listener at a concert performance of Beethoven's *Eroica* symphony experiences something like heroism, pride, elation or triumph. For Aristotle, the purest form of poetic imitation is drama, and the purest form of drama is tragedy.

Aristotle says that: 'Tragedy is an imitation of an action that is admirable, complete and possesses magnitude; in language made pleasurable … performed by actors … effecting through pity and fear the purification of such emotions' (*Poetics*, p. 10). This general definition, especially the last clause, raises serious issues which have been debated heatedly over centuries, and even millennia, and to which we shall return. Before we enter that debate, however, we should note Aristotle's further observations.

He lists six elements of tragedy, some of which seem to focus on the writing of the tragedy, others on the performance (a blurring of distinctions, by the way, which other, later commentators have not always avoided):

1 Plot, that is the action, the story, which, he adds, is enacted by people, actors, as opposed to be being narrated or sung.

2   Character, the way a person behaves (for behaviour defines character); it is important to note that tragedy, according to Aristotle, deals with 'the better type of person', that is royalty, generals, governors, people whose fate is of significance to more than just themselves.

3   Reason, the way plot and character are connected, the logic and coherence of what is presented, and how what is shown is 'likely to happen'.

4   Diction, the speaking of the text.

5   Poetry, the poetic qualities of the text itself.

6   Spectacle, what you see on the stage.

For Aristotle, the most important of these is the plot, which is the imitation of action, the way the events, or incidents, are organised by the playwright. But note that the primacy of plot over the other elements is established through performance:

> Tragedy is not an imitation of persons, but of actions and of life. Well-being and ill-being reside in action, and the goal of life is an activity, not a quality; people possess certain qualities in accordance with their character, but they achieve well-being or its opposite on the basis of how they fare ... So the events, i.e. the plot, are what tragedy is there for, and that is the most important thing of all.
>
> (Aristotle, *Poetics*, p. 11)

Aristotle argues that it would be possible to have a tragedy which contained action but no characters, but it would be impossible to have a tragedy which included characters but no action. Action, it may be noted, is a very wide term, and includes reaction (how characters react to events), for instance, as well as suffering, amusement, fear, and so on.

The action imitated in performance, says Aristotle, evokes and purifies the emotions of fear and pity. 'Purification' is a translation of the vexed Greek word, *katharsis*. *Katharsis* was originally a medical term which referred to the way the body gets rid of poison or other harmful matter. Sometimes, with reference to drama, it has been translated as a purging of fear and pity. The concept is elusive, but it appears to contain within it, for the spectator, both fear ('that could have been me'), and pity (the sorrow we feel for another person in misfortune). And after the event, when the tragedy has closed, we feel cleansed, purged, by the experience. It is this cleansing that tragedy performs which defines the genre for Aristotle. And paradoxically, the moment of *katharsis* (when we weep) is pleasurable.

Katharsis is the crux of Aristotle's view of tragedy. This is what makes tragedy distinct from any other art form. It is also what makes it uniquely powerful.

Since tragedy imitates *action* to evoke fear and pity, plot is its most important element. But the plot is not simply a series of actions bundled up together piecemeal. The arrangement of the incidents is crucial to the tragedy. There are two qualities by which an effective plot may be recognised: first, it must be complete in itself, whole and self-contained; and second, it must have a clear structure, a beginning, a middle and an end. This may not be as simple as it sounds, as different tellings of the story of Oedipus demonstrate.

Box 3.1: Two Oedipuses

First version

Once there was a king of Thebes called Laius, who married a woman called Jocasta, and they had a son called Oedipus. Apollo's oracle foretold that this boy would kill his father and marry his mother. Laius and Jocasta decided to cheat the oracle: the child would have to die. But rather than commit infanticide, they gave the child to a shepherd to leave on the mountainside with its ankles tied together.

However, the shepherd was tender-hearted and gave the baby to another shepherd from Corinth, who promised to bring it up as his own. But in fact he took it to the king of Corinth, who had no children, and who now adopted Oedipus as his son.

Oedipus grew up believing he was the son of the king and queen of Corinth. When he was eighteen, he was told by Apollo's oracle that he would kill his father and marry his mother. Oedipus decided to cheat the oracle: he left Corinth and swore never to return till his parents were dead.

He wandered though the world, and once, at a crossroads, he met an arrogant old man who tried to whip him. Oedipus killed him, and his three servants. He wandered on till he came to Thebes – a stricken city whose king had been killed, and whose crops had failed. Moreover, Thebes was being terrorised by the Sphinx, who killed anyone unable to answer its riddle: What walks on four legs in the morning, two legs at noon, and three legs in the evening? The answer – humans, who crawl before they can walk, and who need a stick in old age – was given by Oedipus, who thereby freed the city from its curse. By acclamation, Oedipus was made king of Thebes, and he married the old king's widow.

For fifteen years, Thebes enjoyed prosperity, and Oedipus and Jocasta had children. Then plague and famine struck again. Oedipus swore to find out the cause of the new disasters, and sent for Tiresias, the blind prophet. Tiresias, in a riddle, implied that the cause lay with Oedipus himself. Then Jocasta told of how her first husband, Laius, had been murdered at a crossroads by a stranger. Oedipus recognised himself in the story. He sent for the old shepherd, who confirmed what had happened. Horrified, Jocasta committed suicide, and Oedipus blinded himself.

Second version

Thebes is beset by famine and plague. The king, Oedipus, determines he will discover why Thebes is suffering, and promises to punish whoever is responsible.

The blind prophet, Tiresias, implies that Oedipus himself is responsible. Oedipus suspects that Creon, Jocasta's brother, has put Tiresias up to this, because he (Creon) wants the throne. Oedipus confronts Creon, but Jocasta is able to still their argument by referring to her child with Laius, and telling them of Laius' murder.

Oedipus is frightened by this revelation. He sends for the shepherd, and while waiting for him talks of his own childhood in Corinth, and the oracle which had foretold how he would kill his father and marry his mother. He reveals how he had tried to cheat the oracle, and how he had killed a man at the crossroads.

Unexpectedly, a messenger arrives with news that the king of Corinth, Oedipus' supposed father, has died, and of natural causes. Oedipus rejoices that the oracle's prophecy has not come true. But then the messenger reveals that Oedipus is not in fact the king of Corinth's son. Jocasta tries to intervene, but Oedipus is adamant for the truth.

The shepherd arrives and tells his story. Oedipus and Jocasta both rush away, only for an attendant shortly afterwards to bring the news that Jocasta has committed suicide and Oedipus blinded himself. The sightless Oedipus now makes his peace with Creon. His daughters bid him goodbye, and he goes into exile. 'Your rule is ended', says Creon.

The two stories are largely the same, but the versions are very different. The first version, which we may call the *fable*, perhaps arouses curiosity, a desire to know what will happen next. The second version, which is effectively the *plot* of Sophocles' tragedy, arouses emotions, perhaps fear and pity, and is the more likely of the two versions to 'grip' us.

The reasons for this are clear. The most obvious perhaps concerns the focus in the telling. The *action* is much more tightly focused in the second version, the tragedy, than it is in the fable. It is self-contained, and its references are organic to the story. Thus, it does away with the Delphic oracle as a character, and also the Sphinx. These may be interesting in themselves, but they do not assist directly in the arousal of pity and fear. The focus also applies to *time*. Whereas the fable covers twenty or thirty years, Sophocles' plot takes less than a day. And similarly with *place*: the fable wanders all over the eastern Mediterranean, but the plot of the tragedy is confined wholly to Thebes.

The two versions may also be compared in terms of their structure. Structurally, the fable is something of a shambles! It jogs along with plenty of strong events – the handing over of the baby, the death at the crossroads, the confrontation with the Sphinx, and more – but it has little shape. The tragedy, on the other hand, is very tightly structured, with a beginning, a middle and an end. The beginning of the tragedy sees the city beset with plague and famine, and the good ruler determined to help his people. The end brings the solution to this problem: Oedipus himself is the problem, which is solved by his blinding and exile, and Jocasta's suicide.

The rhythm of the tragedy is long and strong, whereas the rhythm of the fable is more broken and certainly less oppressive.

The middle section of the tragedy, how the plot develops from the beginning to the end, illustrates the point about rhythm: it may be seen as a straight line driving inexorably towards the conclusion. Certainly, nothing is extraneous. In fact, the middle may be divided into three sections: first, the scenes with Tiresias and Creon, which deal with politics, power and the significance of the problem; second the almost-domestic scenes between Oedipus and Jocasta, in which their pasts are revealed; and third, the scenes with the messenger and the shepherd, in which we learn the truth. It is notable how the first and third sections of the middle balance one another, like two sides of a seesaw poised over the pivot of the scenes between Oedipus and his mother/wife.

We may conclude, therefore, that while the fable behind any plot is likely to be chronological or sequential, the plot itself may jump about, may include flashbacks or omit details, and so on. The plot is the way in which the author treats the fable.

Oedipus the King by Sophocles is an example of what Aristotle considered a successful plot. He believed that tragedy depicted a change of fortune, either from bad to good fortune, or, more likely, from good to bad fortune. The latter, he thought, was the most common and best sort of tragedy, and today tragedy is regarded as dealing almost exclusively with a change from good fortune to bad.

The change of fortune must come about logically, Aristotle also observed, through a connected series of events which follow 'necessarily' or are 'likely'; in other words, they are believable. The function of the playwright or poet is not to say what *has* happened, but what *could* happen. Aristotle allocated a special significance to plot devices which helped to intensify the focus, such as 'recognition' and 'reversal'. Examples of these come from *Oedipus*: first, when the messenger brings news that the king of Corinth has died naturally, Oedipus knows more ('recognition'), but when he adds that Oedipus is not the king of Corinth's son, relief gives way to deeper despair ('reversal').

If Aristotle's views on tragedy have been the most influential, they are by no means the only ones. For instance, he says little or nothing about the profound sense of loss or emptiness we can sometimes feel at the performance of a tragedy. Nor does he notice, as have later critics, that tragedy almost always deals with the protagonist's private world, and that fear and pity seem to be at their most powerful when they occur in family situations. In the Renaissance, tragedy was often considered to be a kind of warning to princes: it depicted the fall of those who abused their power ('When the bad bleed, then is the tragedy good.'). Sir Philip Sidney (1554–86), Jean Racine (1639–99), John Dryden (1631–1700), Georg Hegel (1770–1831) and Friedrich Nietzsche (1844–1900) are among many critics and philosophers of earlier ages who have addressed the question of tragedy, and the literature on tragedy has grown enormously in the last hundred years.

The German philosopher, Georg Hegel, believed that tragedy was the result of the clash between mutually exclusive but equally justifiable causes, such as that between Creon and Antigone in Sophocles' *Antigone*, or that created by the requirement that Hamlet avenge his father, while not committing murder.

Friedrich Nietzsche refined and extended this. In *The Birth of Tragedy*, he asserted first that art was a unique synthesis of dream and intoxication, order and chaos, embodied in the Greek gods, Apollo and Dionysus. Apollo is self-aware, calm, the god of light and the individual; Dionysus is the god of wine, drunkenness, self-forgetfulness and revelry. If Apollo is the guardian of each person's uniqueness, Dionysus unites people and makes them one with nature. Somewhere in the union of these two opposites, Apollo and Dionysus, or in the dialectical clashes between them, Nietzsche argued, tragedy is born.

For Nietzsche, Prometheus, not Oedipus, is the archetypal tragic hero: Prometheus stole fire from heaven to warm and illuminate humankind, for which he was punished eternally. In his ending Nietzsche finds the justice which he asserts tragedy must uphold, for the endless suffering of the hero is matched by the extreme plight of the gods themselves, on the brink of their extinction brought about by the action of the hero. The suffering in both worlds provokes the oneness of heaven and earth, and points to an eternal justice above both gods and humans. In this view, the hero is a 'great soul' who will always, inevitably, strive for what is highest. Prometheus is Dionysian as he strives to unite people, to bring together people and nature, but in doing this he also asserts his Apollonian individualism, his self-centredness. Our humanity is realised only in communion with the world and with people, but we can only reach this distant goal in moments of supreme self-awareness. This, Nietzsche insists, is why tragedy is ennobling, profound and moving.

Nietzsche's *The Birth of Tragedy* gave George Steiner (b. 1929) the title for his work on the subject: *The Death of Tragedy* (published in 1961). Arguing that tragedy depended on a metaphysical view of the world, Steiner suggested that modern rationalism, the result of work by scientific thinkers like Copernicus (1473–1543), Darwin (1809–82) and Freud (1856–1939) had destroyed the basis for true tragedy. We no longer believe in humanity's innate potential for greatness, more especially since the outrages of Nazism and Stalinism, and only the egotistical or the ignorant aspire to tragic status.

This view was countered by, among others, the American playwright Arthur Miller (1915–2005), who attempted to create in his plays heroes who could be called tragic. In Miller's words, each of his significant heroes was prepared to lay down his life to secure 'his sense of personal dignity'. Miller's heroes have an almost Nietzschean will to live, to achieve their humanity, and indeed there have been enough playwrights in the last 150 years to refute the pessimistic notion that tragedy is dead: Henrik Ibsen, Eugene O'Neill (1888–1953) and Federico Garcia Lorca (1898–1936) are three significant modern tragic playwrights.

Tragedy is, perhaps, the supreme philosophical dramatic form. It asks, Why we are here? What is the point of life in a corrupt and corrupting world? Does death have significance? Does suffering bring wisdom? Can we – or should we – challenge Fate? Are we free?

COMEDY

> All tragedies are finished by a death,
> All comedies are ended by a marriage.

So wrote Lord Byron (1788–1824) in *Don Juan*, and although this oversimplifies, it contains more than a grain of truth.

Like 'tragedy', the word 'comedy' in popular usage is not the same as it is when used as a critical term to describe a particular kind of play. Nevertheless in this case, the popular usage – that comedy is something that makes us laugh – may serve as a starting-point for our investigation, partly because comedy has no innovative observer–critic to perform the function Aristotle performed for tragedy; partly also because humans are the only animals which do laugh.

Perhaps the nearest to an Aristotle which comedy can boast is the French philosopher Henri Bergson (1859–1941), whose short monograph, *Laughter*, proved immensely influential. Bergson's thesis was that laughter evolved as a corrective to regulate and order social life. We find those who fail to adapt to the demands of society laughable, because they lack the flexibility which is a sign of human intelligence. The failure to adapt makes them appear mechanical, and the laughter this provokes stimulates them to change their ways. From this developed his idea, often quoted, that the comic is 'something mechanical encrusted on the living'. Thus, a person who is marching mechanically along, eyes front, fails to notice a banana skin in their path. They tread on it and crash to the pavement. This makes us laugh.

But this, of course, raises problems. When a person slips on a banana skin, is it funny or is it actually sad, or upsetting? Is laughter a healthy response to the follies of life, or is it cruel, vicious, uncaring of those who suffer the buffets of fortune? Will someone really reform their walking style because they have slipped on a banana skin? It is sometimes argued that laughter is the only sane reaction to the depressing materialism of modern life, or the capricious whims of cruel fate; equally, it is said that laughter in the face of modern existence is irresponsible and trivialising, that we must face our fate with stoicism and determination, not laugh in its face. Sensibilities change: our ancestors of not so long ago went to the 'lunatic asylum', Bedlam, to laugh at the inmates, whereas today compassion is a more likely response to people with mental disabilities.

This suggests that there are different kinds of laughter. One kind derives from our sense of social responsibility, or our belief in the necessity of good order: we laugh when people contravene the proprieties. This can be as simple as when we see the double meaning in a pun, part of the laughter deriving from the fact that we are pleased with ourselves for 'getting the joke'. It makes us feel superior. This accounts for at least part of our relish of the relationship between Beatrice and Benedick in *Much Ado About Nothing*, which depends on puns and other forms of wit for much of its fun. Laughing because we understand the joke is not unlike laughing at satire, which holds up the follies or vices of humankind for our ridicule. Characters like Corvino, Corbaccio and Voltore in *Volpone* by Ben Jonson (1572–1637), who circle like vultures round the bed of the apparently-dying Volpone, amuse us because their actions are contemptible, beneath us. Our seemingly objective overview makes us feel superior. They contravene the boundaries of propriety and are condemned in our laughter.

Such laughter may also be related to that provoked by the incongruous, which is also not far from Bergson's idea. *Much Ado About Nothing* provides us with an example of this, too: when Dogberry mangles language, we see what he means but cannot express. We are cleverer than he. In *As You Like It*, Audrey's marriage to Touchstone is comic because it, too, is clearly incongruous. And so is the absurdity of the pantomime horse – is it an animal, or two people? And what are two people doing under the blanket horse hide? Part of the laughter we may give vent to when we hear a dirty joke told by a vicar is similarly due to incongruity. But often the incongruity is only visible from a standpoint of accepted social morality, the morality which binds society together. The laughter may be cruel, but it is, at least in intent, corrective, as Bergson suggested. Consequently – and importantly – it is also intellectual. In other words, this comedy is provoked by the way we, as thinking beings, respond to the world, and human behaviour in the world, and how these relate to the social order. It attempts to teach through laughter: we see someone make a fool of themselves, and resolve not to behave like that. Philip Sidney wrote in 1580:

> comedy is an imitation of the common errors of our life, which he [the playwright] representeth in the most ridiculous and scornful sort that may be, so as it is impossible that any beholder can be content to be such a one.
>
> (Sir Philip Sidney, *An Apologie for Poetry*)

Many of the greatest writers of comedy – Jonson, Molière (1622–73), Congreve (1670–1729), Gogol (1809–52) – should be seen as moral instructors, and in their work those who are ridiculed, such as Volpone or Tartuffe, are also often punished. Meanwhile those who conform to social norms and expectations are rewarded, often with a spouse.

This suggests for these morally didactic comedies a structure which both is and is not like that of tragedy. Like tragedy, this kind of comedy moves perceptibly from a beginning (in Aristotle's sense), through a middle to a conclusion; but whereas the typical tragedy shows the fall of a good person from prosperity to disgrace or death, the typical comedy shows a journey in the opposite direction: while the immoral are brought low, the good person goes from ill fortune to prosperity. This is what Byron observed, and what Dante (1265–1321) asserted when he wrote that 'comedy introduces a situation of adversity, but ends its matter in prosperity'. It was this sense of appropriate structure which allowed him to call his epic poem, in which he journeys from Hell through Purgatory to Heaven, *The Divine Comedy*.

But there is another sort of laughter, associated with another sort of comedy, which must also be noticed. That is the laughter which we may call 'feeling' laughter. It is associated initially perhaps with release – release of tension, possibly, or release from the trammels of convention. The laughter the vicar's dirty joke provokes may also be recalled here, for this is, on one level, the laughter of release. Taken further, this is the laughter of 'carnival', as Bakhtin called it, and uses parody, non sequitur, interruption and similar devices to disrupt proceedings, turn hierarchy upside down, and celebrate community and a shared humanity. It demystifies official processes and attitudes, subverts gender roles and enjoys scatological, sexual and other forbidden or indiscreet behaviours. It is found in the snigger, the guffaw, the whoop of delight. Carnival is more than incongruous, for it glories in the 'grotesque'.

The comedy of carnival is also regenerative. It nourishes and renews. As such, it is beyond the kind of morality which prevails in ordered society, and which is at the heart of intellectual or satirical comedy. Carnival is carnivorous and carnal, it exalts red meat and liberated sex – and its typical emblem is the sausage! It turns the oppression of convention topsy-turvy, and encourages licence and excess.

Pieter Bruegel (1520–69) depicted Carnival as a fat, pork-guzzling glutton astride a barrel of beer and opposed by a skinny, fish-eating Lent, personifying fastidiousness and austerity. On stage, this battle finds perhaps its most compelling embodiment in the Italian *commedia dell'arte*. Here clown-servants best their right-thinking bourgeois masters, and young lovers defy their possessive and authoritarian parents to find whatever it is they want – usually sex, sometimes marriage. Shakespeare's comedies obviously have something in common with this, and *The Merchant of Venice* in particular is patterned like a *commedia* play. The miserly old Pantalone-like father, Shylock, loses his sexually excited daughter, Jessica; there is an absurdly self-possessed, ever-hungry and consistently-disobedient servant, Launcelot Gobbo, and much else.

The Merchant of Venice, like other Shakespearean comedies, ends in happy marriages (Portia and Bassanio, Nerissa and Gratiano, Jessica and Lorenzo) which signify reconciliation and a kind of harmony. Marriage, with its implicit hopes for children, is a promise for the future. But comedy is not always as simple as this; it also delights in illicit sex, perhaps especially in foolish husbands tricked by clever, scheming or witty wives, as in, for example, *The Country Wife* by William Wycherley (1641–1715). On one level *The Country Wife* may be understood as satire, but on another, perhaps deeper, level, it is a carnivalesque celebration of human sexuality. The ridiculous and ridiculously jealous husband in *The Country Wife* is a character found in comedies from the earliest Greek comedies to today – the cuckold. Are his exploits, and those of his wife, brought before us merely to teach marital fidelity? Or are they part of something much more subversive – the overthrow of ordered society?

Comedy's attitude to marriage is in fact dangerously ambiguous, and many comedies seem to endorse something like free love. As much as it understands the promise of marriage, comedy also frequently undermines it. Thus, in *As You Like It*, Touchstone's marriage to Audrey will, Jacques prophesies, be full of 'wrangling', since their 'loving voyage is but for two months victualed'. But getting married simultaneously are Orlando and Rosalind, perhaps Shakespeare's most brilliantly conceived and portrayed young lovers, and if any fictional marriage suggests investment in the future, this union is it.

So comedy celebrates those whose relationships are successful as well as those who make a mess of things. Sex, not marriage, is at its heart. Perhaps we can say that comedy celebrates sex – and sex of all kinds! According to Aristotle, comedy grew out of the phallic processions depicted on Greek vases. Men strapped great erect penises to their belts and rampaged through villages, getting exceedingly drunk and generally making mayhem wherever they went. This was the Dionysian rout, the worshippers of the god of wine who brought revelry and disorder to all, and whose life created and expended energy. They are still, perhaps, the embodiment of comedy's deepest urges.

Box 3.2: Ritual and ceremony

Ritual is a way of dealing with the natural but difficult processes of living, especially the 'big' moments in life, transitions involving our place in society and the making of relationships.

The performance of 'rites of passage' – weddings, bar mitzvahs, state openings of Parliament, etc. – moves us from one social position, one kind of relationship, to another. Smaller rituals – the footballer putting on his left boot before his right, the person taking the toothpaste cap off before picking up the toothbrush – seek to provide security, a settling effect. All rituals attempt to control the future.

Ritual is performative (see Chapter 1). Often using costume, choreographed movement, a scripted text, and more, rituals have structures from which their performance may not deviate, because it is in the performance that the ritual becomes effective. The priest places his hands on the suppliant's head, and the suppliant is blessed. The guests blow out the candles on the birthday cake, and the birthday child is recognised as one year older.

Any ritual therefore has a structure, and a function. Ceremony is very like ritual, in that it, too, has a structure, but it lacks a function, it has no real purpose beyond its own performance.

Nevertheless, both ritual and ceremony are like theatre, because not only do they welcome spectators, more importantly, they are both recognisable and evocative. Consequently, theatre uses them. They provide accessible ways of structuring action.

TRAGICOMEDY

In *An Apologie for Poetry*, Sir Philip Sidney deplored plays which

> be neither right tragedies, nor right comedies, mingling kings and clowns
> not because the matter so carrieth it, but thrust in clowns by head and
> shoulders, to play a part in majestical matters, with neither decency nor
> discretion, so as neither the admiration and commiseration, nor the
> right sportfulness is by their mongrel tragicomedy obtained.

Tragicomedy, argues Sidney, provides neither the *katharsis* ('admira-
tion and commiseration' is his version of 'fear and pity') appropriate
to tragedy, nor the energy, the warmth and jollity ('the right
sportfulness'), which comedy properly evokes. It is a form which is
ambivalent, elusive. Perhaps that is why it has (with epic drama,
perhaps) become a dominant form in our insecure age.

It seems that tragicomedy may take one of two forms. First, it
may set a series of contrasting scenes one after the other, a serious
scene following a comic one, another comic scene following that,
and so on. Or second, it may find a way of synthesising the comic
and the tragic, so that each is present simultaneously.

Tragicomedy was first theorised by the Italian writer Giovan
Battista Guarini (1538–1612), whose treatise on the subject
appeared in 1601. Comparing tragicomedy to an alloy, like bronze,
Guarini argued that tragicomedy fused two conventional forms,
tragedy and comedy, by taking something from each, and bringing
them together. From tragedy, he said, tragicomedy borrowed noble
characters, a believable plot line, and 'the danger, but not the
death'. From comedy, it took subject matter which dealt with private,
not public, affairs, complex plotting and a happy ending. In order
to define the objective of tragicomedy, Guarini paraphrased Aristotle:
its aim, he wrote, was to *purge* sadness or melancholy with delight.
Tragicomedy attempted to 'gladden our souls'.

John Fletcher (1579–1625), an English dramatist who was a
youthful contemporary of Guarini, was much influenced by these
ideas, and brought forward his own definition of the dramatic form
in which he made several attempts to write:

> A tragicomedy is not so called in respect of mirth and killing, but in
> respect it wants deaths, which is enough to make it no tragedy, yet

brings some near it, which is enough to make it no comedy, which must be a representation of familiar people, with such kind of trouble as no life be questioned; so that a god is as lawful in this as in a tragedy, and mean people as in a comedy.

(John Fletcher, *The Faithful Shepherdess*, preface)

Fletcher collaborated with Shakespeare on at least one play, but it was Shakespeare writing alone who created perhaps the most perfect tragicomedy according to this definition, in *The Tempest*. Onto Prospero's island are brought a group of people of all classes from his native Milan. Indeed, their leader has usurped Prospero's place as the Duke of Milan, and banished Prospero and his daughter to this island. Now Prospero hopes to end their quarrel. But soon the duke and his courtiers are plotting against Prospero's life. This plot, foiled only at the last moment, exemplifies the idea of danger but not death. Meanwhile, Ferdinand and Miranda, Prospero's daughter, have fallen in love, but there are of course obstacles in their path to the happy ending. And a couple of drunken clowns get up to a series of slapstick adventures with Prospero's monster-like servant, Caliban. The deities Juno, Ceres and Iris appear, and the final reconciliation takes place in a magic circle drawn by Prospero.

In *The Tempest*, the ingredients of tragedy and comedy are not so much mixed as set side by side. A romantic scene involving Miranda and Ferdinand is followed by a 'serious' scene of the courtiers plotting, which is followed by a scene for the clown characters, Trinculo and Stephano. If we were feeling sad, *The Tempest* would perhaps purge our sadness with delight.

But perhaps such purgation is equally likely to occur in the rather different tragicomedies of Anton Chekhov, who honed a form to which many later dramatists have aspired, for Chekhov's tragicomedy does indeed fuse sadness with laughter, sportful guffaws with bitterness and anguish, simultaneously.

The Seagull is the earliest of Chekhov's plays to achieve this, and is still unusual as tragicomedy for two particular reasons: first, because the play ends in a death, and second, because the author himself called it a 'comedy'. It might be argued that *The Cherry Orchard*, for example, is a more precise example of a Chekhovian tragicomedy, but *The Seagull* probably demonstrates the form more vividly.

The tragic elements in *The Seagull* centre on the characters' lives. Treplev's love affair is doomed, and he eventually commits suicide. Nina learns through bitter suffering. Arkadina's lonely, empty life is dependent on Trigorin, Polena is trapped in a loveless marriage and loves Dorn hopelessly, and Masha, too, loves hopelessly, a situation she tries to escape by marrying the shallow schoolmaster, Medvedenko. He is clearly exploited, and though he marries the woman he wants to marry, the union is an utter failure. Trigorin is soulless, and Shamrayev hardly recognises his own irrelevance. All this is at the very least potentially tragic.

Yet the play itself is unquenchably comic. These people are ridiculous, absurd. They behave almost like clowns! And this behaviour actually uplifts our spirits, enhances our life experience. For example, Nina does triumph, in spite of all. Trigorin continues to write, which is what he wants. Arkadina will continue to act. If we take these people too seriously we will be in danger of missing the point, for *The Seagull* invites us to rejoice in and celebrate the variety and the vitality of human life. It is a kind of divine comedy! Comedy is, as has been implied above, energetic, and the characters in *The Seagull* are exceedingly energetic.

It is also worth noting that the people of the play are most ridiculous, and therefore most comic, when they take themselves most seriously, that is, when they are approaching the tragic. For instance, Konstantin's absurd play, which he thinks of as a new manifestation of art, is surely pretentious bosh. Nina imagines that Trigorin is some kind of genius, when in fact he is little more than a hack writer churning out stories for cheap magazines. At these moments, Chekhov manages to find a way of intensifying the tragic and the comic *at the same time*.

This is the height of tragicomedy, and it is behind much of the most fascinating drama of the following hundred and more years: Nobel prize-winning dramatists Samuel Beckett and Harold Pinter are just two of those owing a significant debt to Chekhov.

EPIC

Epic is perhaps the oldest form of literature. The first epics were long songs sung by bards partly to entertain the court or praise the king, but more importantly to provide understanding for just why this king and this people were significant, or even great. Such songs were based in history; indeed in societies which had no writing, epic songs were the only way of retaining the community's history. How accurate they were as such may be questioned. Examples of such epics are the *Iliad*, which describes the long, horrific war from which emerged the victorious Greek people; and the *Odyssey*, dealing with Odysseus' long, difficult journey home after the Trojan War to begin a new, better life. These subjects – war, a journey, a hero – are typical of epic. They justify, or attempt to explain, the origins and purpose of the community to which they refer.

The earliest epic dramas of Western Europe are the medieval mystery cycles, which flourished between about 1300 and 1600. In Britain, there were notable cycles in cities including Chester, Coventry, York and Norwich, and in each of these, the cycle lasted all day. They dramatised the biblical view of world history from the creation of heaven and earth and the fall of Lucifer, through the Old Testament, Jesus' nativity and life, his passion, crucifixion and resurrection, and on to the final judgment day. Thus they justified Christianity. Each episode formed a different play, so there were plays of Adam and Eve, of Cain's murder of Abel, of Abraham and Isaac, and so on. Each playlet lasted perhaps a quarter or half an hour, and each was performed by a different group of people, often the men of a particular trade guild.

In York and Chester, and perhaps elsewhere, the plays were performed from large carts, known as *pagenta*, from which derives our word, 'pageant'. Each cart travelled from one 'station' to the next, stopping to perform the play at each of the different six or eight stations. For the spectator who stayed in one place, therefore, the procession of carts created the whole story of the Bible. The cycle as a whole explained the Christian community of which the spectator was a part. It was effectively the history of Christendom, and showed how we could emerge from the ongoing fight against Satan to reach eternal paradise, depicted at the end of the Dooms-day play, the finale to the whole cycle.

Later, in the Renaissance, epic drama took a more obviously historical shape in history, or chronicle, plays, such as the series created by Shakespeare. The purpose of these was to explain why Tudor Britain was what the Elizabethans conceived it to be – glorious and admirable. The plays showed how out of the turmoil and horror of the Hundred Years War and the bloody Wars of the Roses, the blissfully peaceful and glorious time of the Tudors was born. The rhetoric in *Henry V*, for example, with its references especially to England, is unmistakeable.

With the break-up of the old settled communities by the Industrial Revolution from the mid-eighteenth century onwards, there arose for everyone the problem of how to relate to fractured communities. Romantic epic drama addresses this search for community, either through the stories of sensitive, perhaps heroic, outsiders, as in *Faust* by Johann Wolfgang Goethe (1749–1832) and *Brand* and *Peer Gynt* by Henrik Ibsen, or else through a reaching back to mythical pasts in which community had a mystic significance, as in the *Ring* cycle of Richard Wagner (1813–83) or the Cuchulain plays of W. B. Yeats (1865–1939).

In the middle of the nineteenth century, Karl Marx (1818–83) proposed a different kind of community, neither religious nor national, but based on class. What defined people as social animals, Marx suggested, was their class identity. Believing that the history of the world was the history of the struggle between the classes, he asserted that it was the destiny of the working class to lead society into the future. In consequence of this, and especially after the 1917 Russian Revolution, a new kind of epic drama was created. *Mystery Bouffe* by Vladimir Mayakovsky (1893–1930) dramatised the Revolution as a cross between a mystery play and a comic opera, while *I Want a Baby* by Sergei Tretyakov (1892–1937) questioned genetics as a way towards classless communism.

It is worth noting that these early twentieth-century epic plays, unlike earlier epic dramas, adopted a specifically Marxist standpoint: they no longer simply tried to *explain* the past, they aimed also to seek out the future, especially as it bore upon the structures of class. German epic writers developed this epic form, most notably Ernst Toller (1893–1939) in plays like *Hopla! We're Alive!* and Bertolt Brecht in a series of epic plays, including *Man Equals Man*, *Mother Courage and Her Children*, *The Good Person of Szechuan* and *The Caucasian Chalk Circle*. Brecht also developed a series of theatrical techniques designed to 'alienate' audiences, that is, not to put them off the theatre, but to prevent them from identifying with the central character, and to suggest that what seems eternal is actually mutable. His aim was to make each spectator think about the public problems which his play addressed. For Brecht, *katharsis* was epic theatre's worst enemy. His guiding principle was interruption, breaking the flow of things which encourage us to identify with the protagonist and lull us into acquiescence. To achieve this, Brecht developed a whole system of presentational devices, including bright lighting from visible lamps, a bare stage, the use of placards, songs and much more. Most significant, perhaps, were Brecht's ideas about acting in epic theatre, and these are discussed in more detail in Chapter 5. In Britain, *Johnny Noble* by Ewan MacColl (1915–89) and *Oh What a Lovely War*, created by the Theatre Workshop of Joan Littlewood, provided an epic theatre whose refocusing of British history from a class point of view led by implication towards a different future.

It is worth noticing that attempts to create naturalistic epics have been largely unsuccessful. The Dublin trilogy (*Shadow of a Gunman*, *Juno and the Paycock* and *The Plough and the Stars*) of Sean O'Casey (1880–1964), and Arnold Wesker's (b. 1932) trilogy (*Chicken Soup with Barley*, *Roots* and *I'm Talking About Jerusalem*) may both make for superb family drama, but cannot find a way of relating families to public events: in *The Plough and the Stars*, Padraig Pearse (1879–1916) is no more than a 'tall, dark figure silhouetted against a window', while in *Chicken Soup with Barley* the Battle of Cable Street happens offstage and the Hungarian Uprising of 1956 is a very distant echo.

Even as MacColl's and Littlewood's epics were being created, communism was being revealed as oppressive and repellent. Surely the future did not lie here. As the progressive consensus broke down, different kinds of epic theatre created alternative narratives of our social life from new viewpoints. For example, the end of the British empire provoked a number of 'post-colonialist' epics, such as John Arden and Margaretta D'Arcy's treatment of the King Arthur story in *The Island of the Mighty*, and their six-play re-examination of Ireland's bid for independence in *The Non-Stop Connolly Show*; John McGrath (1935–2002) reinterpreted Scotland's history in *The Cheviot, the Stag and the Black Black Oil*, and Howard Brenton (b. 1942) dramatised colonial oppression, again with direct reference to Ireland, in *The Romans in Britain*. From a feminist perspective, Caryl Churchill created *Vinegar Tom* and *The Skriker*, while from the USA came a two-part epic about the gay community, *Angels in America*, by Tony Kushner (b. 1956).

From all these examples, it is possible to show how epic drama has always been characterised by public concerns: its issues are not private, nor indeed are they social in the usual sense. They are political in a fundamental way, addressing the problem of how we shape our community. Their typical features include largeness of size and scale; frequent use of meta-theatrical devices, such as a narrator, songs, and so on; a hero who tends to be representative, and therefore not particularly interesting as an individual; and a structure which tends to be episodic, relying on fable, montage and gesture for its effect. Twentieth-century epics especially often have open endings, and employ Brechtian alienation techniques, so that spectators are encouraged to consider the issues rationally.

DOCUMENTARY AND AGITPROP

The revolution in Russia in 1917 threw up many strange new artistic forms; in theatre, documentary and agitprop were notable examples, and each owes something to epic theatre.

Most Russian workers and peasants in 1917 were unable to read, but the new authorities needed their support, which would not be forthcoming if they knew nothing of the political upheavals occurring. The first documentaries, therefore, were 'living news-papers', when actors dramatised the news for the benefit of illiterate peasants. The shows were structured like newspapers, with editor-ials (monologues), news items (dramatic sketches), cartoons (clowning), entertainment features (songs and dances), and so on. The political motivation was clear from the start, and the form spread among radical and politically-motivated theatre makers, including the German director Erwin Piscator (1893–1966), the American Federal Theater Project of the 1930s, and Unity Theatre and Theatre Workshop in Britain in the 1930s and 1940s.

These groups usually maintained the political slant and frag-mented structure of the living newspapers, but later documentary play makers sought a more objective 'theatre of fact', such as the original musical documentaries created at the Stoke-on-Trent Victoria Theatre by Peter Cheeseman (1932–2010) between 1964 and 1987. His insistence on the use only of 'primary source material', which included songs, and on the show's creation by the company through an extended rehearsal period, made these historical documentaries a uniquely pure form of the genre.

In the 1990s and 2000s, the form was further developed in Britain, especially by Richard Norton-Taylor (b. 1944), whose *Called to Account*, an indictment of the British prime minister Tony Blair, 'for the crime of aggression against Iraq', took the form of a 'hearing' with councils for the prosecution and the defence, and witnesses giving evidence as in a court of law. The play may be politically-motivated but it uses only what was said in a series of actual interviews by real lawyers in specific offices in London in early 2007. This produced some twenty-eight hours of testimony, which was then edited down by Norton-Taylor to approximately two hours of drama. In performance, actors played the parts of the lawyers, and of the witnesses, who knew their contributions might be used in this way when they were originally interviewed. Other successful examples of the use of edited transcripts of trials or enquiries to create documentary dramas include *The Colour of Justice*, about the Stephen Lawrence murder case, and *The Hutton Inquiry*, about the original Anglo-American invasion of Iraq.

Most documentary dramas, such as these, aim to punch home a political point. This is also agitprop drama's basic *raison d'être*. Agitprop, though resembling the living newspaper in its employment of a mix of sketches, songs, clowning, monologues, and so on, was even more overtly political than the latter. Developed at the same time as living newspapers in the infant Soviet Union, and supported by the Soviet Department of Agitation and Propaganda, agitprop's propaganda aimed to change opinion into support for the Soviet regime, and its agitation aimed to rouse the spectator into political action. Theatres of 'Revolutionary Satire', '*Proletkult*' (proletarian culture) amateur groups, and workshops of communist drama proliferated and took their message across Russia with missionary-like zeal in the early revolutionary years. Later in the 1920s, the Blue Blouse group toured Europe, astounding political activists and theatre radicals alike, and having particular effect on the development of German street theatre groups. But agitprop flourished all across Europe for a few years, including in Britain in the Workers Theatre Movement. It made something of a comeback, too, in the 1960s and 1970s, not only in Britain and some other parts of Europe, but in China during the 'Cultural Revolution'.

It is worth noting that some apparently more conventional plays derive power from their relationship to documentary and agitprop, yet one would hesitate to classify them as such. For example, *Black Watch* by Gregory Burke (b. 1968) dramatises the facts of the deployment of the Scottish Black Watch regiment to Iraq shortly before it was subsumed into the Royal Regiment of Scotland, and also recalls the Black Watch's long history. But it relies not so much on the factual evidence for its effect, as on the visceral fear and horror of real war which it conjures up. It is a throat-gripping drama lived absolutely in the minute.

On the other hand, Theatre Uncut mounts short playlets about specific political or social matters from a deliberately partisan view-point. Theatre Uncut has strong international and beyond-theatre dimensions – it presents shows across the world, from Brazil to Canada, and in theatres and living rooms, on the streets and in community halls – and is a kind of theatrical rapid rebuttal unit. Thus, in 2012, Theatre Uncut produced plays about the Greek economic crisis, about local library funding cuts, about the 'naked rambler' and much more. Moreover these plays are for anyone to perform and any other groups are encouraged to produce them free of copyright fees. Theatre Uncut's website is worth visiting: www. theatreuncut.com

FARCE

Farce is a kind of comedy without serious intent. It is comedy with no moral or didactic purpose. Though as old as any form of drama, farce relies on energy – slapstick, buffoonery, complicated and compromising situations, plotting and scheming characters, rapid action and bawdry – for its success. Many farces deal with extra-marital relationships, cuckolded husbands and tricksters tricked, but its horseplay has little relevance beyond itself. It is largely ephem-eral, though it has provided much theatrical pleasure to audiences of all classes and at all times. Preposterous and boisterous, farce may lack subtlety perhaps because it is a performance, not a literary, genre.

As implied, few farces survive the test of time, though the anonymous medieval French farce of *Maitre Pierre Pathelin* seems to be an exception. The French farceur Georges Feydeau (1862–1921) is often held up as the greatest writer of farce, and indeed at least some of his plays have lasted in the repertoire till the twenty-first century. Notable British farces include *Box and Cox* by John Maddison Morton (1811–91), *Charley's Aunt* by Brandon Thomas (1850–1914), and, more recently, work by Joe Orton (1933–67), Alan Ayckbourn (b. 1939) and Michael Frayn (b. 1933).

MELODRAMA

Melodrama, which means drama with music, dates from late eighteenth-century France, where it expressed something of the French Revolution. Poverty's kinship with virtue and wealth's with villainy are certainly values the form shares with the revolutionaries.

But melodrama may perhaps best be seen as tragedy without a philosophical dimension. Because it was popular during the nineteenth century, when theatre buildings were becoming ever more huge, it has become associated with exaggeration, and the adjective 'melodramatic' is often applied pejoratively to excessive emotion on stage, over-literary dialogue, and hyperbolical gestures. Melodramas used all these, as well as pictorial tableaux, stock characters and spectacular scenic effects. But some of these characteristics may have had more to do with nineteenth-century theatre architecture than with this dramatic form *per se*.

In fact, like tragedy, melodrama almost always deals with domestic situations and private emotions, and the 'melodramatic' trappings are in a sense extraneous to it. In essence, melodrama is probably closer to contemporary television soap operas.

The music which accompanies melodrama intensifies the emotional effect, and it is the emotional effect which makes melodrama unique. Its plots steer swiftly through crime, sex, desire and fear, like dreams or fantasy, and afterwards our pleasure may be hard to justify. What is important is the journey, the emotion as it happens, not the ending. Indeed, some severe critics have scoffed at melodrama's 'happy endings' (though in fact plenty of melodramas have unhappy endings), without understanding its essential dream-like nature.

The greatest melodramatist of the nineteenth century was probably Dion Boucicault (1820–90), famous for his 'sensation scenes', whose best plays, *Arragh-na-Pogue*, *The Colleen Bawn* and *The Shaughraun*, are still revived from time to time.

THE WELL-MADE PLAY

The 'well-made play' (*pièce bien faite*) was developed by the extremely prolific French dramatist, Eugène Scribe (1791–1861). It has no didactic or philosophical purpose, but concentrates on unwinding its plot according to a clear formula. It has five parts: (1) exposition; (2) complication and development; (3) crisis; (4) denouement; (5) resolution. The well-made play tends also to employ dramatic curtain lines to create suspense. Used by many nineteenth-century French dramatists, such as Eugène Labiche (1815–88) and Victorien Sardou (1831–1908), the well-made play continues to provide the basic structure for many successful plays into the twenty-first century.

DRAMATIC FORM DECONSTRUCTED

The French philosopher and critic Jacques Derrida developed the notion of 'deconstruction' which, among other things, suggested the fallibility, indeed the folly, of categorisation. This throws into question the very basis of traditional critical approaches. On the other hand, Derrida's approach has led to a spurt of new, challenging drama, which if it does not coalesce into a 'form' ('postmodernist drama', perhaps), provides nourishment for anyone thinking about problems of form.

Samuel Beckett's playfully entitled *Play* shows three cadavers, or maybe ghosts, in funerary urns arguing about what they did – or what they performed – in life. This is anything but 'play', however playfully presented. Is it a play? It clearly confutes the 'reality' of the corpse in its urn with the live-ness of the actor. It raises the crucial question of where the boundary between action and performance lies, and how we separate real life from the performance of life.

Other plays equally challenge accepted critical ideas. *Rosencrantz and Guildenstern Are Dead* by Tom Stoppard superimposes minor characters on a great tragedy which is happening offstage. The same author's *Travesties* conflates the contradictory worlds of Dadaism, James Joyce's (1882–1941) experiments with the novel form, and ideas for a communist revolution within a structure determined by the leading character's faulty memory and Oscar Wilde's (1854–1900) *The Importance of Being Earnest*. Repetition, contradiction, irony and the undermining of all expectations are the strategies of these plays. The viewpoint presented is constantly shifting, appearance is confused with performance and reality with the performative.

Time, too, loses its accustomed shape. In Caryl Churchill's *Top Girls* and Harold Pinter's *Betrayal*, it goes backwards. In Churchill's *Cloud Nine*, a century takes – oddly – twenty-five years.

Augusto Boal's (1931–2009) anti-Aristotelianism led to his concept of the 'spectactor' (see the section 'Forum theatre' in Chapter 8, p. 188) and Peter Handke (b. 1942) even wrote a play called *Offending the Audience*. Here, a super-normal theatrical situation is set up ('The usual theatre atmosphere should prevail. The ushers should be more assiduous than usual.'), only for the performers, whoever they are – and this is not made evident – to attempt to deny any theatrical reality at all: 'Time is not cut off from the outside world here. There are no two levels of time here. While we are here the earth continues to turn. Our time up here is your time down there.' The audience is acknowledged ('We are not pretending that you don't exist') and the drama admits its non-dramaness. Not only has dramatic form become impossible, the whole basis upon which drama persists is undermined. Dramatic form is an illusion, because drama only explores – and negates – drama itself. 'You have recognised that we primarily negate.'

So a new kind of play emerges, drama as performance material. Martin Crimp (b. 1956) calls for 'each scenario in words – the dialogue – (to) unfold against a distinct world – a design – which best exposes its irony'. Crimp's own plays, and others like *4.48 Psychosis* by Sarah Kane (1971–99) are literally no more than sequences of words, with no speakers identified. These works are teasing, unstable, ironic and self-reflexive. The drama is an exploration in which the audience must make the meanings.

Perhaps the most compelling postmodernist drama (for want of a better categorisation) is *Hamletmachine* by Heiner Müller. This sequence of images in five parts (like the five acts of a Shakespearean tragedy) may or may not conjure Shakespeare's play. Ophelia does a striptease, Hamlet himself suggests that his 'place', if his drama 'would still happen, would be on both sides of the front, between the frontlines, over and above them.' The fact that Müller was living in the totalitarian East Germany of the post-war period may or may not be relevant to our comprehension.

And this is the point. This text has connotations rather than meanings in the old-fashioned sense. Its questions concern the relationship between text and performer, the function of rehearsal, and so on – matters of significance even before performance is reached.

Hamletmachine is very short, its speakers are usually not named, its action is unclear – has Ophelia really drowned herself? Why does 'The Actor Playing Hamlet' say, 'I'm not Hamlet. I don't take part any more'? The text needs the creative input of actors, as well as the imagination of audiences. Heiner Müller appears to be only half serious – or he is at least half serious. This makes his play extremely disconcerting. Is *Hamletmachine* merely a playful fantasy? 'Merely'? Hamlet's crisis of identity becomes the crisis of performance.

And this crisis is at the heart of much 'postmodern' theatre. Forced Entertainment's collaboratively-made presentations, for instance, included *Club of No Regrets* which was 'a layering of diverse voices, actions and objects ... We are catching things not from the point of view of focus but from the corner of the eye', they claimed. They drew on music, fine art, cinema, science fiction, photography, graffiti, street life and more, and they created video installations, internet projects and CD-ROMs as well as site-specific works and children's events.

DIGITAL PERFORMANCE

Much of Forced Entertainment's work, as well as that of other recent companies and practitioners, leads towards digital performance, in which computer technologies have become increasingly important in live performance. They point to a new performance relationship, one between performer and screens on which are projected digitally-manipulated images. At its simplest this might entail a modern dress *Julius Caesar* with, say, Mark Antony's address to the Roman people ('Friends, Romans, countrymen') as a sort of television party political broadcast. But digital performance goes much further than this.

Contemporary theatre has often incorporated digitally-created and manipulated projections, and this may lead to virtual reality performances or performances which are accessed through computer screens. This opens a world of performance hitherto undreamed of. Notably, the possibility of interaction through the computer effectively undermines all previously-held ideas of theatre and performance. Steve Dixon has argued that 'The world wide web is a site of therapeutic-cathartic-overload (which) constitutes the largest theatre in the world'. He points out that almost every action of the computer networks can be seen as performative, including Facebook, personal blogs and the web itself. Here is a vast new spectrum of 'live' performance.

There are already in existence software systems which enable directors and choreographers to use desktop applications to create 'real' performances with the use of computer animation, motion tracking systems and so on. This inevitably raises questions about the relationship of the 'real' body to the 'virtual' body, and of 'real' space to 'virtual' space. The computer easily creates 'digital doubles', exploring in its own terms problems of identity, including mirror reflections, the *alter ego*, the *doppelganger* and so on. Hans-Thies Lehmann (b. 1944) describes *Mare's Nest*, a performance by Station House Opera in which there was

> An ingenious and complex stage setup of two back-to-back video screens, each with a platform and stairs leading up to it and a door through it. The performance consisted of a mix of filmed and live action, so that four people ... and 'their life size doubles inhabit a real and imaginary, half-physical and half-virtual space, often occupying both at once'. In addition the virtual room created on screen was populated by fantasy figures ... that had been filmed near the actual theatre location, thus further confusing the real and the imaginary. The spectators were free to position themselves wherever they wished around this setup and to take in whatever they could or chose to take in. Thus, everyone created their own narrative through the performance but no one was ever able to totalize it.
>
> (Hans-Thies Lehmann, *Postdramatic Theatre*, trans. by Karen Juers-Munby, London: Routledge, 2006, pp.12–13.)

This conflation of stage space and virtual space leads on to the computer's unique potential for interactivity. Via the computer, an artist can make the beginnings of an interactive story which the individual spectator can then change, move on, spoil as she wishes.

The work itself is taken over by the audience. And this brings us inevitably to the video game, 'the most prolific and dramatically effective form of "popular theatre" of the contemporary age'. Indeed the parallels between drama and the computer game are often striking and even disconcerting.

Are we witnessing here the birth of a new form of drama or theatre? Can digitally manipulated drama ever replace 'the smell of the greasepaint, the roar of the crowd'? These questions may become more urgent as time proceeds; but future generations may contemplate them with considerably less surprise – and even alarm – than they seem to arouse today.

POSTDRAMATIC THEATRE

The last two sections of this chapter have considered what has come to be called 'postdramatic theatre'. This has been theorised by the German critic and scholar, Hans-Thies Lehmann. Taking the 1970s as the time when text-based culture, the culture of traditional forms, finally gave way to a pervasive mediatised culture, Lehmann argues that traditional forms of theatre and drama no longer meet the artistic requirements of the age. He examines work by theatre artists already mentioned here, including Heiner Müller, Suzan-Lori Parks and Sarah Kane, Forced Entertainment and Station Opera House, as well as others like Elfriede Jelinek (b. 1946) and Fluxus, to define this new form.

He notes that the prefix 'post' here refers less to after-time than to a rupture with what went before. The form, as he explains it, downgrades the text as such so that performance becomes, not an illustration of a written drama, but a thing in itself, *performance as performance*. Rejecting narrative, postdramatic theatre gives us 'more presence than representation, more shared than communicated experience, more process than product, more manifestation than signification, more energetic impulse than information' (Hans-Thies Lehmann, *Postdramatic Theatre*, p.85).

Lehmann suggests the typical features of conventional dramatic theatre are replaced in postdramatic theatre language by what Elfriede Jelinek calls 'language surfaces' and action by 'states'. Postdramatic theatre deliberately eschews narrative in order to present us with a series of 'dynamic formations'. He notes how many practitioners of postdramatic theatre started out as visual artists, so that it is not surprising that postdramatic theatre often presents human beings as 'gestic sculptures'. He argues that whereas in written drama, the matter in hand proceeds *between* bodies, here it occurs *with/on/to* the body. Thus, postdramatic theatre valorises the moment for itself.

In all this, the spectator's expectations are consistently frustrated or destabilised. The performance relates to the world: Tim Etchells says that Forced Entertainment was trying 'to discuss the concerns of the times', but, he continues, 'in a language born out of them' – that is, not the conventional dramatic language forged centuries earlier. Lehmann describes a performance by Squat Theatre in which 'the audience was placed in a shop with large shop windows, the performers combining their presentation of spoken text with all sorts of activities while another audience curiously observed actors and audience through the shop windows from the street'.

The characteristics which Lehmann isolates as typical of postdramatic theatre include: *parataxis*, that is, placing incidents, episodes, moments of the performance side by side, giving each equal weight, and refusing to point out significances; *simultaneity*, which is the temporal equivalent of parataxis; *musicalisation* of speech, dramatic rhythm and sound; *scenography*, that is, the visual dramaturgy (Lehmann suggests one new kind of text may be 'the text of the staging and *mise-en-scène*'); *physicality*, the vibrancy of the performer's physical presence as such; and the *irruption of the real*, which signifies the consistent intrusion of reality into the performance, and the refusal to inhabit a purely fictionalised world.

By traits such as these – the 'palette of stylistic traits' in Lehmann's phrase – postdramatic theatre is recognisable, and through them it may be seen as a completely new, autonomous dramatic form.

Summary

- Tragedy is a drama which usually shows the protagonist's fall from good fortune to bad. According to Aristotle, tragedy produces *katharsis* – a form of spiritual purification – in the spectator.
- Nietzsche's theory of tragedy centres on a Promethean hero who unites the individualism of Apollo with the sociability of Dionysus.
- Bergson suggested that laughter was stimulated by 'something mechanical encrusted on the living'.

- Comedy either attempts to reform manners through ridicule or celebrates life through energetic licence.
- Tragicomedy mixes the tragic and the comic in a single drama.
- Epic theatre focuses on the social and political dimensions of community, and how the individual relates to that.
- Documentary and agitprop theatre are usually politically-motivated and derive from epic theatre.
- Farce and melodrama are forms of comedy and tragedy without the serious intent of these.
- Some contemporary critics and dramatists have virtually succeeded in destroying notions of dramatic form, thereby undermining traditional critical approaches.
- Digital performance has opened a vast new field for theatre and drama.

FURTHER READING

The most sensible reading about dramatic form is found in the work of original theorists: Aristotle's *Poetics*, translated by Malcolm Heath (Harmondsworth: Penguin, 1996), Henri Bergson's *Laughter*, probably most easily accessed in Comedy: 'An Essay on Comedy' by George Meredith, 'Laughter' by Henri Bergson and 'The Meaning of Comedy' by Wylie Sypher (New York: Doubleday, 1956 and later editions), and *Brecht on Theatre*, edited by John Willett (London: Methuen, 1964 and later editions). Walter Benjamin, *Understanding Brecht* (London: NLB, 1973) is also recommended.

Forced Entertainment's work is described in Tim Etchells, *Certain Fragments* (London: Routledge, 1999). The most comprehensive account of digital performance is Steve Dixon, *Digital Performance: A History of New Media in Theater, Dance, Performance Art and Installation* (Cambridge, Mass: MIT Press, 2007). The very latest developments in performance are theorised in Hans-Thies Lehmann, *Postdramatic Theatre* (London: Routledge, 2006).

Some plays to read: for tragedy, Sophocles, *Oedipus the King*. Two plays from the 1890s represent the two strands of comedy: Oscar Wilde, *The Importance of Being Earnest* is a brilliant satire on social manners and customs, while Alfred Jarry's (1873–1907) *Ubu*

Roi is a carnivalesque riot which has subtle echoes of Sophocles' stern tragedy. For epic theatre, the plays of Bertolt Brecht are the obvious choice, either *Mother Courage and Her Children* or *The Caucasian Chalk Circle*. William Shakespeare's *The Tempest* and Anton Chekhov's *The Seagull* are superb examples of contrasting types of tragicomedy. Contemporary plays mentioned here include: Gregory Burke, *Black Watch* (London: Faber & Faber, 2007) and Heiner Müller, *Hamletmachine* (New York, PAJ Books, 1984).

4

THEATRE AND HISTORY

THE NECESSITY OF HISTORY

Nothing is more ephemeral than theatre. Last night's show has vanished almost as if it had never been. True, the costumes are gathering dust in the wardrobe, there are a few photographs in ageing scrapbooks and a yellowing poster or two with their corners curling over: but not much else beyond memories.

Yet if our present is to mean anything to us, we must know about how we arrived here. If you don't understand what happened yesterday, you will not be able to understand today. And in living, as someone has pointed out, we all operate as historians all the time: we try to understand what has happened in our own lives so that we can make sensible choices about the present and the future for ourselves. The same holds good for the theatre. We need to make sense of the past.

Theatre history, therefore, first and foremost explains what theatre is at the moment. It is worth studying in order to understand better how theatre speaks. Theatre interprets and images human experience: the theatre historian scrutinises how it does this so that not only will old plays be adequately appreciated, but – more importantly – so we can learn from our forbears and thereby make better theatre ourselves. More than that, theatre history attempts to stimulate appreciation of the special qualities of the theatrical event, and illuminates the relationship between that event and the wider world within which it happens.

Michel Foucault (1926–84) urged that we should describe the present by analysing the forces which have created it. Following Nietzsche, he called this the 'genealogy' of our time. The questions such an approach would seem to demand of theatre include, What is theatre for? How does it intervene in reality? What is dependent on it, or what does it depend on? Though questions like these can hardly be answered in a chapter – or a book – like the present one, nevertheless some of the things said below may begin to address such problems.

Perhaps the first thing to say about history is that it is usually recorded through narrative. Narrative seems to be a way of thinking which is inherent in the way the human mind works. We explain things through narrative (X annoyed Y, so Y got angry and threw a stone which went through the window. The homeowner appeared and chased X and Y down the road …), which is why history is usually presented in such a mode. The problem is that an historical event, or even what happened between X, Y and the homeowner, is not in fact a story: we tell it as if it was in order to be able to grasp it. The historian is on one level a teller of tales, like a dramatist. Narrative gives meaning to events, but there are dangers in this, as will become apparent later in this chapter. For now the comparison between historian and dramatist is worth pursuing, for both create narratives to explain cultural, political, even psychological realities. But how they tell the story is central to each of their projects, as a glance at a historical drama such as *King Johan* by John Bale (1495–1563) will demonstrate.

Box 4.1: *King Johan*: rewriting history

One reason for examining theatre history is that theatre itself has proved a particularly powerful vehicle for challenging accepted versions of history. Examples of this from the twentieth century include Bertolt Brecht's *Mother Courage and Her Children*, which effectively confronted conventional interpretations of German history, which saw the Thirty Years War as the seedbed of benevolent capitalism, as well as the beginning of Germany's ability to take its place as a leader of nations. This interpretation seemed to justify Bismark, the First World War and even Hitlerism, but was effectively demolished by Brecht's insistence that the Thirty Years War actually demonstrated the German love of violence, and that in fact it had helped only the rich, leaving the less well-off victims of oppression not rectified for centuries. A second example is *Oh What a Lovely War*, created by Joan Littlewood and her Theatre Workshop, which was crucial in changing perceptions of the First World War. Where before it had been regarded as a more or less honourable victory, *Oh What a Lovely War* presented it as dishonourable carnage motivated by greed and carried through with supreme incompetence.

Perhaps the first historical play to challenge accepted versions of history was *King Johan* by John Bale. Not only did this play radically reinterpret the role of King John in English history, it also crystallised the moment of change in English drama, from a basically medieval and Catholic form to a basically Renaissance and Protestant one. In essence, we may say this was exemplified by an increasing awareness of the individual as unique, with opinions, preferences and desires which were their own: a huge psychological shift, which is discernable both in Bale's politics and in his dramaturgy.

King John (1167–1216) was (and still is) a controversial figure. His struggles against the pope in the early thirteenth century made him a key figure in English political discourse in the sixteenth century, and especially during the reign of Henry VIII (1491–1547), because Henry wished to break with the Catholic Church. John had been interpreted by all previous British historians, who were of course Catholics themselves, as calamitous. But in the 1530s Henry VIII established a Protestant Church which paid no allegiance to the pope in Rome. However, when his daughter, Queen Mary (1516–58), acceded to the throne in 1553, she reinstated Catholicism as the national religion – only for her successor, Elizabeth I (1533–1603), to return the country to Protestantism. These vicissitudes were deadly serious, and many people suffered exile, and even execution, for adhering to the 'wrong' faith.

A central question became: is salvation a matter for the Church, or a matter for the individual? Protestantism put increasing emphasis on the individual, and sermons described how an individual soul could be tempted, and how it could be saved. This scenario – temptation, a fall, and ultimate salvation – became the basic pattern for 'morality' plays, which flourished for perhaps a hundred years from the late fifteenth century. Their basic impulse is didactic, and their focus the individual soul.

The means by which the moralities addressed personal temptation and salvation was allegory, an embodying of abstract ideas in physical form. Thus death could be presented allegorically as an old man with a scythe. He could lead a Dance of Death, dragging each individual along behind him. The method could be extended. Our other problems could also be embodied, and represented by characters who attach themselves to us and are called Poverty, Despair, Covetousness or Sensuality. The drama is in the way we cope with, or resist, them, until we finally meet Death. We, too, as central character, are allegorised – as representative of the individual soul, we become Everyman, or Mankind, or something similar. And allegory also allows simple but effective symbolic staging, as when, in *King Johan*, Sedition is carried on stage by those who 'support' sedition.

The central attraction for audiences of morality plays came to be the Vice, a devilish figure, disrespectful, outrageous, subversive, and frequently obscene or shocking. This created a problem for the morality play makers – the character of Vice was clever, comic and full of energy, and therefore far more attractive than the stodgier characters representing the virtues. Sedition, the chief Vice in *King Johan*, cannot stop laughing at one moment: 'Hold me, or else for laughing I must burst!' Virtue never behaves like this.

The morality plays were presented by small professional companies – six or eight men – who performed in great halls of mansions or colleges. The acting area – 'stage' would be too grand a name – was at the bottom of the hall, in front of the screened-off kitchen, while the audience sat at tables, including the head of the household on the dais at the top. The minstrel gallery was usually conveniently situated above the kitchen. It was an informal arrangement, which put the emphasis on spectacle and tableau rather than detailed realism, as in the use of costume, which was highly emblematic. Thus, Justice was presented dressed in red and carrying a sword, while Truth was in white and held a book. The arrangement enabled the spectators, sitting at their tables with food and drink in front of them, to consider the ideas in the play, rather than become too personally involved.

John Bale was a major practitioner in this theatrical world. His life was extremely colourful, and is the subject of John Arden's novel, *Books of Bale*. He was a parish priest in the 1530s and became Bishop of Ossory in Ireland in the 1550s. But between these appointments, he had at least one spell in prison, and spent years in exile on the continent. In the late 1530s, as Henry VIII was forcing Catholicism out of Britain, he led a professional acting company which presented most of the twenty or more plays he wrote. When he died in 1563, it seems he was revising *King Johan*, perhaps for a new performance for Queen Elizabeth.

Bale's influence on the development of English drama has often been underestimated, and especially in the way it followed a different course from that of the continent. Where other British morality plays, even the great ones like *Magnificence* by John Skelton (1460–1529) and *Ane Satire of The Thrie Estaitis* by Sir David Lindsay (c.1485–1555), are fundamentally conservative, Bale's are radical and progressive, both in content and in form. From his earliest plays, such as the lost *The Knaveries of Thomas Becket*, Bale promoted the new Protestant cause of Martin Luther (1483–1546), exemplified in England by the policies of King Henry VIII. His method in *King Johan*, who struggled against Rome apparently as Henry VIII was doing, is to introduce real historical characters into the morality play framework, thus paving the way for the later, greater Elizabethan chronicle and history plays.

Bale's Vices represent Roman Catholicism: the Devil in his *The Temptation of Our Lord* is disguised as a monk, but in *King Johan* this identification is much more specific. The allegorical becomes the individual. Sedition is revealed as the Archbishop of Canterbury, who then disguises himself as Good Perfection. Dissimulation is also Simon of Swynsett who poisons King John. One important consequence of these equivalences is that the Vices become less attractive, and the 'message' of the play is strengthened.

In *King Johan*, the Widow England, oppressed by Sedition (the Roman Catholic Church) appeals for protection to King John. The struggle is long and arduous between the virtuous king and his agents, who correct the erring characters Clergy, Nobility and Civil Order, and the greedy agents of the power-hungry Pope, who finally succeed in poisoning him. While the villain, Sedition (Archbishop Stephen Langton, (c.1150–1228)), is promoted to sainthood by the Catholic Church, Imperial Majesty (though not King John, who has died) reconciles the people. Bale thus presents an alternative narrative of the reign of King John. What had been usually seen as disastrous, Bale presents as a time of social cleansing of society and would-be renewal of the body politic. In order to achieve this, not only do the symbolic and abstract characters have to become named individuals, as Protestantism's focus on personal salvation receives an emphatic dramatic expression, but the usual morality play structure is also modified in the interests of what Bale purports to present as historical accuracy (actually, of course, extremely contentious history). John (like Henry VIII) is not so much tempted by, as the victim of a particularly vicious plot: his story is more that of an innocent traduced than one of an everyman tempted, falling and ultimately saved.

Thus Bale not only reconfigures history with this play, he also discovers a new dramatic form – the history play – which will become a significant component of the coming Elizabethan theatrical summer. It is crude, over-long and for significant stretches frankly boring: but it is a major achievement, still under-regarded in most theatre histories. A further consequence, by the way, which is perhaps not so welcome, is that Bale's political intervention alerted the authorities to the power of drama, and prompted them to insist on their right to censor plays, first through the office of the Master of the Revels, and then the Lord Chamberlain, whose power continued until 1968.

As the example of John Bale's *King Johan* makes clear, theatre history, like the above, should refer not only to the development of the theatre, but also to the society within which it operates and with which it interacts. It is then clear that history does not simply narrate the past, it interprets it. We should always ask: whose history is it?

Thus, just as in the sixteenth century there were Protestant views and Catholic views of King John's reign, so today we must ask: whose history are we telling? For example, most history recorded in most history books is written by white, male, heterosexual, middle-class historians. But is theirs the only possible viewpoint? Suppose we look at events from a woman's perspective? In Shakespeare's time, a woman could be queen, evidently, but not an actor. What about the servant's perspective on events? Or a black person's? Or someone who is not heterosexual? Some of the following exercises in Shakespearean history might therefore be interesting. Compare Shakespeare's treatment of Aaron in *Titus Andronicus* to his treatment of Othello. Compare the performance of Paul Robeson (1898–1976) as Othello with that of Laurence Olivier (1907–89). What did any of the female actors who have played Hamlet (e.g. Sarah Bernhardt (1844–1923), Asta Nielson (1881–1972), Frances de la Tour (b.1944)) bring to the role? How might Shakespeare's depiction of Jack Cade in *Henry VI Part 2* appear to a *sans-culotte* of the French Revolution? Or to an anti-Gadaffi rebel in Libya in 2011?

'New Historicism' is in some senses a way of seeking these comparative views of history. It suggests there is no ultimate historical 'truth' to be found, only a series of perhaps interconnecting reverberations. From this position, the plays of Shakespeare, for instance, must be seen less as works of great drama than as documents of their time, just as other cultural products of the Elizabethan age such as street ballads or miniature paintings are. For the New Historicist, the context, and specifically the *historical* context, is crucial to any examination of a performance or piece of theatre. And the key element in this contextualisation is often taken to be the structures of power in the given society, structures which the performers themselves may be ignorant of or may discount, yet which inevitably colour what they do. The New Historicist asks: how is power shown to be distributed (even if it is unacknowledged) in this performance? How does it operate? Who is marginalised? Who has knowledge? Such questions may be addressed equally of the performed text, and of the group of performers of the text.

But, however appealing this approach may be today, we should also realise that the methods of historians change. From about 1850 till the second half of the twentieth century, the 'positivism' of Auguste Comte (1798–1857) prevailed in historical research and thinking. This approach suggested that 'facts' would 'explain' the 'truth' about the past, and all the historian had to do was to unearth all the facts, and an objective truth would become apparent. Since Comte's day, we have begun to doubt the notion of 'objectivity': the 'objective' explanation of gravity given by Sir Isaac Newton (1642–1727) was overturned by Albert Einstein's (1879–1955) theory of relativity. We think now that cultural perspectives alter views of the same past events (as Bale's did of King John). The 'silent', that is, those without a voice in society – the poor, the marginalised, the 'others' – often have very different interpretations of what has happened. It is the voices from 'below' or 'beyond' the dominant groups in society which point, for example, to colonial oppression, the exploitation of working people or the victims of racism or sexism, and their experiences put different interpretations on events. Theatre history can uncover how common social assumptions of particular historical periods about, say, gender, may underlie specific plays, and also how the drama often challenges such assumptions. This may be the case with *Twelfth Night* (though of course there is no suggestion that this is all *Twelfth Night* is about).

Box 4.2: *Twelfth Night*: Shakespeare and gender

William Shakespeare probably wrote his sequence of 154 sonnets in the early part of the 1590s. They are mostly addressed to a young man, whom Shakespeare begins by urging to marry, but whom he soon finds himself passionately attached to. The story of the sonnets is complicated by the existence of a 'dark lady', whom both the poet and his young male beloved become entangled with. Theirs is a complex love triangle, which is further aggravated by other characters, such as the 'rival poet', who make more or less fleeting appearances in the sequence. The sonnets are notable because they show Shakespeare involved in intense love affairs, in which the gender of the *dramatis personae* is obviously of slight importance.

At this time, Shakespeare wrote *The Two Gentlemen of Verona* in which two male friends become involved with two women, and act out a series of more or less acceptable love episodes. All four of the central characters in this play were played originally (as Shakespeare knew they would be) by young male actors, so that the confusions of gender are mapped onto the confusions of love. It is a potent mix, but one which Elizabethan theatre had already begun to explore. *Clyomon and Clamydes*, possibly by Thomas Preston (1537–98), *Gallathea* by John Lyly (c.1554–1606), *Soliman and Perseda*, perhaps by Thomas Kyd (1558–94), and *The Scottish History of James IV* by Robert Greene (1558–92) are just some of the plays which include women who dress as men and which therefore, willy-nilly, explore problems of gender representation. *James IV* in particular explores the sexual dimension to this gender swapping, when Lady Anderson, wife of one of the Scottish lords, finds herself attracted to Queen Dorothea when the latter is disguised as a boy. What appears here to be a lesbian relationship is considerably more complicated than this, because both women are played by male actors, and one of them is playing a woman dressed up as a man.

In Shakespeare's *The Two Gentlemen of Verona*, the friendship between Valentine and Proteus clearly has an underlying homoerotic strand, which is partially concealed by Proteus' situation at the opening of the play – he is betrothed to Julia. But when Valentine leaves him, and himself becomes engaged to Silvia, Proteus deliberately interferes, coldly discards Julia and prevents Valentine's match. Indeed, he comes close to raping Silvia. But Valentine, witnessing the assault, offers her to him to show how deep his love for Proteus is. It is a shocking episode, which any production which shies away from the homoerotic implications of Valentine and Proteus' relationship cannot present convincingly. Although the play ends more or less conventionally, it is Shakespeare's presentation of the depth of sexual desire intertwined with the problems caused by gender confusion which remains in the memory from a staging of the play.

Throughout the 1590s Shakespeare continued his exploration of this theme. One of the finest, and most disturbing, examples of this is in *As You Like It*, when Rosalind, a woman played by a man, accompanied by Celia, also played by a man, courts Orlando. Rosalind disguises herself as Ganymede, an androgynous male, in order to pursue this courtship, a masquerade which is further complicated when Ganymede plays Rosalind in a 'pretend' marriage with Orlando. Here a man plays a woman playing a man who plays a woman, in order to fulfil his – or her – sexual desires. Perhaps the most complicated, as well as perhaps the most satisfying, of these explorations by Shakespeare comes in *Twelfth Night*, a play which revolves round Viola, a young woman (played by a man), who disguises herself as Cesario, a young male page. She becomes the object of the sexual desire, first, embarrassingly openly, of the Lady Olivia (played by a man, of course) and simultaneously, covertly, perhaps without his even being aware of it, of Duke Orsino. Orsino had initially imagined he loved Olivia, and had sent Cesario to court her on his behalf, thereby setting in motion this strange, exciting, impossible love triangle. It is of course incapable of resolution so long as love is believed to be dependent on gender. Actually, as Shakespeare knew well from his own experience recorded in the Sonnets, love depends on person, while gender is merely a performed attribute of any person. Viola's is the supreme performance of gender on one level, and precisely why such performance is deceptive on another.

Shakespeare's resolution to the problem of Viola/Cesario's dual singularity is to divide her/him in two, so that both her/his more conventionally-minded lovers may be satisfied. He creates an identical twin for Viola in Sebastian. It is a question whether in fact Shakespeare knew that twins of opposite sex cannot be identical. If he did, it is a subtle and amusing irony. But even without this, the ease with which Olivia can transfer her desire from Cesario, a woman disguised as a man, played by a man, to Sebastian, and Orsino can transfer his affections from Olivia to Viola, indicate the fragility of gender identification. It is too complex, and too subtle, for such a simple resolution. At a deep level – one which perhaps many spectators never consciously realise – the happy ending of *Twelfth Night* therefore depends on the dissolution of the problems, and anxieties, of identities bound up in gender. As Olivia and Sebastian and Orsino and Viola move smoothly, happily into the sunset, our joy springs from the understanding that it is the person, not their gender that makes them loveable.

HISTORICAL EVIDENCE

Historical evidence is of two kinds. 'Primary' evidence – artefacts and documents, for example – and 'secondary' evidence – that is, later interpretations of these primary sources. Both are of interest to the historian, but they do not provide the same kind of historical evidence. For the purposes of this chapter, we may confine the discussion to primary sources.

Theatre buildings provide a starting-point for historical evidence beyond the play text – ruined theatres like the ancient Greek theatre at Epidaurus, excavated theatres, like the Elizabethan playhouses on the south bank of the Thames, the Globe and the Rose, and still-functioning old theatres like the little Georgian theatre in Richmond, Yorkshire, built in 1788. Buildings often determine acting styles, and the history of acting, especially the controversies raging round matters such as how far the actor should 'live' the part, and how far the role should simply be 'presented' (discussed in Chapter 5) is also a fruitful site for 'primary source' research.

Then theatre generates all sorts of documents. Much can be learned from play scripts themselves, from how the play is written, in verse or prose, the kinds of characters presented, whether stock types or psychologically individualised, and the dramatic forms favoured at the time. Beyond play scripts are other documents: diaries, for instance, such as that of Samuel Pepys (1633–1703), who wrote on 3 January 1661: 'To the Theatre, where was acted *Beggar's Bush*, it being very well done; and here the first time that ever I saw women come upon the stage.' Other diaries, like that of Henry Crabbe Robinson (1775–1867), shed light on other periods of theatre history, and some actors, such as William Charles Macready (1793–1873), also kept diaries containing important information. These are complemented by memoirs, especially the memoirs of professional theatre practitioners, from Colley Cibber (1671–1757), whose *Apology for the Life of Colley Cibber* was published in 1740, to Joan Littlewood, author of *Joan's Book*, published in 1994, and beyond. Whether to believe every word of such documents is, of course, a matter for debate. Often such works are transparently self-justifying, or deliberately sensational, or varnished in some other way, and their contents sometimes remind one of the oral traditions of the theatre, which however may also provide interesting source material. They cover everything from traditional stage 'business', to reports of Shakespeare playing the Ghost in Hamlet, to Stanislavsky weeping during rehearsals for *The Village of Stepanchikova* by Fyodor Dostoyevsky (1821–81) at the Moscow Art Theatre. The account by Ellen Terry (1847–1928) in her memoirs of her meeting with Henry Irving (1838–1905), with whom she formed a famous and highly successful stage partnership later in her career, may serve to put this material in perspective, though that is not to say that the historian can afford to ignore it:

> One very foggy day in December 1867 – it was Boxing Day, I think – I acted for the first time with Henry Irving. This ought to have been a great event in my life, but at the time it passed me by and left 'no wrack behind.' Ever anxious to improve on the truth, which is often devoid of

all sensationalism, people have told a story of Henry Irving promising that if ever he were in a position to offer me an engagement I should be his leading lady. But this fairy story has been improved on since. The newest tale of my first meeting with Henry Irving was told during my jubilee. Then, to my amazement, I read that on that famous night when I was playing Puck at the Princess's, and caught my toe in the trap, 'a young man with dark hair and a white face rushed forward from the crowd and said: "Never mind, darling. Don't cry! One day you will be queen of the stage." It was Henry Irving!' In view of these legends, I ought to say all the more stoutly that, until I went to the Lyceum Theatre, Henry Irving was nothing to me and I was nothing to him.

> (Ellen Terry, *The Story of My Life*, London: Hutchinson,
> 1908, pp. 72–73)

Another kind of diary or memoir which may be extremely useful for the historian is the minutes or other records of business dealings. A particularly significant example of this is that kept by Philip Henslowe (c.1550–1616), lessee of the Rose Theatre in the 1590s, and later leading entrepreneur of the theatre who built the large Fortune Theatre in 1600. His Diary records all his dealings with playwrights, actors and others, and provides unusually keen insights into the theatre of Shakespeare's time. Newspapers sometimes provide unexpected evidence of theatrical mores, as for instance in some nineteenth-century court reports of spectators whose behaviour in the theatre had brought them before a magistrate; and sometimes, too, sensitive theatre critics' descriptions of productions or actors can bring the apparently-dead to life. Here, for example, is a description from *The Times* of Harry Corbett (1925–82) as Richard II in 1955:

Mr Harry Corbett's king is not merely effeminate, and cruelly capricious, his sudden fluctuations from arrogant self-assertion to cringing submissiveness are from the outset symptoms of insanity. In his downfall a latent streak of religious mania grows into a monstrous obsession. For the deposition scene he shambles on in a coarse and ragged robe and gives away his crown with a crazy cunning. In the dungeon at Pomfret he is tethered by a chain round his ankle like the dangerous lunatic he evidently is.

> (*The Times*, 18 January 1955)

Newspapers often seem almost as ephemeral as theatre performances, but they may contain valuable insights like this. As may theatre posters and other forms of advertising, programmes and similar material.

Any piece of historical evidence, however, must be carefully considered before it is simply accepted for what it purports to be. Caution needed in the treatment of individuals' memoirs has already been mentioned. The historian will want to wonder why a particular piece of evidence has survived when other evidence has been lost. Who produced this witness? Why? What were they trying to do, or say? Who stood to gain? Some documents may be interpreted in more than one way, and neither may be 'wrong'. It should also be remembered that things decay – and some things decay faster than others. And some things never decay.

Most historians now recognise that their own value systems inform their historical narratives. This can be especially apparent in the language the historian uses, for language itself is value-laden. If, as suggested earlier, the historian is somewhat like the novelist – or the playwright – in trying to make sense of researched material by constructing a narrative out of it, it is worth noting that this narrative will be created in words – that is how the meaning is drawn out. But the language itself is not neutral. The reader, too, brings value systems, prejudices and expectations to any examination of history, and this, too, must be taken into account.

And beyond their own value systems, historians must also be aware of the value system of the play being studied, or the theatre, or the period. This may reflect the values of the director, or the author, or of the time or the society, or indeed a mixture of these. In the examples given in this chapter, I have avoided drama not in the English language, and drama not from the greater British Isles. I venture into Irish history, multiculturalism and the British Sikh community, in order to illustrate how modern theoretical approaches may illuminate particular theatrical events, and how these events interact with social and historical concerns surrounding them. How far these narratives reflect merely my own values must be a matter for the reader's conjecture or interpretation.

Box 4.3: *Cathleen ni Houlihan*: theatre and nation

Frantz Fanon (1925–61), brought up in the French colony of Martinique, examined the concept of 'nation' in a number of significant ways. Recognising that nationalism was a progressive force for downtrodden colonial peoples, he also demonstrated that it was oppressive and reactionary – and usually violent – when harnessed by imperialism. Yet he argued that, paradoxically, it was only through violent struggle that imperialist oppression could be defeated. He further suggested that in the nationalist struggles of subjected peoples, intellectuals and artists had a crucial role to play, not least in developing a necessary cultural identity.

In 1891, the leader of Irish nationalism, Charles Stewart Parnell (1846–91), died, and in the decade that followed Irish opponents of British rule felt themselves often confused and unsure how to move the cause of freedom forward. Nationalism developed a number of strands: there was, for example, something of a political resurgence of the old Fenianism associated with men like John O'Leary (1830–1907), and there was also a kind of cultural revival led by younger intellectuals such as Douglas Hyde (1860–1949), a future president of Ireland, which was manifested in a renewed interest in the Gaelic language, and a new emphasis on traditional features of Irish life, such as Gaelic sports like hurling.

The Irish literary renaissance also developed at this time, spear-headed by the young poet W. B. Yeats, who wrote in an Anglo-Irish idiom to attempt to define the Irish identity or character. Yeats dreamed of an Irish theatre, but had not the wherewithal to translate his dreams into action until in 1897 he met Lady Augusta Gregory (1852–1932), whose enthusiastic support created both the financial and the organisational means to realise the dream. Together they established the Irish Literary Theatre, with its own journal, *Samhain*, which Yeats edited. A major aim was to counteract, indeed destroy, the stereotypical stage image of the Irishman as a feckless, happy-go-lucky ne'er-do-well, with a shamrock in his button-hole and a shillelagh in his hand, who spoke with a lilting blarney which made him actually a brutish buffoon. This stereotype is typical of what Edward Said was to define, many years later, as the 'Other', the objectification of the subjected people in order to deprive them of cultural and artistic energy and identity. Yeats and Gregory wished to articulate genuine Irish aspirations, and thereby restore a measure of dignity to the Irish people. For them, Ireland was a tragic heroine, not a drunken clown, and they started writing plays to assert what they regarded as the true soul of Irishness.

At the same time, an Irish National Dramatic Company had been created by the brothers William (1872–1947) and Frank Fay (1870–1931), the latter of whom attacked Yeats' apparent escapism, and more or less challenged him to create a play that would 'rouse this sleeping land'. Yeats responded with *Cathleen ni Houlihan*, written jointly with Lady Gregory in 1902. As their Irish Literary Theatre foundered, the two groups amalgamated to form the Irish National Theatre Society, with Yeats as its president. Their inaugural production, on 2 April 1902, at the Hall of St Theresa's Total Abstinence Society, Clarendon Street, Dublin, consisted of a double bill of *Deirdre* by 'A. E.' (George Russell, 1867–1935), and *Cathleen ni Houlihan*. It was the latter which made a resounding impression.

The play has been criticised for its brevity and its lack of subtlety, but these apparent faults have also been described as ballad-like simplicity and economy. Set in 1798, the year of Wolfe Tone's (1763–98) unsuccessful rising against the English, the play depicts a peasant family fussing about the wedding arrangements for their son. They are interrupted by the entrance of a fierce old woman bewailing the loss of her 'four fields', and her passionate call for young men to help her recover them inspires the young bridegroom to leave his mundane life and his bride, and follow her. The play's call for total sacrifice, its promise to merge the individual's identity into something larger, perhaps more significant, and its glorification of possibly doomed heroism all give it a romantic and poetic force which is intensified when it becomes clear that those who answer the call are transformed, as the Old Woman herself is transformed: at the end she becomes 'a young girl (with) the walk of a queen'. To respond to Ireland's call is to energise one's nobler self. For the Old Woman is the Shan Van Vocht, the symbol of Ireland, and her four green and beautiful fields the four provinces of Ireland – Ulster, Munster, Leinster and Connaught.

Somehow Yeats was able to persuade the famously-beautiful Maud Gonne (1866–1953), best-known as a fire-eating nationalist orator, and the object of his passionate but unrequited love, to play the part of the old woman. William Fay did not approve, and rehearsals were disrupted by her not infrequent absences, but when it came to the performance, she was inspired. Indeed, the play's influence probably owed as much to her as it did to Yeats or Lady Gregory (in fact Lady Gregory was not even in the audience, having departed for Venice a few days earlier). Gonne's powerful stage presence, amounting to genuine charisma, as well as her reputation as an uncompromising fighter for independence, gave her performance a mesmerising quality, which some put down to her turning to the audience to address them, rather than her on-stage partners, with her most passionate lines. The packed house – 300 or more spectators in the tiny hall – responded with passionate excitement.

Cathleen ni Houlihan held up to its audiences a heroic, romantic vision, it offered the young of Ireland a possibility, a gesture, and showed how the past affected the present, and might affect the future. It retained an honoured place in the Irish nationalist theatre's repertoire, and was frequently performed over the next decades, though never again with Maud Gonne in the leading role. But its continued popularity suggested how the theatre might be useful to militant and progressive nationalism, and how nationalism can imbue theatrical performance with passion. Theatrically it perhaps crystallised the desire for an Irish drama which led to the founding of the Abbey Theatre, funded by Miss A. E. F. Horniman (1860–1937), and with William and Frank Fay as leading participants. The Abbey was instrumental in discovering and presenting the plays of J. M. Synge (1871–1909), who was to join Lady Gregory and Yeats in a management triumvirate, and it was to provide a model for both provincial and national theatres later in the twentieth century.

Irish nationalism and Irish drama each drew strength from the other. It was a difficult relationship, quarrelsome but undoubtedly productive. Literature searches for truths about people and nations, where politics seeks concrete ways to achieve hopes and aspirations. It was perhaps no coincidence that when the Irish nationalists took up arms in rebellion at Easter, 1916, many of their leaders were playwrights. Pádraic Pearse was not only a schoolteacher but a quite prolific playwright, and James Connolly (1868–1916), the trade unionist and Marxist, wrote and produced plays to teach his followers specific political lessons. Thomas MacDonagh's (1878–1916) *When the Dawn is Come* was staged at the Abbey Theatre, and he and Joseph Mary Plunkett (1887–1916), together with MacDonagh's brother, John (?–1961), who also fought in the Easter Rising, and the playwright, Edward Martyn (1859–1923), founded the Irish Theatre in Hardwick Street, Dublin, where Pearse's plays, among others, were presented. Even later leaders, such as the mayor of Cork, Terence MacSwiney (1879–1920), who was to die after a seventy-six-day hunger strike, wrote plays. And the Easter Rising itself was highly theatrical – a romantic gesture, heroic, perhaps, but with no hope of succeeding. Yet it so fired the country that in less than a decade twenty-six counties of Ireland were freed from the British yoke.

Years later, when an old man, W. B. Yeats still agonised over *Cathleen ni Houlihan* and its consequences:

> All that I have said and done,
> Now that I am old and ill,
> Turns into a question till
> I lie awake night after night
> And never get the answers right.
> Did that play of mine send out
> Certain men the English shot?

The answer to Yeats' question is: probably, yes. And if so, does it not demonstrate the power of theatre in shaping national consciousness?

DRAMA AND SOCIETY

Following the ideas of Hans Robert Jauss (b. 1921), one way of seeing theatre history is to examine the way society has received drama. Plays offer different experiences to different spectators at different times. As society changes, so our view of the past changes too. The way Shakespeare's plays have been received over the centuries illustrates this clearly. In the later nineteenth century, what was most valued in Shakespeare's plays was his ability to create 'character'; in the first decades of the twentieth century, it was his poetry and his imagery which seemed to capture the imagination; later in the century, he was prized for his political insights; and so on. This may tell us more about the nineteenth and twentieth centuries than about Shakespeare and his society: thus, it is not that the twentieth century lost the idea that Shakespeare's characters were interesting, it was that people then became more interested in other features of his work.

We attend the theatre in a state of expectation, a state which depends on our earlier experiences of going to the theatre. And theatres produce plays which will respond to this expectation, that is, what they think their audience can accept. Jauss argues that the audience's expectations form a 'horizon' within which they will interpret what they see. A play which exceeds that expectation, or breaks the pre-formulated horizon, may be either rejected (as was, for instance, *Waiting for Godot* by Samuel Beckett) or acclaimed as a masterpiece (as was *Rosencrantz and Guildenstern Are Dead* by Tom Stoppard). In any case, the new work gradually alters the potential audience's perspective, the horizon changes. A significant work, like *Waiting for Godot* or *Rosencrantz and Guildenstern Are Dead*, is like a driver, moving us, the passengers, towards new horizons, so that we see the whole landscape differently. In the landscape's new config-uration, we come to value the work which has effected this change as a 'classic', and when we see it next time we re-evaluate it, and our interpretation changes. Thus, dramatic history may be seen as a matter of social evolution: it is concerned to identify how and why the expectations of the audience change.

This makes theatre history at least partly consonant with a wider social history. Indeed, plays have been seen as sites wherein social forces struggle for dominance in a sort of microcosm of a society in flux. Most good plays include contradictory impulses – progressive, reactionary, liberating, dissentient, subversive, whatever. In this case, the context is as important as the text, which is on this level an attempt to intervene in social processes, contending with existing power structures, and often seeming both to endorse and to resist the insidious tentacles of social or political power. Perhaps this ambiguity is at the heart of the continuing debate about Peter Brook's production of *The Mahabharata*, examined here. What does the performed text do within the whole consortium of social and cultural relations?

Box 4.4: *The Mahabharata*: intercultural performance

In 1985, Peter Brook presented *The Mahabharata*, a play created from the ancient Indian epic, which is probably also the world's longest poem. The furious reception accorded to this production across the world crystallised significant debates about intercultural perfor-mance, 'orientalism' and postcolonialism, especially as these applied to theatre makers. This section therefore examines a particular moment in history when these crucial issues confronted the theatre world.

To begin at the beginning, it is important to know that the *Mahabharata* is more than a poem, it is an epic which is also a cornerstone of South Asian civilisation. It was probably composed, or put together, over a period of time 2,000 years or more ago. Supposedly made originally by the sage Vyasa, grandfather of the poem's heroic figures, it was handed down for centuries from one generation to the next by word of mouth.

The thrust of the ideas in the *Mahabharata* derive from Hinduism, or perhaps they inspire Hinduism. The formative Hindu religious text, the *Bhagavad-Gita*, is spoken by one character, the disguised god Krishna, to the hero, Arjuna, immediately before the final battle. The story of the *Mahabharata* tells of the struggle for dominance between two sets of cousins, the Pandavas and the Kauravas, but branching out from this and included in it, at least in the fuller versions, are all sorts of other stories, and stories within stories, with more or less direct relevance to the central fable. The *Mahabharata* is therefore the source not only of religious and devotional wisdom, but also of many folk tales, legends, songs and, significantly, of dramatic performances. It is important to understand that there are many *Mahabharatas*, stories, dances, dramas and so on, and none of them is what we might term 'original'. The *Mahabharata* is multidimensional: no version is complete, all are relative, and part of the richness in each version is the density of the intertextual references.

Pertinent to the central arguments about the status and ownership of the *Mahabharata* is the fact that in every part of the Indian sub-continent, stories from it have been acted and danced, presented by glove puppets and marionettes, and made the subject of picture books and cartoons. Peter Brook himself noted that everywhere in India people loved the *Mahabharata*, and everywhere they had their own tradition of performing it. A brilliant outsider's description of one such tradition has been given by John Arden in 'The Chhau Dancers of Purulia', reproduced in his book, *To Present the Pretence*. To this may be added other examples, such as the classical dance of Manipur, in the northeast of India, which presents the stories as soft, flowing dances, sinuous and beautiful, or the equally resonant traditional dance of Orissa, in eastern India, in which the dancers are more sculptural and the dances more staccato. The *Mahabharata* is also traditionally performed beyond India, for instance in Muslim Java in Indonesia, where its fundamental Hinduism has been replaced by Islam, and the leader of the victorious Pandavas converts to the religion of the Prophet before he dies. Who owns this *Mahabharata*?

Such traditional performances reward anyone researching them. Two further examples may be considered in a little more detail, for they too shed light on the cultural problems under discussion. First, the version made over centuries by the Tharu people of the Dang Valley, in south-western Nepal, which is called *Barka Naach*, or 'Big Dance', and is essentially a devotional puja in honour of the Pandavas. The *Barka Naach* tells the story of the *Mahabharata* through a combination of dance, mime and song, and the performance is (or was) believed to assure a good harvest. Two days of *puja* precede the Big Dance, and there is also an additional day of devotion afterwards, so that the whole lasts for four days. After the main performance in the central Tarai, the fertile lowlands of the country, the performance is carried to other villages, and each village chooses which of the episodes in the enormous whole will be performed for them. A cycle of performances takes fifteen years: after the first performances have been given, they must be repeated five years later, and then again after another five years. There is no set date for the next cycle to begin.

The *Barka Naach* subdivides the epic into a number of discrete episodes, or plays, each lasting over an hour, and consisting of songs and choruses. The songs are sung by soloists, whereas the choruses are sung by all the performers. The texts bear the hallmarks of the oral tradition, featuring repetition, formulaic phrases and so on, and the individual roles are passed down from father to son. The episodes are sometimes at variance with the usual story – for instance, in the *Barka Naach*, Yudhishthira, the eldest of the Pandavas, plays the game of dice with Duryodhana, not with his uncle Sakuni, though Sakuni is there to give advice. The *Barka Naach* also includes delightful episodes, as when Arjuna teaches the courtiers to dance and make music while dressed as a woman, and comic, as in Bhima's fight with an elephant, which typify the freshness and range the *Mahabharata* is able to comprehend.

Better known, and as stimulating, are *Kathakali* versions of the stories. *Kathakali* is the classical performance form from Kerala, southwest India, and seems to have derived from ancient Hindu ceremonies. As a form *Kathakali* crystallised in about the seventeenth century of the Christian era – roughly contemporaneous with Shakespeare. *Kathakali* is an amalgam of dance drama and popular theatre. Performers are highly trained in acting and dancing, especially in the mudras, or finger movements, which can signify almost anything. The actors do not speak, but only communicate through the mudras. The characters are symbolic types, recognisable from their striking make-up and costumes. The make-up is bright and heavy – green for heroes and gods, and red and black for villains, but with many variations, such as Hanuman (the monkey god) who has a white beard and complicated red, black and white patterns on his face. The costumes are highly decorative, including sometimes over fifty yards of cloth under thick woollen jackets, the heaviness of which is probably responsible for the classic *Kathakali* rhythmic swaying movements, and characters also wear fantastic headdresses.

The stage has no scenery, but a curtain is held up by stage assistants before the performance begins and whenever powerful characters appear. The new character peers over the curtain, often making weird sounds accompanied by drumming and music, before the curtain is slowly lowered and the scene commences. Two drummers at the back of the stage accompany the action and two singers tell the story which the actors present. A performance traditionally begins in the evening, and continues until dawn, preceded by propitiatory rites and dances, and as the night proceeds, the rhythms speed up until the climax comes at dawn amid frenzied drumming and noise. The action develops in three modes, narrative passages, sung dialogue – accompanied by the actors' mudras – and passages of gesture and dance without sung accompaniment. *Kathakali* is renowned for its songs, or ragas, formalised in structure, but extremely versatile.

As might be expected, *Kathakali* includes in its repertoire many dramas drawn from the *Mahabharata*, but unusually for traditional Indian theatre, the authors of the various plays are known. Thus, *Kalyana Saugandhika*, which tells the story of Bhima fetching a rare flower from Hanamun's garden for Draupadi, is by Kottayath Tampuran (1645–1716); *Kiratta*, in which the god Shiva tests Arjuna, and which includes a furious and exciting boar hunt, is by

Irrattakulangara Rama Varier (1801–45); and perhaps the best known of the *Kathakali Mahabharata* plays, *Duryodhana Vadha*, which tells how Duryodhana tries to undress Draupadi, but which Krishna prevents by making the cloth she is dressed in endless, and concludes with the extraordinary scene of Bhima drinking Dussasana's blood before killing Duryodhana, was written by Vyasakara Aryan Narayanan Moosad (1841–1902). *Kathakali* dramatises stories from other traditions, too, and its versatility is shown by the fact that a *Kathakali* version of *King Lear* was created in the late 1980s.

It is against this background that we should consider Peter Brook's controversial European production of *The Mahabharata*, first performed in 1985. Brook saw the *Mahabharata* as an anonymous and poetical history of humankind: he wished to 'suggest' India, to create 'a flavour' of India, but to bring to this something 'from beyond India'. The *Mahabharata*, he argued, could only have been created in India, but it carried a more universal poetical sensibility. David Williams (b. 1957) wrote of his production:

> This *Mahabharata* presents us with a dense narrative of immense moral complexity and metaphysical ambiguity, exploring the most profound and primordial of human themes: self-discovery, the forces of moral and personal determination and predestination, man in society and man's destruction of that society. While resolutely refusing any easy answers – politically, psychologically, morally – it constantly gives flesh to a positive attitude in the face of a contradictory plurality of experiences, within which personal and universal are indissolubly intertwined.
> (David Williams, *Peter Brook: A Theatrical Casebook*, London: Methuen, 1992, p. 354)

Brook's production was marked by its theatrical brilliance and equally its unexpected simplicity. It deliberately developed Brook's belief that theatre should aim to communicate across all sorts of cultural divides, and that this could be achieved if the work was presented honestly enough, openly enough and simply enough. All traces of the 'actorly' and the 'theatrical' must be done away with, he believed.

Performed initially in a quarry in Avignon, so that the finale was happening as the sun came up, rouging the quarry's stony sides, this *Mahabharata* deliberately utilised an international – or supranational – range of traditions and styles, each determined only by what seemed appropriate to, and truthful for, that particular moment in the story. The international cast cut through almost all expected conventions and presented something seemingly unique in Western theatre history. This included Ryszard Cieslak's (1937–90) blind and furious Dhritarashtra; the suicide of Drona, symbolically depicted by him pouring a bucket of blood over his own head; Arjuna's chariot represented by a single wheel (with all its connotations); and the arrow, fired by Arjuna and physically carried by Krishna from the bow of the hero towards the virtuous Bhishma, slowly, slowly, till it reached its target, when there was a great rush of shouting and excitement. These were only a few of the multitude of diverse, extra-ordinary moments, and were set in the context of Brook's simple storytelling technique, which was used with tact and imagination.

It could be added, by the way, that Brook's has not been the only attempt by Western theatre to present the *Mahabharata*: in 2007, for instance, Sadler's Wells, London, presented a version created by Stephen Clark, Nitin Sawhney and Stuart Wood, with some visually beautiful moments and a few echoes of traditional Indian *Kathak* dance, but spoiled perhaps by bland, typically 'West End' music. Nevertheless, British audiences came to see it, and approved it. But it was Peter Brook's version – perhaps because it was such a thea-trical revelation – that attracted a critical frenzy.

Brook was accused of cultural rape, while also being hailed as the creator of the twentieth-century theatre's most spectacular achieve-ment. He was guilty of cultural imperialism, it was asserted, stealing the cultural 'property' of the developing world for his own (Western) ends, ripping the epic from its context, and losing the underpinning Hindu social understanding and cosmology. By decontextualising the *Mahabharata*, Brook had, it was argued, robbed it not only of its resonance and its complexity, but even of its meaning.

Brook's defenders countered that his production had in a sense sought at least some of this. Translating such an enormous work into a theatrical language inevitably involved simplifying, finding a basic, and therefore culturally decontextualised, theatrical idiom for the work. It was only because of this urgent need to simplify, embedded in Brook's *modus operandi*, that the production was possible. But it was further suggested that the apparent simplicity was actually deceptive, that the theatrical signs thus produced were in fact highly suggestive and challenging to a theatrically literate audience.

It was clear from the argument, and from the passion with which it was conducted, that the production had raised, in extremely stark fashion, problems of intercultural exchange and transmission, of what has become known as 'Orientalism', and of the globalisation of culture. The disputation continues.

It seems worth suggesting that the *Mahabharata* in any version raises profound issues. These range from the psychological – problems of addiction, for instance, and of the need to sink to the lowest level in order to regain personal control – to the political – concerning the sharing of power, and the impossibility of dividing a naturally unified land (examples range from divided Ireland through the Palestine–Israel conflict to the division of India and Pakistan) – and the spiritual – most obviously in the Hindu significations. How does consideration of these problems sit with the 'ownership' of stories? For many, what is important in this argument is the way myth – in this case, the *Mahabharata* – works to evoke and to enlighten, how performativity ensures that the original story, whether presented as an epic poem or a dramatic production, constantly renews itself, and how everyone who sings the song of the *Mahabharata*, and everyone who performs it, recreates it, makes it new, ensures that it is alive in the contemporary world.

The argument between critics and practising artists continues. The last word here goes to the well-known Indian painter, Nalini Malani (b. 1946), who has been attacked, like Peter Brook, for mingling Western and Eastern myths in her work: 'The way I look at it, together we all inherit the rich histories passed on to us from the past. Our points of reference, ideas and values are not confined by man-made borders.' (*Nalini Malani*, Irish Museum of Modern Art, n.d., p. 40).

The debate about the *Mahabharata* asks the question directly: where does the play, or the institution of drama itself, fit into the ongoing discourses of power, or knowledge (for the two are closely interlinked)? Is the play part of the process of institutionalisation which is ongoing in contemporary society? Is it helping to train and shape obedient and conformist individuals, 'docile bodies', which

Foucault argues power is exercised in order to produce? Or is it resistant to this? The answer may be that it does both, usually at different moments in its performance, sometimes perhaps simultaneously.

Foucault, the most significant forerunner of New Historicism, also argues that power operates through continual classification, re-classification, surveillance and intervention. The power of religion, for instance, is exercised through moral imperatives and 'right' behaviour, including behaviour in a religious building. Thus, rape cannot be committed within a temple. The two categories – 'rape' and 'temple' – are mutually exclusive. Yet rape is committed in the temple in *Behzti* (*Dishonour*) by Gurpreet Kaur Bhatti (b. 1969), the subject of the final example in this chapter. This play confronts problems of 'truth' – orthodox truth, and the apparently contradictory but no less valid truth of the dissident. Where Foucault would maintain that all 'truths' tend to be repressive, it is also the case that not all truths are equal, that some tend to respond more readily to the structures of power and knowledge. We may ask, does a play like *Behzti* resist these structures?

Box 4.5: *Behzti: dishonour*

On 9 December 2004, *Behzti* (the Punjabi word for 'dishonour') by Gurpreet Kaur Bhatti was presented at the Door, the studio theatre of the Birmingham Repertory Theatre. Set in a Sikh temple, or *gurdwara*, the play deals with a woman in her fifties, Balbir Kaur, and her grown-up daughter, Min, who discover that Balbir's deceased husband, Min's father, had a homosexual affair with one of the elders of the temple, Mr Sandhu, who is also guilty of sexually abusing young girls. During the play, Sandhu rapes Min. At the end, Balbir and another of Sandhu's victims assassinate Sandhu with a Sikh ceremonial sword. The *gurdwara* was home to cover-up and corruption.

Subtly structured, beautifully controlled, this play is in no sense the melodrama which such a brief summary might suggest. It employs language with a sardonic, vernacular accuracy, including comic but reverberative West Midlands immigrant argot, and it contains a number of characters who are interesting, often exasperating and always understandable. The play is ultimately about people in power exploiting those without power, the young, the vulnerable, the members of the community least able to fend for themselves.

The Birmingham Repertory Theatre had for some years before this struggled to find a way of responding to the multi-ethnic community which the city had become in the second half of the twentieth century. It consistently employed actors of Caribbean and Asian origin, and mounted a number of plays addressed specifically to this constituency. How successful this policy was may be questioned. Typical were, perhaps, *East Is East*, a fairly vapid comedy, and *The Ramayana*, an Indian classic epic which was given spectacular treatment, though it played to sparse audiences and might raise some of the questions suggested in the section on the *Mahabharata* above. Nevertheless, it was an honest policy, which in 1998 was extended to the newly-founded Door studio theatre attached to the Rep. The policy here was to present work by new writers, many of them radical and from minority groups, and by the time of *Behzti*, premieres by over fifteen different writers had been staged. It was a space for new ideas and different approaches.

But clearly on this occasion trouble was foreseen. In a note written weeks in advance of the opening, Bhatti wrote: 'In a community where public honour is paramount, is there any room for truth?' In other words, the structure of the society depicted in the play was one which was a natural home to deceit and hypocrisy. Representatives of the theatre visited and discussed the play with leaders of Birmingham's Sikh community, who however seem to have misunderstood the purpose of the discussions, and imagined that they were being offered some sort of control over the production. Their basic request was that the setting should be changed from a *gurdwara* to a community centre. Perhaps they understood that the impact of the play would hardly be the same if the setting were altered in this way.

Once the play began its run at the theatre, peaceful Sikh protesters picketed the theatre. The performances continued. On Saturday 18 December, some 400 Sikhs attacked the Birmingham Repertory Theatre. Audience members and theatre employees were jostled and threatened, and the demonstrators tried to enter the building and, being held back by some eighty-five police, nearly half of them in riot gear, threw missiles and smashed windows. Part of the city centre by the theatre was cordoned off, 800 people were evacuated, including the audience at the main theatre's Christmas production, *The Witches* by Roald Dahl (1916–90), and the performances of both this and *Behzti* were cancelled. On the Monday following these scenes, the theatre announced that it was ending the run of *Behzti* there and then, despite the fact that many tickets had been sold for future performances.

'The mob has won,' proclaimed the *Birmingham Post* the next day. 'It won't be long ... until the book burning begins'. This possibly hysterical reaction was nevertheless in key with many of the protests which were sparked across Britain, and the play received massive support from the worlds of the arts and academia, and indeed was supported by many Sikhs. The theatre had broken no law, it was pointed out, and nor had the author. It was the protesters who had set off fire alarms, thrown missiles and smashed windows; it was the protestors who had broken the law. Yet they appeared to have been rewarded. It was noted that the city council had failed to intervene, the police had failed to protect the theatre-going public, the Repertory Theatre had failed to honour their contract with Bhatti, and the Sikh leaders had failed to restrain their too-enthusiastic followers, or in many cases even to condemn the violence. Meanwhile, Bhatti's family were threatened with violence, and Bhatti herself faced with apparent abduction and murder.

Of course, if the play had not touched a sensitive nerve, it and its creator would not have been menaced by such treatment. That nerve was the setting, as the Sikh leaders had suggested before the first performance. To a Sikh, the *gurdwara* is the doorway to the *Guru Granth Sahib*, the supreme spiritual authority in Sikhism. The *Guru Granth Sahib* is a text, a holy book, rather than a living person, but it is conceived as the embodiment of all the gurus and revered as a living spiritual guide. It contains not solely Sikh holy writings, but also writings from other religions – Islam, Hindu, Kabirpanthi and Ravidasi. The *gurdwara* is thus not the same as a church or a mosque or a synagogue, for it holds the *Guru Granth Sahib* itself which is essentially sacred. In the *gurdwara*, this holy book is placed on a raised dais and covered with an ornate canopy, while the people sit on the floor, lower than it.

To set a play about sexual abuse and exploitation, and even a sort of ritual murder, within this kind of temple is thus hugely offensive to those who accept Sikhism. Nevertheless, the liberal principle of the right to freedom of speech and expression demands that the play should still continue. The theatre's determination to give voice to invisible communities and exploited individuals is wholly honourable. But it may not be as simple as it seems. What if the individual is a dissident within the 'invisible' community, and does not actually represent it? How is the outsider – the theatre – to know? Clearly, terms like the 'Asian community' or 'ethnic minority' are far too vague, for each group contains many and various subgroups, individuals, attitudes and so forth. In the Sikh community, there are certainly generational and gender-related tensions, which Behzti itself explores. It is worth noting that young Sikh women in particular supported Gurpreet Kaur Bhatti. Furthermore, the individual's freedom of expression must be set against the community's right to be treated with respect. Sensitivity to minorities must be a principle if we are not to repeat the Nazi horror. Besides, many Sikhs – and others – argue that freedom of speech is the merest hypocrisy in twenty-first-century Britain, when abusing people on grounds of their colour or race is not tolerated – and more than one television personality has lost their position as a direct result of apparent racism.

It is also worth suggesting that the social trauma which Behzti provoked was because the play was not just about Sikhism. Bhatti herself has pointed out that religion and drama have collided for centuries, and this play surely applies to Christianity, say, or Islam, at least as much as to Sikhism. The Roman Catholic Church has certainly not yet lived down the horrific revelations about its many priests who have sexually abused young and vulnerable believers, and it may not be coincidence that the Catholic Archbishop of Birmingham condemned Behzti and welcomed its cancellation. And though the abuses depicted perhaps apply most clearly to religious groups, abuse of this kind has also been depressingly prevalent in boy scout groups, television studios, care homes and other places where vulnerable young people are available to sexual predators. Religion is not the only institution, perhaps, which gives disproportionate power to its leaders, who are not subject to any sort of democratic control. All this is to suggest that this play is not simply about one small minority group, but has far wider implications than were often discussed when it was current news.

Finally, it is worth pointing out that the key objection to Behzti was centred on the fact that the play was set in the gurdwara. But in fact it was not a gurdwara, it was a wood-and-canvas stage setting. The wood-and-canvas setting was a metaphor, an image, it was not an actual temple. And the people performing were actors, not actual people. No real rape was committed, no real execution was done. A play is play, not reality. But maybe the play came too close to suggesting that religious observance, too, is actually performance, and this, at a deep level, undermined the authority of religious leaders. The implications of the *Behzti* affair are clearly complex and have not yet died away.

Looking at the theatre's past is thus complicated, but nevertheless it should provide us with fun as well as insights. The more we think through historical moments, trends and events, the more clearly do we see how to shape the questions we need to ask of the past. All interpretations are partial, must be constantly reviewed, and are always liable to change, which does not mean that we should not continue to try to interpret the past. Theatre history shows us how the theatre may speak to, and for, our generation. It shows how theatre responds to reality, and by provoking us to rethink our morality, our responsibilities and our identity, it may produce a new reality.

Summary

- The history of theatre is important because:
  - it shows how history speaks;
  - it shows how we can learn from history to make better drama now;
  - it provides a 'genealogy' of contemporary theatre.
- Theatre history also refers to the society in which its works were made.
- Primary historical evidence includes:
  - play texts;
  - archaeological evidence from old theatre sites;
  - documents (diaries, memoirs, etc.)
- Theatre historians and their readers need to be aware of how their own value systems may inform their judgments.

- By examining how particular plays have been received in the past, we see how plays include progressive as well as reactionary elements.
- We need to ask: how and where does drama fit into the ongoing discourses of power?

FURTHER READING

The most comprehensive overview of the subject of this chapter is probably Thomas Postlewait, *The Cambridge Introduction to Theatre Historiography* (Cambridge: Cambridge University Press, 2009), though it must be admitted that the going here is sometimes quite tough. Thoroughly stimulating is *Theatre Histories: An Introduction* by Philip B. Zarrilli, Bruce McConachie, Gary Jay Williams and Carol Fisher Sorgenfrei (London: Routledge, 2006). An excellent, more traditional history of theatre is O. Brockett, *History of the Theatre* (Boston MA: Allyn and Bacon, 1995). Also useful is any general guide, such as *The Cambridge Guide to World Theatre* edited by Martin Banham (Cambridge: Cambridge University Press, 1988).

For the theatre historian, seeking and finding the resources for her work can be daunting. Local libraries, perhaps especially local university or college libraries, often have interesting original material; and so do local theatres. For the English researcher, *The Directory of Performing Arts Resources* compiled by Francesca Franchi (London: Society for Theatre Research and the Theatre Museum, London, 1998) is invaluable. And for research beyond Britain, *SIBMAS International Directory of Performing Arts Collections* under the general editorship of Richard M. Buck (Haslemere: Emmett Publishing, 1996) is even more extraordinary, with resources in 173 countries from Afghanistan to Zimbabwe listed.

There are also many societies for theatre research which can be accessed via the internet: The Society for Theatre Research, Irish Society for Theatre Research, American Society for Theatre Research, Theatre Research International, The International Federation for Theatre Research, etc.

The plays examined in this chapter are: John Bale, *King Johan*, in *Four Morality Plays*, edited by Peter Happé (Harmondsworth: Penguin, 1979); William Shakespeare, *Twelfth Night* (many editions);

W. B. Yeats, *Cathleen ni Houlihan*, in *Collected Plays of W. B. Yeats* (London: Macmillan, 1960 and later editions); Jean-Claude Carrière, *The Mahabharata* (London: Methuen, 1989), which is also available on DVD; and Gurpreet Kaur Bhatti, *Behzti* (*Dishonour*) (London: Oberon Books, 2004).

5

ACTING

A BODY IN SPACE

The actor is unlike any other artist because his own body is his instrument. The painter has a canvas and brushes, the musician a violin or guitar; the actor only has his or her own body. The Russian director and actor, Vsevolod Meyerhold (1874–1940), expressed this as an algebraic equation:

$$N = A_1 + A_2$$

when N is the actor, and A1 is his understanding and A2 his physical capability.

The fact of the actor's own body as his instrument leads to paradoxes. For instance, the actor's body is real, but it performs, or presents, a fictional body; this fictional body, however, clearly has a physical reality. The relationship between these two bodies is constantly problematic. It raises, acutely, questions of identity. Theatre asks: Whose body? Whose identity? Most especially this is relevant to questions of gendered or sexual identity (see the section on *Twelfth Night* in Chapter 4, p. 81), but it is also true that the body's actions encapsulate and incarnate social power structures.

The actor, in presenting her body on the stage, is therefore at the heart of theatre's discussion of identity and the self. In life, the sense of self first appears in a child when they begin to locate themselves in a physical body in space. The body's surface, the skin, is understood as the boundary of the self: it enables a person to define themselves as a distinct entity. Thus, the body is not simply a physical something, it is the embodiment of a person's individuality. The problem with this concept, however, is that the body itself is porous, not only obviously in the head and the genitalia, but in the sweat pores and so on. Moreover, it may be asked precisely where the body ends: are hair and nails part of the body, even though we cut them off? What about tattoos, or make-up? The borders, in other words, are extremely unclear so that it is virtually impossible to create an absolute distinction between me and not-me. It seems that our subjective identity can only ever be partial.

Today the body is seen as a fundamental site of cultural, social, psychological and political struggle. No longer is the old Romantic notion of the mind as superior to the body accepted; first, because our mind is in our body, and second because the materiality of the body is as capable of making meanings as the intellect is. This it does, in both culturally specific and more widely symbolic terms, through posture, gesture, movement and so on. Studies of 'body language' reveal how, willy-nilly, the body expresses cultural values in movement, gestures and physical rhythms. In law courts, school and church as well as in work and at home, our bodies are expressive. We may compare the stage's revealed body with that displayed in sporting contests, strip shows, life drawing classes, etc. This was first explored practically in the 1960s and 1970s, especially in the work of a number of women performance artists, including Yoko Ono (b. 1933), Laurie Anderson (b. 1947) and Meredith Monk (b. 1942), who pioneered the use of the body as the raw material.

Their work leads naturally to a consideration of the disabled body, which has often been stigmatised in the past, and which often seems to have no place at all on the stage. In our society, conceptions of the normal tend to brand anything not normal, and this especially applies to the physical self. But in earlier times, 'normal' was not much considered: as far as the body was concerned, the concept of the 'ideal' implied that all bodies were flawed, the able bodied as much as the disabled. Lennard J.Davis (b. 1949) compares our responses to *Venus de Milo*, the statue with no arms renowned for its physical beauty, with a living woman without arms. And we may ask: is 'wholeness' possible in a fragmented world characterised by shifting and fragmented identities?

People with disabilities have been repressed, victimised, and institutionalised, and still are. Theatre in particular has often turned its back on disabled actors. Their bodies are deemed not to match what theatre requires. Yet this discrimination has been faced and outfaced by Graeae Theatre, who have fought the fight for disabled actors in Britain for many years, and their standard of production and performance has shown up many better-known 'mainstream' companies. They were founded in 1980, and now have their own premises, the Bradbury Studios in London, with rehearsal rooms, studios, offices and so on. The company is named after the three Graeae sisters, who shared one eye and one tooth between them in Greek myth, and their memorable productions have included such diverse work as Molière's *Georges Dandin*, Kane's *Blasted* and *Bent* by Martin Sherman (b. 1938), as well as adaptations of *The Hunchback of Notre Dame* and *The Iron Man* by Ted Hughes (1930–98), all with companies of disabled actors. Graeae's spirit is perhaps best characterised by their 'Rhinestone Rollers' group's Christmas presentation, *Sequins and Snowballs*, in which their wheelchair dancing troupe rock 'n' roll into the night! Graeae's success has significant implications for our consideration of the body as present on stage.

Michel Foucault suggested a power relationship between the watcher (such as a gaoler) and the watched (the prisoner), and the male 'gaze' became a much fought over battleground. (See the section on 'The gaze' in Chapter 8, p. 192.) The watcher 'fixed' an identity, wanted or not, on the watched, the object of the gaze. But theatre was able to provide a new dimension for this relationship: whereas in life, as suggested, the watcher usually has power over the watched, in the theatre the actor, who performs a *fictional* identity, may play with, undermine, even contradict the identity the watcher wishes to construct for the 'character', and thus the watched may be able to impose on the watcher. In the theatre, matters are perhaps not so simple as in life!

The complication may stem partly from the fact that the actor is always quoting, never doing something 'for real'. If the actor's body is the centre of the experience of performance, it is a body which in its movements, poses, attitudes, gestures, is only 'pretend', is always a metaphor for something else.

Box 5.1: Clothes and costumes

If the boundary between our bodies (our selves) and the world outside our bodies is blurred, one obvious manifestation of that threshold may be found in the clothes we wear. They cover and conceal much of our physical bodies (and all that our bodies represent in terms of our personal identities), but they also show us to the outside world. Clothes are a sort of meeting place for our private and public selves, an extension of the body, but not actually part of it. They combine uniquely personal expression and social conformity.

Clothes also have their own conventions, usually embedded in the dictates of the fashion industry, but still encoding all sorts of cultural and personal statements through their systems of semiotics. They may be symbolic, aesthetic, or bear the marks of status; as uniforms, they may indicate our oppression or demonstrate group identity. Fashionable clothes may make the wearer stand out, but they may also help the wearer to conform. Unfashionable clothes manifest an attitude to society just as surely as do fashionable ones. People who dress differently, whether by overdressing or by unnecessary shabbiness, often shock us, and sometimes seem to threaten us. Clothes – or costume – can also be a key to understanding the framing of a performance (see Chapter 1).

These are seminal ideas which must inform the work of the theatre costume creator.

THE PARADOX OF ACTING

The question of how far actors merely 'pretend' and how far they 'live' their parts – and how far they should attempt one or other of these courses – has always been at the heart of debates about acting.

The problem was perhaps most forcefully stated by Denis Diderot (1713–84), a critic, philosopher, journalist and playwright, in a brochure called *The Paradox of Acting*, published in 1773. Though part of an ongoing debate in France, Diderot's pamphlet was also written after watching the English actor, David Garrick (1717–79), entertain a Parisian drawing room by presenting the counterfeit of a series of differing emotions, none of which he was feeling himself as he showed them. This was acting wholly without feeling, and it crystallised Diderot's views. He begins the essay (which is written in dialogue form) with a challenge: 'If the actor were full, really full, of feeling, how could he play the part twice running with the same spirit and success?' His answer is clear:

> Before he cries 'Zaïre vous pleurez,' or 'Vous ferez ma fille,' the actor has listened over and over again to his own voice. At the very moment when he touches your heart he is listening to his own voice; his talent depends not, as you think, upon feeling, but upon rendering so exactly the outward signs of feeling that you fall into the trap. He has rehearsed himself to every note of his passion. He has learnt before a mirror every particle of his despair.
>
> (Toby Cole and Helen Krich Chinoy, *Actors on Acting*, p. 164)

Diderot's ideas were developed 100 years later by another French theorist, himself an actor of the highest quality, Benoît Constant Coquelin (1841–1909). Coquelin conceived the idea of the actor having a 'double personality' (from which Meyerhold derived the algebraic formula quoted earlier). Coquelin's 'first self' was the player who conceives the character, while his 'second self' became the instrument who presented the character to the audience. Coquelin criticised heavily his English contemporary, Henry Irving, for his willingness to seek effect, an overacting, as Coquelin saw it, which sprang from Irving coming too close to 'living' the passions of the character he was presenting. Irving's riposte, delivered in a lecture given in Edinburgh in 1891, asserted that the emotional faculties inevitably followed the brain in presenting 'passion', and quoting Hamlet ('in the very torrent, tempest, and (as I may say) whirlwind of your passion, you must beget a temperance that may give it smoothness'), he added that the only difference between the actor's presentation of passion on the stage and its reality in life lay in the actor's 'discretion'. Then he set out a challenge of his own:

> Diderot laid down a theory that an actor never feels the part he is acting. It is of course true that the pain he suffers is not real pain, but I leave it to anyone who has ever felt his own heart touched by the woes of another to say if he can even imagine a case where the man who follows in minutest detail the history of an emotion, from its inception onward, is the only one who cannot be stirred by it.
>
> (Henry Irving, *The Drama Addresses*, London: Darf Publishers, 1989, p. 158)

The debate has continued. To 'live' the part remains for many actors the ultimate goal, and there is undoubtedly an almost trance-like state which actors sometimes achieve during performance which seems like 'being' the character, and which appears to transcend the actor's own reality. It is a state somehow beyond the self, and yet in some way the self is also clearly present – if only in the body (which is one reason why the body is so central to all thinking about acting). It is also clear that during performance, the actor is not herself, and yet she is not not herself; and while she is also not the part, she is not not the part either. The actor and the character are both somewhere betwixt and between. This is comparable to the audience which does not believe what it sees, but does suspend its disbelief. The double negative is significant, and not the same as a positive.

Acting resides somewhere between the kind of self-exposure which the best performance art entails and the total possession of the shamanist. Like both these, acting is framed in time and space, but while it involves something of the showing of the one, it also involves something of the being of the other. This is the eternal paradox of acting.

Different styles of acting prompt different solutions to the paradox, and it is to different styles that we now turn.

REALISM IN ACTING

In the late nineteenth century, an intellectual revolution was taking place in Europe and America. Thanks to the work of men as different as Charles Darwin, Friedrich Nietzsche, Karl Marx, Hippolyte Taine (1828–93) and Claude Bernard (1813–78), new ideas and discoveries were radically changing the way life, society and the individual were understood. The intellectual ferment heavily influenced developments in the novel by writers such as Fyodor Dostoyevsky, Emile Zola (1840–1902) and others, and the fine arts, especially the work of impressionists like Edouard Manet (1832–83) and Paul Cézanne (1839–1906). But the theatre, addicted to 'old forms' like melodrama and pantomime, seemed to lag behind.

What was needed, as Zola, for instance, volubly argued, was a more 'natural' form of theatre, both in play writing and in play presentation. Truth to life in the theatre would enable audiences to engage with the significant ideas of the moment, and drag the theatre out of its apparent dark age. In fact, by the 1880s the move towards naturalism was beginning, first in the prose plays of modern life by Henrik Ibsen, which took notions of heredity and environment, class division and the exploitation of women in bourgeois society as their themes, and then in the productions associated with the German theatre company of the Duke of Saxe-Meiningen (1826–1914). His work was followed by further experiments in naturalism on the stage in Paris by André Antoine (1858–1943), in Berlin by Otto Brahm (1856–1912) and in London by J. T. Grein (1862–1935). But it was in Moscow, in the Art Theatre founded there in 1898 by Konstantin Stanislavsky (1863–1938) and Vladimir Nemirovich-Danchenko (1858–1943) that naturalistic acting was properly explored and developed, and attempts were even made to codify it into a system.

Stanislavsky's system was formulated over more than a decade of work. During this period, his ideas changed, he learned from experience and he created new institutions – notably the First Studio of the Moscow Art Theatre in 1912 – to conduct his experiments. At no time was he satisfied with it, and at no time did he consider it was finished and complete. It was a practical system to be tried and applied by the professional actor, consisting of principals and exercises which were of varying degrees of use. Nevertheless, the system is still the basis for all attempts to act 'naturally' on stage or screen, and underlies the work of any actor who attempts to inhabit – 'live' – her part. And, Stanislavsky believed, it is applicable in any dramatic circumstance, however absurd, futuristic or fantastic.

The system consists of two parts. In the actor's work on himself (sic), the actor works to develop physical control, especially her ability to relax physically (that is, to eliminate all forms of physical tension), and the ability to focus the attention, or concentrate. In addition, the system explores how the actor may train her imagination. To assist the actor to 'believe' in what she is doing, Stanislavsky introduced a kind of mental lever, which he called the 'Magic If'. 'If this were real' – then what? (See the 'Play' section in Chapter 1, pp. 1–7.)

Complementing the actor's work on himself, which was essentially private, was the actor's work on the role, in which the private work is applied to text and character. Stanislavsky believed that all actions stem from feelings. In other words, our inner experiences lead to our external actions. So, for example, he believed that if a person saw a bear, she would be frightened and the fear would prompt her to run away. Thus he wished to penetrate the inner experience of the dramatic character and then to find a way to make that inner experience real for the actor. This he believed would stimulate the actor to 'true' action (as opposed to something merely play-acted). One solution for this was the 'Emotion Memory', which on a simple level merely requires the actor to remember feeling an emotion similar to that of the character; but soon came to involve a 'sense memory', too. In this, the actor thinks of how particular sensations affect her – for example, how the smell of frying bacon makes her feel nostalgic, or the sound of church bells makes her sad – and then transfers this to the moment of acting. So, if the actor needs to feel nostalgic, she will fry some bacon in the Green Room before entering the stage; or, more likely, an actor who needs to feel sad will spend minutes in the wings before their entry, not thinking about feeling sad but listening, in their memory, to church bells. Later this method was largely discarded as unreliable and likely to bring with it unwanted corollaries.

More and more Stanislavsky came to believe in the efficacy of objectives to produce actions. He noticed the difference between lighting a fire, and lighting a fire to get warm. In the second of these, the actor's justification ('to get warm') makes the action interesting, truthful. Thereby he discovered that justified actions create believability.

During the first period of rehearsals, therefore, Stanislavsky insisted that the actors sat round a table, and worked out their objectives. First they discovered the play's 'superobjective' – why the playwright had written the play, his 'message' in over-simplistic language. Each character, too, had a 'superobjective', an overriding motivation in life, such as the drive to make money, to beget children, to prove one's intelligence, or whatever. Such 'superobjectives' – and all other decisions about the performance of the play – were modified and informed by the 'Given Circumstances' – that is, where the events take place, and the time in which they happen, as well as all the biographical details which can be gleaned about each character. The Given Circumstances also take note of the circumstances of production – the stage, the style, the ideas of the director, and so on.

The work round the table then became more detailed. The play was split into episodes and each episode was split into 'bits'. A bit – usually no more than three or four lines long – contained a single action, and each action had to be justified. In other words, for each bit, the actor finds an intention or task, and this is what stimulates (or justifies) the action. Thus, though in the episode one character may want to seduce the other, and that is her main objective, the seduction must be broken down into its component bits, each comprising one step in the process. The intentions or tasks for the successive bits might be: to help him relax, to put him at his ease, to make him feel important, to cut out the outside world, and so on. Each intention stimulates a particular action, which is the nub of that particular bit: she takes his coat, offers him a cup of coffee, asks after his mother, closes the curtains, and so on. Each action must be in response to a specific intention. This is the iron rule of the Stanislavsky system: no action may be performed unless for a reason.

What is more, as Stanislavsky noticed, it is in the process of fulfilling the tasks that the 'character' appears. To begin by desiring to create an angry person, or a timid person, or whatever, approaches the problem from the wrong end. Stanislavsky argued that if the actor got each intention right, and then each action right, the character would be there. As Aristotle noted, character is displayed in action, not the other way round.

Only when all the preparatory work round the table had been completed was the process of 'embodiment' commenced, and actors were allowed to stand up and begin 'blocking' the scenes. The factors which were of especial importance now were the 'through-line' of actions, which had to be logical and coherent, the 'inner truth', sometimes called the 'subtext', in which the intentions and tasks were kept alive, and the tempo rhythm, that is, the way the whole part is constructed and played, its overarching physical architecture.

This sketched outline of the Stanislavsky system perhaps indicates some of its complexity and detail. Any actor who uses it properly finds it testing and hard work – for many, it is too hard, and they take short cuts. But for those who do use it, it is a revelation. Interestingly enough, after decades working on the system, Stanislavsky himself moved on from it in the 1920s and 1930s to what has come to be called the 'Method of Physical Actions'.

This was an attempt to make the work of the actor less cerebral, more dynamic and immediate. In this method, the actors read the play, or the scene, together, and discuss it, focusing on *what happens*, as well as the characters' objectives, the given circumstances, and so on. But then, without more ado, they get up and try to recreate the scene through improvisation.

The first improvisations are usually short and perhaps rather strange; the actors may break down, they may omit more than they include. But after the first attempt to create the scene, they return to the script, re-read it, compare what they did with this original, and then try again. Slowly the work becomes more interesting. The actors begin to find the rhythm and structure of the scene, where the telling conflicts happen, the action and the counter-action. They may need different props, or to spend time discussing the author's language or rhythm. And they improvise again. The process is also known as 'Active Analysis' because the analysis is done not round the table as in the basic Stanislavsky system, but through action. This method has become more and more popular as it has become better known, so that now it is probably true to say that it has largely superseded the original Stanislavsky system.

After the Moscow Art Theatre visited New York in the early 1920s, one of Stanislavsky's most brilliant young actors, Richard Boleslavsky (1889–1937), stayed behind, and began teaching what he understood to be the Stanislavsky system at his Laboratory Theatre. His work in turn inspired a group of young Americans, led by Harold Clurman (1901–80), Cheryl Crawford (1902–86) and Lee Strasberg (1901–82), to establish the Group Theater along what they imagined were the lines of the Moscow Art Theatre. In the 1930s they were responsible for some of the most memorable productions in American theatre, and they developed actors like Lee J. Cobb (1911–76) and Stella Adler (1901–92) whose realism was a revelation. After the Second World War, they founded the Actors Studio in 1947, where the 'Method' was developed, especially by Strasberg who led the Studio for over three decades. His work laid a heavy emphasis on emotion memory, especially in the context of Freudian psychology, and evolved its own language – 'spine' for the character's 'superobjective', 'beat' (perhaps from Boleslavsky's Russian-inflected pronunciation) for 'bit', and so on. The Actors Studio produced a high number of America's best-known actors, including Marlon Brando (1924–2004), James Dean (1931–55), Dustin Hoffman (b. 1937), Robert de Niro (b. 1943) and Al Pacino (b. 1940).

Box 5.2: The psychological gesture

Michael Chekhov (1891–1955) was the nephew of the playwright Anton Chekhov. Michael trained as an actor and performed especially notably at the Moscow Art Theatre's First Studio, and later at the Art Theatre itself under Stanislavsky's direction. His Khlestakov in Gogol's *The Government Inspector* in 1921 was particularly acclaimed. In 1928 he emigrated to the West where he did much teaching of acting and developed his own system. This clearly owed much to Stanislavsky, but also depended on a number of original ideas. One of the best known of these was the Psychological Gesture.

The Psychological Gesture (PG) is the key to the actor's will, what drives her creativity. It is essentially a strong, well-shaped but simple movement – a gesture which uses the whole body. The actor thinks about the character in detail – the 'superobjective', the events the character participates in, her desires, actions, rhythm – and finds a movement to express all this. The movement is repeated several times. It embodies the quintessence of the character.

Chekhov recommended that the actor should start to make a PG with the hand only, to discover how it might express the character's essence – a grasping movement, perhaps, or a clenching of the fist, a droopy movement or a stretching out. This is then extended to include both hands and arms, the torso, and finally the whole body. The PG must be strong, clear and clean: it should partake of the nature of an archetypal gesture or movement.

The PG is the means by which the 'creative intuition' intervenes between the actor and the drudgery of reasoning out how the character works. It is a way of activating what has been called the actor's 'body-think' mechanisms. A PG can be made from the very first fleeting impression of the role. Later, it will be modified, changed, scrapped and created anew, as rehearsals proceed.

Chekhov further suggested that a PG can be made not just for the character in the whole play, but also for specific scenes or even parts of scenes. Sometimes the actor finds a block at a particular moment in rehearsals. Chekhov argues that by returning to and working with the PG at such moments, blocks to progress can be creatively removed.

CREATIVITY AND TRADITION

A strong contemporary acting style comes from popular traditions which have existed through the ages. In the West, for instance, there have been all manner of histrions, mimes, skomorokhi, cabotins, lords of misrule, Jack Puddings and others who have created theatre in pubs, market places, barns and village squares. Their plays were rarely fixed in the sense of being scripted, and were infinitely adaptable to the circumstances of the performance. The performers were often travelling showmen, or clowns, frequently illiterate, and they relied on quick-witted extemporisation, circus skills, spectacular effects, music, song and a good deal of interaction and banter with the audience. Their shows never pretended to realism, and they used the typical techniques of the oral performer; that is, they used a specific sort of improvisation which was neither purely spontaneous nor derived from a play script. They learned how, as a company, they could jointly tell a story they all knew – though a synopsis was as likely as not hanging up backstage – and they did this through a technique a little like a preacher preaching his favourite sermon from notes, or like somebody telling a joke – the plot is always the same, but the words and phrases and rhythms differ with each telling. Such performances leave little behind, but something of their flavour can be gained from looking at pictures like Bruegel's Flemish Fair, and something of their significance can be gleaned from the ideas of Mikhail Bakhtin about carnival. (See the section on comedy in Chapter 3, p. 53.)

The best known example of such theatre is the Italian *commedia dell'arte*, which flourished for two and a half centuries from about 1500. *Commedia* was essentially a broad and non-realistic style of performing. Its appeal was visual as much as verbal, and in performance it always acknowledged its audience. The performers often wore masks and usually played the same part in play after play – *commedia dell'arte*'s favourite characters included Pantalone, the old miser, Arlecchino, his servant, il Dottore, the lawyer, Flavio and Isabella, the young lovers, and Capitano, the braggart soldier. *Commedia* plays, which exist as scenarios, not fully-scripted dramas, were designed to allow the actors to use their many skills, including mime, tumbling, dancing, singing and playing musical instruments, as well as speaking the speech and performing their *lazzi*. These, according to Dario Fo (b. 1926), were all kinds of 'stage business ... situations, dialogues, gags, rhymes and rigmaroles which they could call up at a moment's notice to give the impression of on-stage improvisation'. Significantly, Fo continues:

> This repertoire had been prepared and assimilated through the experience of an infinite number of performances, of different shows, of situations worked out directly on the audience, but the central fact was that the majority were the result of study and careful preparation.
>
> (Dario Fo, *The Tricks of the Trade*, London: Methuen, 1991, p. 8)

Acting in this tradition often seems slapdash and untidy; in fact, as Fo makes clear, it is carefully and expertly prepared. And, indeed, acting in this style is not as easy as it looks. Characters need their every action justifying, as in the Stanislavsky realist tradition, but the actions themselves are larger than life. The fact that they often accommodate the audience suggests that these performances are located in reality, not realism. This is an actors' theatre *par excellence*.

In the early twentieth century, Vsevolod Meyerhold in Russia developed a training system for modern actors to develop this style of acting. Like Dario Fo after him, Meyerhold insisted on the importance of rigorous training, and set up the first studio in theatre history to formally explore possible means to do this. He called his classes 'Scenic Movement' and centred them on the body in space.

Key to this was his understanding of the *commedia dell'arte* actors' 'play', which was comparable to a child's play (see Chapter 1, p. 2): for the child, play is 'real', but it involves copying. The child never tries to 'be' mummy or daddy, it copies, recreates their movements, intonations of the voice, and so on. Characterisation is thus a form of physical expression, as was the case with the *commedia dell'arte*, whose masks were similarly characterised by patterns of movement and gesture. But Meyerhold devised a whole series of 'set roles', timeless on one level, but relevant to the contemporary world, such as the simpleton, the intriguer, the father figure, and so on. Each set role had its own '*emploi*', its typical way of expressing itself through movement and rhythm, and it was from this common base that 'character' was developed. Moreover, a role might employ different 'set roles' in different situations as the character entered different situations – at one time a father figure, but at another an intriguer – just as in life we 'perform' different roles in different situations. Meyerhold was perhaps the first practitioner to experiment with this idea of performing life. (Again – see Chapter 1, p. 8.)

Meyerhold's training methods were worked out as he went along, exploring especially the technical aspects of acting – exits and entrances, the use of props, and so on. For him, acting was controlled by rhythm – spatial rhythm (the body on stage and in relation to other actors, any scenery, and so on) and temporal rhythm ('musicality', the way a scene 'flows', and the necessary pauses and surges). His students performed exercises, such as 'Shooting from the Bow', the 'Leap on the Chest', and the 'Slap in the Face', almost dance-like explorations of physicality in space. Some of these were developed into what he called 'études', such as 'The Hunt', in which 'Shooting from the Bow' featured prominently. And the études then fed into the student's actual acting practice. According to Igor Ilinsky (1901–87), one of Meyerhold's most brilliant pupils, his system, known as 'Biomechanics',

> combined the gymnastic, the plastic and the acrobatic; [it] developed in the students an exact 'eye'; [it] enabled them to calculate their movements, to make them meaningful and to coordinate them with their partners; and ... helped them to move more freely and with greater expressiveness in the stage space.
>
> (Igor Ilinsky, *Sam o sebe*, Moscow: Iskusstvo, 1961, p. 155)

Balance, physical control, rhythmic awareness, both spatial and temporal, and responsiveness to the partner, to the audience, to external stimuli, are the defining factors of the biomechanically trained actor, and they are the attributes needed for acting creatively in this popular traditional style.

Meyerhold's student, Sergei Eisenstein (1898–1948), best known as a film director, with the writer Sergei Tretyakov, developed Biomechanics into a system which they called 'Expressive Acting'. This was derived from Eisenstein's influential theory of 'The Montage of Attractions', which theorises popular theatre performance as a series (or montage) of unexpected theatrical shocks (or attractions). An attraction might be anything from a soliloquy to an acrobatic stunt, an exotic costume to a comic song. Expressive Acting initially consisted of a number of apparently unrelated skills such as dance, storytelling and circus skills. Tretyakov's theories of stage speech, which involved emphasising consonants at the expense of vowels to develop 'verbal gesture' and a 'vocal mask' for each character, were also practised. But, following the physical and gymnastic ideas of François Delsarte (1811–71) and Rudolph Bode (1881–1970), Expressive Acting, like Biomechanics, integrated the actor's various skills in the physical. It provided also that actors should not only master physically difficult, and even dangerous skills, but that they should then be able to deform them, thus making them expressive. (A man with a limp is more interesting, and 'expressive', than a man who walks perfectly, Eisenstein asserted.) The actions then had to be 'sold' to the audience, in the manner of circus artists 'selling' their acts. Characters were to conform to what Eisenstein called 'typage', developed like Meyerhold's 'set roles', from *commedia dell'arte*, and performers were to have an 'attitude' towards their material. Eisenstein and Tretyakov's theatre was thus to be tendentious in the best sense. It was carried into silent films, and can be seen in performance in, for example, Eisenstein's *Strike*.

Another acting programme to suit this kind of theatre – creative but playful, and relying on popular tradition – was devised by Ewan MacColl and Joan Littlewood when they established Theatre Workshop in Britain after the Second World War. Their aim was the creation of an all-round actor who could dance, sing, speak verse, tell jokes and perform simple acrobatics. They insisted, first, that their actors studied theatre history and theory, and also politics, for their theatre was as tendentious as Eisenstein and Tretyakov's.

Their physical training began, as Stanislavsky's did, with learning to relax, and from this they put considerable emphasis on movement skills. They developed their own exercises involving walking, hopping, skipping and running, and developed more from their under-standing (gleaned from books) of the Eurhythmics of Jacques-Dalcroze (1865–1950). They also discovered the famous etchings of characters from the *commedia dell'arte* by Jacques Callot (1592–1635), and used them as the basis for more fantastical movement work. In 1947, they contacted Rudolf Laban (1879–1958), and he seconded to the company his assistant, Jean Newlove (b. 1922), who developed an extraordinary range of Laban-based movement work with Theatre Workshop's actors.

Meanwhile, MacColl and Littlewood devised a wide range of breathing and voice exercises, as well as enlisting help from a sup-portive trainer of opera singers, and they were the first British theatre practitioners who worked systematically on the Stanislavsky system (again as far as they understood it from Stanislavsky's translated books). Littlewood also became particularly adept at devising games and improvisations to integrate the elements of their work, to ready it for productions, and she gave her actors exercises which involved playing the same scene in different styles, thereby deliberately extending their range. It was a programme which enabled Theatre Workshop to become twentieth-century Britain's most radical, and probably most accomplished, theatre group.

Like Meyerhold and Eisenstein, Joan Littlewood admired early movies, many of which were able to capture popular theatre styles. This was especially true of comedies like those of Charlie Chaplin

(1889–1977) and Laurel and Hardy (1890–1965; 1892–1957). Dario Fo, whose plays won him the Nobel Prize for Literature, but who was yet better known as a performer, acknowledged the influence of Chaplin on his work, though he traced his artistic ancestry back to the medieval strolling Italian *giullare*, or comedian. Fo largely rejected formal training systems, though he did train with the French mime teacher Jacques Lecoq (1921–99), and he insisted on the importance of a physical 'warm up' in preparation for a performance, and in strenuous and critical analysis of it afterwards. But Fo was clear that his audience was his most helpful teacher, and quarrelled with Diderot's ideas because, he said, Diderot had no experience of performing, especially to popular audiences.

Fo's most creative work was marked by what he called 'Grammelot' and by mask work. Grammelot was a kind of medieval gibberish, useful for parodies and for satirising pomposity, but also extremely funny in its own right when performed well. Characteristically, it forces the actor to work with his hands, his face, his body, and Fo's exuberant physicality ideally suited its use. Equally, he was suited to working with a mask, for a mask, too, forces the actor to express his meanings through his body: the pelvis, Fo asserted, was the centre of the masked actor's universe. His international success demonstrates clearly that this style of acting retains enormous power and resonance.

ALIENATION

This book has suggested in several places the idea that we 'perform' our lives. We 'perform' the family breakfast, we 'perform' taking the kids to school, we 'perform' the diligent worker in the office, and so on. This enables us to isolate what we do, that is, to 'alienate' it, so that we may analyse, question, debate it. This is exactly what one kind of contemporary acting, usually associated with Bertolt Brecht, seeks to do.

Though he was primarily a playwright and director, he had much to say about acting, and was interested in actor training. What he looked for was a 'naïve' actor, one who would simply 'report' the action to the audience, so that the audience could analyse and judge it. This was, in essence, the theatrical transaction as Brecht saw it.

Although he never spelled out what an actor training regime might look like, Brecht did devise a fairly coherent approach to the production of the play, and from this it is possible to uncover the essence of the 'Brechtian' actor. For Brecht, the process of production begins with a 'naïve reading' of the script, when all the actors and stage assistants gather and the play is read round – that is, each new speech or stage direction is read by the next person in the circle. No-one makes any attempt to characterise, and the stage directions are read out with as much interest as the spoken words. Even the characters' names which prefix the speeches are read out. From this reading – or several such 'naïve readings' – discussion and investigation of the play begins. The actor must remember what impression the play first made on her, especially what surprised or shocked her. She must then go on to consider what is interesting about the play from various points of view, including historical, political, social, moral and even aesthetic. Not only must the results of these discussions be evident in the final performance, they must inform the actor's approach to the character's 'super-task', that is, how the character fits into this overall perspective. The 'super-task' also involves the actor recognising the contradictions in the character, which would help her to objectify the character, so that it is presented as fragmentary, contradictory, following not a logical or coherent path, as in the Stanislavsky system, but a zigzag, inconsistent path.

The second phase in Brecht's production process centred on the 'blocking' – that is the positioning of the actors on the stage, their groupings, movements, and so on. Brecht never came to rehearsals with the blocking planned, but spent weeks, even months, in rehearsal, working on the blocking cooperatively with the actors. He sought absolute clarity from moment to moment, and believed that if the blocking was clear enough, a spectator behind a pane of glass, who could therefore not hear the dialogue, would still be able to follow the progress of the story.

For blocking purposes, each scene was split into 'processes'. A process was a short but complete entity, probably a single interaction between characters. The processes accumulated to make the story – one thing after another. When a process ends, because that particular interaction has ended, the scene reaches a 'nodal point', and the process is interrupted. A nodal point is a moment of decision, when the scene changes direction. Brecht developed an exercise for actors when a nodal point was reached, called the 'Not ... but ... ' exercise. When the actors reached the nodal point, they were to stop and say 'Not' and then to play out what did not happen next for a few seconds or minutes. Then they stopped, played the scene up to the nodal point again, when they again stopped. Now they said: 'But', and proceeded to play out the next process. This gave them a physical understanding of these moments when a character makes a decision, or things change in some other way.

The point where the process meets the nodal point was sometimes described as the 'gest'. The gest was a key moment when the characters' attitudes were truly revealed. It might be shown in a pose, in a movement, in an interaction between characters. Brecht emphasised the social dimension of the gest. He pointed out that a man cringing from a fierce dog might in itself be a gest, but its social content only becomes clear when it is understood that the man is a tramp who is constantly harassed by the watchdogs of the selfish rich.

Obviously the idea behind these practices was to help the actor to 'alienate' the play from the audience, so that the audience could concentrate on the content. Brecht developed other rehearsal exercises to the same end. For instance, he might ask his actors to rehearse in the past tense (not 'I love you', but 'I loved you'), in the third person (not 'I loved you' but 'He loved her'), or adding 'he said' or 'she said' after each speech (not 'he loved her' but 'he said he loved her'). He asked actors in rehearsal to swap roles, and he got those who had to sing to speak against the music. These, and other devices, were all to help distance the action, to help the audience to make judicious assessments of it. The German word he used for the effect he desired was *Verfremdungseffekt*.

Finally, Brecht insisted on as many run-throughs of the production as possible, since it was in these that the actors could consolidate the contradictions in their parts, judge and understand the rhythms, ensure that the story was completely clear, and so on. In the end, the performance was to be 'quick, light and strong', and the dialogue to be tossed between the actors like so many balls. Then the events would be properly alienated, and the matter placed before the audience ready for judging.

Box 5.3: The street scene

Brecht's best known description of his new form of acting was his 'Street Scene'. In this, an old person crossing the road is knocked down by an oncoming vehicle. The witness must demonstrate what happened, and this demonstration illustrates the kind of acting Brecht wanted.

First the witness shows the pedestrian walking along, leaning on a walking-stick, a little out of breath. He does not look before stepping into the road. Then the witness shows the driver, who takes his eye off the road at the critical moment. The demonstration shows each character's level of responsibility for the accident.

The witness is not a highly trained actor. He may not have, for example, a stick to lean on, but may just mime this. It may be better if the demonstration is not perfect, because what is important is that the police, or jury, or whoever is the audience, understands what happened, and is not distracted by the brilliance of the performance.

There is no attempt to create an illusion in the street scene. Never does the witness 'live' the action. If it is necessary to embellish the scene – for instance, if the old person was limping – then that should be added. But only matters which add to our understanding need be presented. Even if one of the characters in the demonstration became emotional, there is no need for the witness to be emotional, though the witness may raise her voice or speak loudly if that is relevant.

The point is that this 'theatre of the street' is socially useful.

ACTING IN THE HOLY THEATRE

There is a kind of theatre in which the essential metaphor swerves into something altogether fierier, something which demands that the actor perform virtually as herself. It is closer to performance art, perhaps, or shamanism. Antonin Artaud (1896–1948) called this the 'theatre of cruelty'; Peter Brook's name for it was the 'holy theatre', when 'the invisible takes possession' of the performer, and 'through him, it will reach us'. (Peter Brook, *The Empty Space*, p.47.)

This is a theatre of direct experience, rare but terrifying, for it aims so to scorch its audience with uncontrolled shock, physical pain, true torment as to scour them into purity. It provides a physical experience addressed to the senses rather than the intellect, with the aim of taking its audience through a physical experience to a purity and spirituality beyond. For the actor who must take the spectators on this journey, a 'performance' can be extremely painful as well as emotionally draining. Nevertheless, some of the most exhilarating and awe-inspiring performances of the last hundred years or so have come from actors working in this style of theatre.

Artaud himself advocated an end to speech which conveyed rational sense. He wanted his actors to scream, bark, shriek, whisper, howl, groan, he wanted incantation, whistling, sweet harmonies, 'weird and violent words and … wild, piercing, inarticulate cries' (Martin Esslin, *Antonin Artaud: the Man and his Work*, London: John Calder, 1976, p. 9). To this end he devised a series of exercises for actors, which emphasised the use of the diaphragm, the chest and the head, first in a series of breathing exercises, then as a spring-board for utterance. By mastering breathing, Artaud suggested, the actor developed the means to master emotion, and the exercises moved from breathing to shouts and on to rhythm.

Further exercises involved long improvisations, including animal impersonations and also tests of the imagination as actors were asked to be fire or the wind, or to enact a dream, to achieve intensity without premeditation. Out of this would come a new understanding at a visceral level of the 'language of theatre', not merely the vocalised shouts, hisses, growls and so on, but also the physicalisation of anguish which Artaud saw as a condition of con-sciousness. The actor must act with her whole body, and through mime, mimicry, gesture and pose achieve the quality of dance, using the body itself as the first and crucial hieroglyph of meaning. The actor must therefore be able to slither, stride, stamp, sway without forethought, stretch her arms out or up, or pump them like a marathon runner, wag her head or topple it sideways, flirt, rage, find a frenzy within which to lose herself. The actor embodies secret, almost unknown feelings, desires, drives and fears which can pass unimpeded into the entranced spectator.

Artaud's prescriptions may seem impossible to follow, and indeed his own record as a practitioner is undeniably weak. But his ideas have inspired some of the most challenging and brilliant performances in the years since his death, in performance art, in pop music concerts, and in more conventional theatrical settings.

The Theatre Laboratory which flourished in Poland in the 1950s and 1960s, led by Jerzy Grotowski (1933–99), considerably extended Artaud's ideas. Especially in the early 1960s, after years of work, they presented a series of extraordinary productions which depended very largely on the intensity and commitment of the actors. Playing deliberately to tiny audiences – they did not admit more than one hundred spectators to a performance – they developed what Grotowski called a 'poor theatre', one which focused on the actor and did away with reliance on huge budgets, multiple props, expensive settings and the like. The audiences at the Theatre Laboratory sat with Faustus round his 'last supper' table, or looked down into the room where the Constant Prince was tortured. The actor was asked to 'open up', to 'emerge from himself': his job was seen as being to offer an invitation to the spectator in 'an act of love'. Grotowski was extremely keen on actor training, but this meant not so much the acquisition of skills as ways to remove personal obstacles, what he called a '*via negativa*', to an utterly open performance. If this theatre was therapeutic, its function to 'integrate' its spectators' lives, the actors were seen as priests or healers, who had to understand that they would gain nothing from the experience, but that they would have to give much. At its best, this theatre provided some of the most extraordinary acting performances in Western theatre: Ryszard Cieslak, for instance, in *Akropolis*, seemed to achieve a state of trance, in which the externalisation of his internal suffering enabled him somehow to become both subject and object of the work.

One of Grotowski's assistants in the early 1960s was Eugenio Barba (b. 1936), who set up his own experimental company, Odin Teatret, in 1964. His work moved Grotowski's Artaudianism in a new direction. He became interested in the quality of the actor's energy, and in the actor's 'presence'. He invented exercises – for instance, modifications of Meyerhold's Biomechanics – only to discover that, for him, conventional training concerned not how to act so much as how to define the self. Having worked on the margins of society in India and South America, Barba's work explored performance vocabularies shared by performers from many different cultures. He became interested in such fundamentals as how a performer stands, the space the performer occupies, and the actor's energy and physiology. In this, his internationalism of performance is like that of Peter Brook. Brook's work, too, has explored fundamental cultural exchange through performance in African villages, as well as the use of an invented language (*Orghast at Persepolis*) and a 'Theatre of Cruelty' season in London in 1964. Brook's attempts to strip away 'style' are paralleled by Barba's search for a theatre language which exists outside cultural referents.

A final example of Artaud-inspired theatre was the New York Living Theater of Julian Beck and Judith Malina. Beck was vehemently opposed to conventional actor training, preferring, with his collective of performers, to explore elements of physical theatre. The company's ceremonial and ritualistic productions often involved strenuous audience participation, for which the actors trained, but, like Artaud, Beck and Malina saw their works as rites of purgation which worked for spiritual change. The Living Theater influenced other American companies in the later twentieth century, such as the Open Theater of Joseph Chaikin, the Performance Group, later the Wooster Group, and the Bread and Puppet Theater of Peter Schumann (b. 1934).

THE MASTERY OF MOVEMENT

There was a time, fifty or more years ago, when British actors were famed for their statuesque qualities: not only did they possess stiff upper lips, the rest of their bodies were stiff as boards as well. That has largely changed now, and most actors understand the importance of learning dance – tap, jazz, modern – doing yoga, or perhaps martial arts like T'ai chi, or the Alexander Technique.

Instrumental in changing attitudes in the British theatre was the German-born refugee from Nazi Germany, Rudolph Laban, whose influence, even when unacknowledged, has been pervasive. His best known book is probably The Mastery of Movement, but his most extraordinary achievement was probably to formulate a notation which would record precisely danced or other movement. This could be read like music, so that a dance could be reconstructed simply from Labanotation, or kinetography as he called it.

From an actor's point of view, Laban's work is significant because he investigated the principles of movement, and asked the question: what is the purpose of any movement? Like Stanislavsky, he was concerned with the performer's intention, or objective. He asked, first: Why is the performer moving? The answer to this would suggest the answer to further questions: Where is she moving? How should she move? and What kind of energy should she use in the movement? Thus, the expressive quality of movement is derived from its intention.

Laban also explored the implications of the personal space within which the performer operates, and suggested the kinesphere, a kind of imaginary bubble, around the performer to define this. This was then related to the three-dimensional cross, through which the performer relates to space around her: the horizontal forward-and-backward dimension, the horizontal left-to-right dimension, and the vertical up-and-down dimension.

Considering the flow of movement, and the efforts required for them, Laban analysed movement through its direction in space (basically, whether it was direct or indirect), its speed or timing (fast or slow) and its weight (heavy or light). These indices led him to what he called the 'Eight Basic Efforts', as follows: (1) the punch, which is direct, fast and heavy; (2) the slash, which is indirect, fast and heavy, as when you slash with a sickle at a hedge; (3) the press, which is direct, slow and heavy, as when you push a car; (4) the wring, indirect, slow and heavy, like wringing out a wet towel; (5) the dab, which is direct, fast and light, as in throwing a dart; (6) the flick, indirect, fast and light, as when you flap your hand in front of your nose to disperse an unpleasant smell; (7) the glide, which is direct, slow and light, like a graceful ice-skater moving slowly in a straight line; and finally (8) the float, which is indirect, slow and light, like a leaf falling on a still autumn day.

Any performer who can master these eight efforts and apply them is beginning to discover how to physicalise a role.

SPEAKING A TEXT

Voice training is now seen as an essential ingredient in actor training, and work done by teachers like Cicely Berry (b. 1926), Patsy Rodenburg (b. 1953) and Nadine George (b. 1944) have helped very many actors to achieve their potential. Understanding how the voice works should – but does not always – begin with finding out something about the speech organs, in order to isolate them and begin to control their functions. Basically, the speech organs may be divided into three: (1) the respiratory system, that is, the lungs, the windpipe and so on; (2) the larynx, vocal cords and glottis; and (3) the articulatory system, the nose, lips, tongue and so on. The actor also needs to learn to hear herself as she speaks.

It is also useful for an actor to know how to analyse speech. For instance, even so simple a thing as a syllable becomes elusive once one tries to pin it down. A working definition is that a syllable is an audible movement of the respiratory muscles. So 'Good morning' is three syllables. But actually, of course, we usually say something more like 'uhh-ning' which is still three syllables, but only one of them is clearly audible, one is blurred and one inaudible. Yet it is likely that this utterance will contain three movements of the respiratory muscles. Similarly, syllables may be stressed or unstressed, which involves different kinds of effort in the muscle movements. Try saying 'men', and then 'dimension'. The syllable pattern provides one sort of rhythm to speech.

The voice is an extremely versatile instrument, with a variety of ways of making what is spoken dynamic. These include volume, which depends largely on the force of the air expelled from the lungs; tempo, the speed at which the speech proceeds; continuity, that is, the flow, the use of pauses, any hesitations and so on; rhythm, which all speech possesses, that is, the recurrence of two or more (or the expectation of more) movements, usually to do with word stressing (it is worth noting that rhythm in English is stress-timed, rhythm in French and many other languages is syllable-timed); tessitura, the range of notes the speaker employs; pitch, the speech melody, or voice gesture; and register, that is, the 'tone of voice', whether it is breathy, tight, falsetto, or what, often indicating the emotional state of the speaker. The actor should try to understand and take control of all these.

Many voice exercises help actors to 'free' their voice, and there are exercises designed to aid clarity of speech, and to articulate consonants and vowels. Actors also learn how to adapt their voice to whatever space they are in. Much good voice work, of course, depends on realising the character's intentions, and Laban's eight efforts can also be used to help the actor to speak. A phrase or a line can be 'punched' or 'floated' with very different results.

Finally there are simple techniques actors use to help them, like deciding whether a sentence is a statement, a question or a command. If a sentence is to have only one stress, where should that stress fall? It is interesting to stress different words in the same sentence to see how different meanings may be obtained. It is also worth remembering that nouns are the most important words in terms of carrying the sense of a sentence, and that, in probably three-quarters of all speech, it is the nouns which are stressed.

Summary

- The actor's body on stage is at the heart of the theatrical transaction. It raises problems of identity in a uniquely theatrical way.
- The question of whether and how far an actor should 'live' a part has been debated for centuries, and is not yet settled.
- The Stanislavsky system is the basis for most realistic acting.
- An alternative, more spectacular, physical and improvisational tradition derives from popular theatres.
- Bertolt Brecht's system of acting depends on self-conscious performing to 'alienate' the audience, that is, to help them judge the actions presented.
- 'Holy theatre' actors test the limits of their own endurance and commitment in the intensity of the performance.
- The basics of movement and speech are also crucial weapons in the actor's armoury.

FURTHER READING

Probably still unrivalled as a book which covers all aspects of acting is Toby Cole and Helen Krich Chinoy, *Actors on Acting*, (New York: Crown Publishers, 1970). Robert Leach, *Makers of Modern Theatre*, (London: Routledge, 2004), covers the main styles of contemporary acting in detail.

The following specialised books are recommended, but there are many others which investigate this endlessly fascinating subject: Konstantin Stanislavski, *An Actor's Work*, (London: Routledge, 2008); Bella Merlin, *The Complete Stanislavsky Toolkit*, (London: NHB, 2007); Edward Braun (editor), *Meyerhold on Theatre*, (London: Methuen, 1969, and later editions); Bertolt Brecht, *The*

Messingkauf Dialogues, (London: Methuen, 1965, and later editions); Antonin Artaud, *The Theatre and Its Double*, (London: John Calder, 1970, and later editions); Jerzy Grotowski, *Towards a Poor Theatre*, (London: Methuen, 1981); Rudolf Laban, *The Mastery of Movement*, (Plymouth: Macdonald and Evans, 1980); Cicely Berry, *Voice and the Actor*, (London: Harrap, 1973).

6

DIRECTING

HISTORICAL

In theatre history, the twentieth century is notable for the rise to pre-eminence of the director. Before that, whoever it was who arranged the actors on the stage, their exits and entrances, as well as executed all the other tasks the contemporary director is asked to do, seemed of small importance. The increasing importance of the director was probably one response to the 'crisis' in the theatre of the later nineteenth century referred to in Chapter 5 (p. 111).

Before this, it seems that the play was 'directed' by the playwright. The word 'wright' means 'maker', and certainly in ancient Greece the play was not considered 'made' until the performance was over. The scripts contain no stage directions (frustratingly for later producers as well as scholars) because the authors directed the performers – solo actors and chorus members alike. Indeed we know that the *Choregos* (financial backer) paid the author and the chorus to rehearse, sometimes for months before the performance.

In the medieval period, the mystery plays seem usually to have been under the direction of a 'pageant master' who was responsible for 'bringing forth' the plays. 'Bringing forth' included not only directing the actors, but also 'bringing forth' the wagon upon which they would perform. A well-known miniature painting,

'The Martyrdom of St Apollonia' from *The Hours of Etienne Chevalier* by Jean Fouquet (c.1420–c.1481), depicts scaffold stages or grandstands surrounding a theatrical presentation of the martyrdom, supervised by a proto-director with stick (a sort of cross between a magician's wand and a conductor's baton) and book in hand. In England, by the time of Henry VIII, it seems that it was possible for local town leaders to hire mystery play scripts for performance, and it is known that professional actors were hired to appear in, and almost certainly 'bring forth', some mystery plays. In France, the pageant-master and poet Jean Bouchet (1476–1557), wrote that he was responsible for designing the stage and scenery, as well as stands for spectators, contracting carpenters to construct them, casting and rehearsing the plays, as well as acting himself, finding and hiring doorkeepers, and making announcements to the audience.

As with the Greek theatre, the playwright in Shakespeare's theatre was probably ultimately responsible for the staging of the play. Perhaps the best fictional portrait of a playwright–poet is Shakespeare's Peter Quince in *A Midsummer Night's Dream*, who struggles to control his actors' exuberance in order to be able to 'make' the play. He assembles the acting company, explains the play briefly to them, casts them and gives out the 'parts' to the actors. Before the twentieth century, it was common practice for the actor to be given no more than his or her own part, written out on a long scroll, with the cue (three or four words) from the previous speech to show when they begin speaking. That was all the actor was expected to attend to. Quince also arranges rehearsals, makes a props list and directs the actors, indicating where they enter and exit, correcting their pronunciation and discussing their character's place within the story. Shakespeare probably did much the same for the King's Men at the Globe Theatre, and later in the century we know that the French playwright and actor, Jean-Baptiste Poquelin Molière, directed his own plays because he shows himself doing so in *The Impromptu of Versailles*.

By the eighteenth and nineteenth centuries, the responsibility for staging a play in the theatres of Europe fell largely on the shoulders of the actor–manager. In England, David Garrick, Edmund Kean (1789–1833), and Henry Irving were among the famous actors who staged plays to ensure they themselves were squarely centre stage when they were on, with most of the lighting directed at themselves, too. Irving would rehearse for up to six hours without a break even for lunch. He sat in the auditorium, explained what he wanted and then insisted on every intonation and every move conforming precisely to this. Patiently he went over and over a scene until it was exactly as he wanted it. He rehearsed himself (in the central role) at home, and used an 'extra' to stand in for him during rehearsals. The company never saw his performance until the final dress rehearsal.

Everything was to change in the last decades of the nineteenth century, perhaps with the rise of naturalism, when audiences wanted something subtler, or at least different from, what soon became thought of as old-fashioned theatricality. Naturalism demanded an ensemble of actors whose stage rhythms and stage actions seemed 'natural'. For this, an outside eye was required, one which was unbiased towards particular characters and which could create a true semblance of 'real life'.

THE GREAT DIRECTORS

As already implied, it is arguable that the history of the theatre in the West since about 1875 is the history of a series of outstanding directors. One of the problems of constructing such a history, however, is that what goes on in the rehearsal room, the director's private laboratory, as it were, is rarely accessible to those outside it. True, some directors have written diaries of productions, and some actors have too; there are prompt-books available (such as Stanislavsky's for *The Seagull*) and model books (such as Brecht's for *Mother Courage and Her Children*), not to mention photographs, anecdotes and more. Nevertheless, much about the work of the great directors has remained infuriatingly elusive, and matters mentioned in this section are more by way of notes towards further investigation than anything else.

It is generally accepted that the first company to employ a director in the modern sense was the Duke of Saxe-Meiningen's company. Saxe-Meiningen himself had strong ideas about how the drama should be presented, and he employed Ludwig Chronegk (1837–91) to put them into practice. Chronegk was something of a despot, drilling his actors mercilessly, but he achieved a degree of authenticity, as well as a standard of ensemble playing which was a revelation. In particular, he insisted that every actor in a crowd scene was individualised and occupied on stage, thereby ensuring that every member of a stage crowd was 'real'. Chronegk influenced the naturalistic directors who came after him – André Antoine in France, Otto Brahm in Germany, and above all Konstantin Stanislavsky in Russia, who developed his system in the first two decades of the twentieth century (see Chapter 5, p. 111–114).

Once these men had established the primacy of the director, their apparent addiction to naturalism (which, by the way, they would have disputed) fomented rebellion against their form. Leading these younger directors were Edward Gordon Craig (1872–1966) and Vsevolod Meyerhold. Craig was perhaps the first to call for the absolute dominance in the theatrical process of the director, who, combining this with designing the production as well, would become a 'theatre artist', who would produce the unity which he saw as crucial if the art of theatre was to reach its full potential. This was a symbolist theatre, one based on ritual and abstraction, which would attain spiritual significance. In his most notorious advocacy, Craig therefore called for actors who would be little more than puppets, 'übermarionettes' he termed them, who would follow the theatre artist's vision.

More practical but no less original was Meyerhold, whose most significant contributions to theatre practice, both still probably under-appreciated, were, first, the concept that the actor's performance could be like a human being's life, a sequence of performances, an idea far ahead of its time and only now coming to be properly explored (see Chapter 1, p. 8); and second, his method of working, which he called the 'theatre of the straight line', because of the way dramatic meaning was processed. First, the text created by the author is 'assimilated' by the director. His assimilation is then passed on to the actor, who assimilates this. Finally, the actor reveals his assimilation of what the director had given him to the spectator in performance. The playwright's ideas are the parameters within which the director conceives the production; the director's ideas are the parameters within which the actor creates his character; the character is what is presented to the audience. It is, as it were, a straight line from playwright, through director and actor, to spectator, as opposed to the more usual process in which the playwright (or, more accurately, the play text) and the director effectively constrict what the actor does.

By 1920, it is possible to say that the director was in his (and it usually was 'his') pomp in Western theatre. In the USA David Belasco (1853–1931) bestrode the theatre scene, especially in New York where he mounted a series of popular realistic melodramas, many at the theatre bearing his own name. Max Reinhardt (1873–1943) in Germany was a more substantial figure artistically. An extremely prolific director, he was also capable of genuinely original work, and made an impact on many forms – legitimate theatre and cabaret, realism and expressionist theatre, and embodied at least some of Craig's ideas probably more successfully than Craig himself. Thus, his attempts to liberate theatre from literature and his frequent use of settings conceived architecturally, as well as his preference for a thrust stage, were all part of a coherent artistic vision. He directed a number of German theatres, including the Neues Theater on Schiffbauerdamm, Berlin, and the small Kleines Theater, and then the Deutsches Theater, Berlin's most significant theatre, in conjunction with the small Kammerspiele. He founded and ran the Salzburg Festival from 1917, and was director of the Theater in der Josefstadt, Vienna. In addition, he founded and ran his own school for directors. He seemed to be equally at home with all sorts of drama, including both his subtle chamber productions of realist works by the likes of Henrik Ibsen, Gerhart Hauptmann (1862–1946) and Arthur Schnitzler (1862–1931) and his ground-breaking productions of expressionist dramas by, among others, August Strindberg, Carl Sternheim (1878–1942), Reinhard Sorge (1892–1916) and Reinhard Goering (1887–1936). He consistently directed Shakespeare, finally and most memorably, perhaps, in the 1935 Hollywood film of *A Midsummer Night's Dream*, and he created extraordinary spectacular shows, often outdoors, including *Oedipus Rex* at the Circus Schumann in Vienna in 1910, repeated at Olympia in London the following year, and the medieval *Jedermann* (*Everyman*), adapted for the Salzburg Festival by Hugo von Hofmannsthal (1874–1929), and performed in front of the ancient cathedral. These productions showed Reinhardt's development from Saxe-Meiningen's crowd work, for now not only was every member of the huge crowd individualised, they were welded into a breathtaking whole through mass choreographed movement. Reinhardt's energy was prodigious, and partly showed in such creations. When the Nazis came to power in 1933, Reinhardt donated his theatres to the German people and left Europe for the USA, where he worked for the last years of his career.

Perhaps in the end more influential, but of a style and temperament exactly the opposite of Reinhardt's, was Jacques Copeau (1879–1949), who was also, however, something of a follower of Edward Gordon Craig, whom he met in 1915. Two years before that he had founded the Vieux-Colombier theatre in Paris, dedicated to anti-realism and poetic simplicity. What Copeau wanted was little more than the actor on a bare stage, and he explored mime and physical theatre extensively when these were hardly known. He staged mostly classics, especially Molière and Shakespeare, as well as some new plays, but his work was interrupted by the First World War. In 1917, as part of their propaganda effort, the French government sent him and his company to New York, where they remained until 1919. In 1920 they re-formed in Paris, but by now actor training was coming to be more and more significant for Copeau, and in 1924 he withdrew with some of his followers to Burgundy where he converted to Catholicism. Here he and his most industrious follower, Suzanne Bing (1885–1967), developed a training scheme based on control of the breathing, natural gymnastics and the 'noble' (or neutral) mask. The group, or 'brotherhood' as Copeau called them, were known as Les Copiaus, and performed irregularly, presenting mostly medieval and *commedia dell'arte*-style pieces in open air settings. The emphasis was on simplicity, improvisation and ritual, sometimes using neutral masks and usually on a bare stage. The group dissolved in 1929, and in 1936 Copeau returned to Paris, working with the Comédie Française from 1936 to 1941, the last year as director. Copeau's influence on the development of French theatre was incalculable, not only through his own companies, and the Compagnie des Quinze, formed in 1931 out of Copeau's 'graduates', but also through the work of many individuals whom he taught or worked with, including Charles Dullin (1885–1949), Louis Jouvet (1887–1951), Copeau's nephew Michel Saint-Denis (1897–1971), Valentine Tessier (1892–1981), Etienne Decroux (1898–1991), and at second hand, as it were, Jean-Louis Barrault (1910–94), Jacques Lecoq (1921–99) and many more.

Box 6.1: *The Storming of the Winter Palace*

The Storming of the Winter Palace was staged on 7 November 1920, three years to the day after the Bolshevik revolution. It was a unique production performed in and around the real Winter Palace in St Petersburg, and involving over 8,000 performers and probably over 100,000 spectators. It was a huge re-enactment of a seminal event in Russian history, and many of those who had been involved three years earlier recreated their historical roles in this mass spectacle.

The whole event was coordinated by nine men: five assistant directors, three directors – Yuri Annenkov (1889–1974), Alexander Kugel (1864–1928) and Nikolai Petrov (1890–1964) – and one overall directorial supremo, Nikolai Evreinov (1879–1953). Evreinov was a playwright, director and theatrical theorist, whose concept of drama in life often pre-empts contemporary performance theory (see Chapter 1) in uncanny ways. *The Storming of the Winter Palace* was therefore a high point in his career, being a theatricalisation of life perhaps without previous precedent.

The performance represented the final battle between the Whites (the Provisional Government and its forces) and the Reds (the Bolsheviks), and included a dramatic chase across the square, and the storming of the actual palace with fireworks and trucks full of soldiers, bicycle corps, cavalry and vast crowds of communist-inspired workers.

The whole was clinically worked out and directed. As one participant noted, the drama spectacle was much better organised than the actual storming of the Winter Palace, which was chaotic and even anticlimactic. All the participants in the spectacle were strictly controlled by the directors. Each director or assistant director controlled one group, and each group was divided into subgroups, each with its own leader, who was an actor in the piece. These leaders were rehearsed in the evenings for three weeks before the performance. The mass of the actors were simply told the plan of action before the performance, and then had to follow their leader. Evreinov sat on a raised platform in the centre of the huge square, and coordinated and orchestrated the performance by field telephone, light signals and motorcycle couriers. Apparently the only real hitch occurred when the telephone link to the battleship on the river was broken, and a motorbike despatch rider had to be sent to order the cruiser to stop firing its guns.

As a directorial creation, *The Storming of the Winter Palace* was probably unique, not only as a piece of original theatre but as an operation carried out with almost military precision and intelligence.

THE CONTEMPORARY DIRECTOR

The term 'director' used to be synonymous with 'producer', but now the latter term is taken to refer more specifically to the business management of a production. In the contemporary theatre the director has overall responsibility for all the artistic elements of the production. This includes the text itself – its arrangement, any cuts and so forth – as well as casting, rehearsals, staging, the *mise en scène*, lighting, music, costumes and make-up, and above all the 'key idea'. It is therefore more or less essential for the director to know at least something of other areas of theatre practice; but she should also know something of fine art, music, philosophy and literature, and she should know theatre history, and be able to use it creatively. Moreover, the director should be able to deal with people, to communicate and inspire. The orchestra conductor is sometimes compared to the theatre director, but the conductor is there at the performance, in control as the director cannot be.

From this it follows that a person with a craving for power is unlikely to make a good director. Sometimes it is argued that the best directors were once actors, like Stanislavsky, Meyerhold or Joan Littlewood, but neither Brecht nor Peter Brook were ever actors. There seems to be no ideal way of becoming a director. Some are actors or stage managers who want to direct, some are university graduates who like theatre, others have nothing more than their ambition with which to arm themselves. Some directors are tyrants, others are enormously democratic; some are artistic revolutionaries, others extremely conventional, even timid. Directors once tended to work from the text, which was their anchor and starting-point, but this is less acceptable in the twenty-first century, and actors, too, realise there is more to a production than speaking the text. This is partly as a result of the work of contemporary directors, the best of whom have an energy and drive to innovate that is transforming theatre and relations among its practitioners. Some of those whose work is worth discovering are: Peter Fomenko

(b. 1932), Ariane Mnouchkine (b. 1939), Tadashi Suzuki (b. 1939), Robert Wilson (b. 1941) and Robert Lepage (b. 1957).

A figure of importance in many European and American theatres, and of growing influence in Britain, is the *dramaturg*, a German title which has slipped into English. The dramaturg's first job is to do with ensuring the play-worthiness of the text, which places her somewhere between the playwright and the director. The dramaturg is the person who makes the script stageable. 'Adaptations' of work, often translated work, are often made by dramaturgs. She also works on context and content, dramatic structure and character psychology, the play's themes, and its technical demands and qualities.

Beyond this, the dramaturg will often assist with casting. She will probably attend many rehearsals and even direct certain scenes or actors. She is likely to inform participants about the play and its circumstances, and may also liaise with the designer, the stage manager and others. She will prepare the programme and may oversee the publicity. It is sometimes claimed that the truly successful dramaturg is a co-author of the play, or the production, and there have been court cases in the U.S.A. when the dramaturg's position has been vigorously examined. The question cannot be resolved here, but the fact demonstrates the importance of the position.

For British would-be directors there is little properly rigorous training available, though other countries do provide training, and there are very well established three-year courses for actors. The next section of this chapter is in no way 'a training', of course, but at least it points to the way the basic conventional directorial role is usually fulfilled today. Of course, the more experienced or imaginative the director, the less likely she is simply to follow this pattern. The aim here is to suggest something of the complexity of the director's contribution to modern theatrical production. What follows, therefore, is mostly practical, and should be read in conjunction with the previous chapter about acting and the following chapter on scenography. As the director is the effective hub of everything, her work inevitably overlaps with those others.

Box 6.2: Film director, stage director

Many directors from the theatre have made films, and some film directors have worked in live theatre. The two media are not the same, however, and few directors have mastered both. The greatest exception to this generalisation is probably the Swedish director Ingmar Bergman (1918–2007). His name came to be associated mostly with the cinema, and certainly his huge output of films, including *The Seventh Seal*, *Wild Strawberries*, *Cries and Whispers* and *Fanny and Alexander*, was as impressive as anybody's in the twentieth century. But he began his career in the provincial theatre before the Second World War, and over the next sixty or more years he directed an extraordinary number of highly acclaimed and exciting stage productions, so that his stage career should be regarded as just as significant as his career in films. For many years he made a film in the summer, and returned to the Stockholm stage to direct one or two plays in the winter.

In his early twenties Bergman 'shouted a lot' and 'made trouble', according to the author and director Erland Josephson (1923–2012), 'but he was already a professional'. In these early years he experimented widely with political drama and physical theatre, and staged plays both in intimate surroundings and on very large stages. He directed plays by, among others, Shakespeare, Molière, Ibsen, Tennessee Williams, and especially August Strindberg, and for three years from 1963 was director of the Royal Dramatic Theatre in Stockholm. Here he was responsible for far-reaching reforms to a thoroughly conservative cultural institution, and he also created a number of startling productions. In the 1970s he returned to the Royal Dramatic Theatre, where his work on plays by Strindberg was particularly admired, and after a stint with the Munich Residenztheater, he returned for a third spell to Stockholm in the 1980s.

Though he was an author and playwright himself, most of his theatre work investigated the acknowledged pinnacles of Western drama. He used the text as a jumping-off point for radical reinterpretation, seeking always the heart of the playwright in his frequent reworking of texts for contemporary performance. Encouraging actors to achieve a raw honesty, his productions were still filmic in a visual sense, dense and often pregnant with agonising uncertainty. His *Miss Julie* by August Strindberg, for instance, seen at the Edinburgh International Festival in 1986, was riven by striking images – the blinding ice-white dawn, for instance, in which the preening Jean tormented the eponymous heroine, and the use of a simple basin from the kitchen draining board as a kind of symbolic prop. It was theatre of extraordinary immediacy and power.

One of Bergman's actors, Gunnel Lindblom (b. 1931), said of working with him: 'I felt he really understood what I was trying to do. You didn't have to show him something exquisite: he saw the work in progress and saw what it could become.' Perhaps that is why he was able to make such an impression in both media.

FIRST TASKS

The first job of the director is to choose a play. The choice will be constrained by a number of considerations, including financial (though there are ways round a lack of money), the performance space available (though this can usually be adapted), and the technical resources of the theatre and required by the play. The director may also want to consider what actors are available to her, or what designer or scenographer she would like to work with. Is the acting company large or small? What is its gender balance? Can this be alleviated by double casting or cross-gender casting? What audience is expected? The audience at a West End commercial theatre will not be interested, perhaps, in what might appeal to an arts centre audience in a university town. The relevance of the play to the community within which it is to be performed is worth considering. Bertolt Brecht sometimes used an exercise in which the company had to think of why a chosen play might relate to different communities – say, a crofting community in northern Scotland, a group of trade unionists, a youth club audience, and so on. In the end, the most significant factor will be – and probably should be – the personal enthusiasm the director feels for the play.

Having chosen the play, the director will usually be responsible for negotiating the performing rights if the author is alive, or has died fewer than seventy years ago. Once permission has been granted, scripts must be organised, and if the play is in copyright and in print, this usually means that printed scripts must be bought. There must be enough scripts for the stage management team as well as the actors.

Before the actors gather for the first rehearsal, it is usual for the director to have meetings with the scenographer or her team – set designer, costume designer, lighting designer and so on. Who these are is generally the director's choice, and it is the director's task to enthuse them and arouse their creativity. If possible (and it is not always possible if the rehearsal period is a mere three weeks or so) the scenographer, or the team, should attend some rehearsals. The ideal is for there to be enough time for the scenographer to attend a week or two of rehearsals and then start to work on the basis of the director's and actors' creative work, and the two sides of the production proceed in complement with each other. But this is rarely feasible.

It is more important for the stage set to be workable for the actors than for the designer's visual brilliance to be displayed. But it is also important to recognise that the setting is not merely a background, but something closer to an environment which makes its own contribution to the meaning of the performance. The director must discuss with the designer not only how these general principles apply, but also how each scene will be staged, and how the design will facilitate this. The relationship of lighting, costumes and props to the set must also be discussed: Is a doorway too narrow for the passage of a crinoline? Can the necessary light reach that dark corner? A clear and clean stage setting is usually the ideal, with nothing too fanciful about it, unless that is required by the script. Shakespeare, Brecht, Beckett – all require little more than an empty space, though it is also true that a cluttered stage may be inspiring, as with *The Caretaker* by Harold Pinter.

The director also needs to ensure at this stage that matters such as publicity and the design and content of the programme are in hand, and should also decide about intervals in the performance. The interval vitally affects the rhythm of the production. Though August Strindberg advocated performance without intervals, in fact more than about ninety minutes without any break is unfair on at least some theatregoers. The concentration span of most spectators is hardly this long, and many will need a toilet break, or simply to stretch their legs, if they are to get the best from their experience at the theatre. Conventionally, and for good reasons, the second 'half' of the performance is usually shorter than the first 'half'.

Auditioning and casting are crucial for the director. Auditions must be carefully planned so that the qualities the director is seeking are most likely to be evident, but the good director will remember that most actors are actually extremely nervous when they attend an audition. Some directors find it helpful to ask actors to consult the script before auditioning. The commonest audition asks the actor to present two contrasting speeches, one from a classical play, and one from a modern play, but not everyone would agree this is the most useful format for an audition. Some directors audition by 'work-shop' – games, exercises, improvisations, and so on – which demonstrates the actors' abilities to work with others, to focus energy and to respond to problems. Sometimes an actor may be asked to perform a scene or a speech from a play she has recently performed, and then perhaps to criticise this performance. Some directors like to chat to those who audition for them, to find out what kind of person they are, whether they would work together easily, and so on. An actor might then be asked to discuss a performance she has seen, so that they show their artistic sensitivities and criteria. Perhaps actors might be asked in advance to read the play and to prepare something which expresses a theme or an idea or a piece of narrative, and to perform this in any way they like without resorting to the text – they could mime, dance, sing, whatever, thus demonstrating imagination and versatility.

The director needs to watch not just 'how good' the actor is, but to notice mannerisms, vocal or other tricks, and so on, and to consider how any actor will fit into the company as it shapes up. Not only will they 'get on' socially, but how will this actor's skills complement those of the other actors? This is a little like picking a football team: one goalkeeper is enough, but perhaps two strikers are needed. Moreover, it may be wise to avoid casting people who loathe each other (though sometimes there are dividends from such daring!). To cast actors who have trained at the same school, or who have worked together before and share a theatrical 'language', or are in other ways professionally compatible, is often sensible. The idea is to create an ensemble. The best actor may not be the best person for this particular cast.

Indeed, as far as casting is concerned, the best directors are often prepared to take risks. A significant factor, though one which is hard to judge, is whether the director believes she will be able to find the sources of the actor's energy. Typecasting of the old-fash-ioned kind is largely a thing of the past: actors in the nineteenth century virtually always played the same types – the 'heavy man' played the villain, the 'juvenile leads' played the hero and heroine, the 'low comedian' played the comic servant, the superbly-named 'walking lady' and 'walking gentleman' played secondary parts, like the faithful friend, or the villain's agent, while an actor called 'general utility' played whatever speaking parts were left; 'super-numeries' played non-speaking parts. Today, most directors have assimilated Brecht's observations: 'As if all cooks were fat, all pea-sants phlegmatic, all statesmen stately. As if all who love and are loved were beautiful. As if all good speakers had a fine voice.' Edmund Kean was small but often played heroic parts. Stanislavsky was extremely handsome, yet he rarely played lovers. Does Estragon have to be old? Does Henry VI have to be white? There are many different Vanyas, Blanche DuBoises. After fewer than five minutes, audiences stop noticing whether the actor's physical fea-tures seem conventionally appropriate. Directors should – and often do – take risks in casting. And surprisingly often, the risks justify themselves.

BEFORE REHEARSALS

Meanwhile, the director's own preparation for the production should be well under way. Indeed, the good director will already have spent much time researching and thinking about the produc-tion. She will not have discovered all the answers to all the pro-blems in the play, for many of the juiciest of these can only be solved creatively in rehearsal with the actors, but she will have begun to focus on some of them. For instance, she will try to discover where the play's energy comes from – Astrov's desire or Serebriakov's selfishness? Lady Macbeth's craving, or Malcolm's resilience? Perhaps both of these, and some other sources as well. What is the play's key idea, what was the bee in the playwright's bonnet when she wrote the play? Only one key idea is permitted, or the production will seem unfocused. For *The Seagull*, the key idea might be: 'Love is destructive, it works like a narcotic.' It might equally be: 'Those we admire (writers, actors, etc.) have feet of clay.' Neither of these is wrong, and both could be regarded as themes. Nevertheless, for the play to possess a clear core, one only must be chosen as key, and all the other facets of the play subordinated to it.

The key idea may lead to the central problem of 'director's theatre', that is, that the production can become a vehicle for the director's 'concept'. While the former should animate the production, the latter too often becomes a sterile fetish.

The director needs to read the play several times in order to be able to consider problems like its energy sources, and its key idea, effectively. In her series of readings, she makes notes. Initially, what is her first impression of the play? Next morning, what can she remember of it? The answers may come in useful later. After each successive reading, the director will make random notes, jot down odd details, suggest to herself possible themes, even note down a few quotations. Thoughts, ideas, themes begin to emerge. To return to *The Seagull* momentarily, where do the ideas about love, about conservation, about the future fit in the overall pattern?

Then, the director needs to be sure she knows the meanings and the pronunciation of unusual or problematic words, names or phrases. She needs to become certain about the place and time of each scene, and the overall chronology of the play. She will consider cutting the text, and though this is in general not to be encouraged, in certain circumstances, depending on the play, the potential cast and the intended audience, cuts may be necessary. At this point, too, the director will begin to have ideas about action, stage pictures, rhythms – this is inevitable, and so long as these are not regarded as final decisions, such thinking is useful. What is to be avoided here is too much thought about 'character' (anyway an unhelpful conception, as suggested in Chapter 5, p. 113), or 'blocking', which will come later.

The director also needs to understand the dramatic form of the play, and how it will inform her work, for this will help to determine much about her approach. Furthermore, if the director knows that it is, say, a tragedy that she will be directing, the unsystematic thoughts which are bubbling in her brain may acquire some order. Not that she needs at this point to strive for order. Disparate thoughts may be unrelated or unreconciled one with another now. But inevitably some order will gradually emerge from the chaos, and a knowledge of dramatic form will help to focus the key idea. It will help to determine whether the production of, say, *Hamlet*, will mark it as a political play, a psychological study, a thriller, or a philosophical dilemma dramatised. It could be any of these, or something else entirely. But again, it must be stressed that it can be only one thing at a time. One of the arts of directing consists of knowing when to postpone a decision – usually a tactical matter – and when to decide, especially about overall strategy.

Once the key idea has become clear to the director, she begins to wonder how to realise it. The answer to this question will determine the style of the production: naturalism, surrealism, outré, lyric, physical, intense, whatever. Style might be regarded as the dynamo of the production. It comes from within the production, not necessarily from the play script as such, and is the conduit through which the deep content is brought to light. This, it should be noted, is not the same as stylisation, which is something laid over the style, like icing over a cake. The director's next research work, which is sometimes carried out with – or even by – the actors if time permits, involves discovering everything possible about the clothes, manners, food, entertainments, morals and so forth of the group of people whom the play concerns in the chosen time and place. Research should be done on the author and her circle, and the director (and the actors) should try to saturate themselves in the ambience of the period – read some novels and some poetry, become familiar with the language of the time, as well as the art, music and ideas. The more specific such research is, the better.

By now the director is in a position to start making up her book. The script needs to be interfaced with blank pages on which will be written all sorts of notes opposite the appropriate moment in the written script. (A good example is S. D. Balukhaty, *'The Seagull' Produced by Stanislavsky*, New York: Theater Arts Books, 1952.) Some directors make columns on the blank facing page, a column each for the character's intentions, actions and other ideas, or maybe for lighting effects, sound effects and so on. Others colour code their notes. Most directors just scribble as and when they need to. By the end of the production, a few pages may still be relatively empty; others will be dark with notes made over other notes and beside others. The notes should indicate where an episode begins and ends, and indeed the 'bits' within the episode, perhaps with a caption or title for each bit (and for each episode), indicating what actually happens. The director's notes will also include matters such as intentions and actions (see Chapter 5). For the director, an intention should include another character or characters: 'to shame him', 'to make him laugh', 'to get rid of her'. The action consists in the method of fulfilling the intention: 'by pointing a finger', 'by joshing him', 'by threatening'. There may also be an activity which the director will want to note: 'while setting the table', 'while picking her fingernails', and so on. The blank facing pages gradually fill up as the production continues.

REHEARSALS

When rehearsals begin, it is the director's job to create a haven within which the actor feels safe to experiment, to make a fool of herself, to dare to do something unexpected. Here the play will be opened up, deep mined, mapped. A good working atmosphere is one in which the actor feels she is trusted, and in which no contribution, however footling from however insignificant a member of the cast, is treated contemptuously. The director must encourage the actors to feel excited by the play, and must be able to take advantage of any unplanned or fortuitous moments in rehearsal. She creates the situation, the atmosphere in which the actor can create, and she prompts, cajoles, stimulates, strokes, asks questions, flirts to draw out whatever the actor has to give.

A rehearsal is an investigation. If all the answers were obvious, there would be no point in rehearsing. Of course, mechanical matters must be taken care of – entrances and exits, fights, routines, and these must be practised from early in the process, but it is a process, one which Anne Bogart (b. 1951) has described as being like a ouija session: 'You place your hands on the pulse and listen. You feel. You follow. You act in the moment before analysis, not after.' She also suggests that a rehearsal is a little like a date – as you go towards it, you don't know what will happen, but it will be exciting, arousing, challenging … (Anne Bogart, *A Director Prepares*, London: Routledge, 2001.)

The director is endlessly flexible and patient. She pays infinite attention to what goes on in the rehearsal room. She is here, present, now. She is interested in the play as a play, in the actors as human beings, in the acting space as space, in the process of performance creating. She should not follow the script all the time, but should watch, and watch from different places to obtain a full picture of what is happening. What emerges during a good rehearsal emerges spontaneously, is never pre-planned. The director's most practical concern is the focus. Her job is to focus the work of the actors, which, by the way, may be achieved by way of lighting, or stage scenery, as well as by acting skills of one sort or another. The director needs to know what focusing tools to employ.

It is therefore important that the director does not evade the problems which arise. Problems may energise those who face them, they may force actors to develop new artistic strengths, and when a problem is overcome there is a true sense of achievement. The one problem which is exclusively the director's is the difficult actor. It is wise not to criticise any actor, but rather try to work with them. An actor's problem may stem from vanity, or be the result of over-sensitivity, or of a too-well-developed fear of disapproval or failure or mockery. The director should never try to face the actor down, particularly in front of others, or make her feel foolish. Patience and attempts to understand must be the watchwords at all times. The director does well to remember that it is the actor, not the director, who faces the audience.

The correct atmosphere in the rehearsal room is assisted by sensible practice in the basic day-to-day arrangements. The rehearsal room should be clean and uncluttered. Should the windows be open? Is the radiator on? These matters can be attended to in advance. If the rehearsal takes place on the stage, is it possible to light it with more than simply the gloomy working lights? Three and a half weeks – the usual time in the professional theatre for a play to be rehearsed – is not much time for creative excitement to be generated (every other theatre has envied the many months which are, or used to be, available at the Moscow Art Theatre and the Berliner Ensemble). Scheduling needs to be precise and economical to use time efficiently; the rehearsal programme, by the way, may be worked out with the stage management. Moreover, deadlines should be notified early – two weeks for any deadline is not much to ask. For example, when must lines be learned by? This should ideally not be too early, since this can set preconceptions too firmly, fix intonations, and so on, thus impairing receptivity and creativity. When will props be available? Again, this does not always need to be very early: the actor pays attention to the glass when it is finally substituted for a paper cup. When will sound be used first? When will costumes be tried on?

In rehearsals, particularly in the early period of rehearsal, when the director is learning about the actors, and the actors are learning about the director and about each other, many directors begin with warm-up games and exercises, to help actors to become focused, relaxed and energised. Sometimes warm-ups might concentrate on breathing and voice exercises, at other times they might be more energetic, and involve trust games, concentration exercises, or dance and movement exercises. Warm-ups repay time spent on them in the way actors will then approach their tasks in rehearsal.

The first rehearsal usually consists of a read-through of the play by the actors. This should be seen as a sort of open sesame to who knows what? Some directors mistrust the first read-through (Nicholas Hytner (b. 1956), director of Britain's National Theatre, called the first read-through of Shakespeare's *Henry IV* 'an unpleasant ritual that has to be got through'), partly because it may put pressure on the actors, who 'ham' their reading, or try to make a 'character' before they know the play, or the director's approach. Furthermore, not all actors are good at sight-reading – some indeed suffer from dyslexia – whereas, contrariwise, some actors with long experience of radio may read 'too well'. But the read-through does enable actors to wrestle with their parts for the first time in public, especially if they are encouraged not to act, but to talk the script, to address it to the director, or to the other actors. It enables actors to hear their potential partners, and it may also give an early indication of the production's running time. The director makes no comment on the reading as such; she will spend the rest of the first rehearsal discussing the play's key idea, its context, the author's attitude, themes and ideas, style and rhythm. This is probably the best moment to indicate the stage set, too, either by showing the designer's model or at least some sketches of it.

Many directors like to conduct two or three readings before they do anything else, and discuss them after each reading is complete. Others get down to more detailed work round a table and only read the whole play again when it seems right. The round-the-table discussions, certainly for naturalistic plays, are where the results of the director's research are most likely to be raised. The aim of this discussion work, at least if the play is not being given its premiere, is not to find some different 'take' on the script, but to find the truths embedded in it. The director in these sessions is almost like a teacher, relentlessly probing with questions the actors' responses to the text. First, the actors will define their 'super-objectives', and these need to be reconciled to the play's key idea as formulated by the director. What are the given circumstances? How does your character spend the day? What is the layout of the house? (The set and costume designs must be available during these discussions.) Actors begin to create biographies for their characters, with the aim of 'justifying' what they do. Finally, the play is split into bits, and the intentions and actions of the character may be discussed bit by bit. Once or twice during this process, or perhaps only at the end of it, the whole play is read again, perhaps this time with interruptions where points of discussion or clarification are necessary.

The round-the-table sessions are vital. They must be open, honest, engaging, and not (as too often happens) merely form a veneer of democratic discussion to cover the director's desire to dominate. How long these sessions last is a question properly only decided in the actual rehearsal process. For many, the longer they last, the stronger they are, and when the actors finally do get up from the table, they are bursting for some action. This can provide a hugely profitable shot of energy when 'blocking' begins. Sometimes it is a good idea to block a section or two, and then return to the table. It must be appreciated by all that the moment the table work gives way to this embodiment of the action is nerve-wracking for all concerned: actors are frightened to lose the comfort of the chair and table, but directors too are nervous that their hopes will be dashed, or their discoveries turn to dust.

'Blocking' is the name given to that period of rehearsal when the actors and director, in collaboration, find the basics of how the play will be staged, how the actors will use the set and the stage space, what sorts of rhythms will be workable for the various sections. The less the director can impose on the actor in this phase of rehearsals, the better. The blocking aims to create visual patterns and suggest emblems of relationships, and sometimes some of this is significantly in the director's mind already. Many directors, for instance, use groupings from paintings – a Bruegel peasant wedding, Leonardo da Vinci's (1452–1519) *The Last Supper*, and Michelangelo's (1475–1564) sculpture of the Pietà have all been used by leading directors as the basis for effective stage pictures. Significant moments may also be at least partially conceived in advance by the director: Richard III woos the Lady Anne over her husband's coffin, not alongside it; Serebriakov and his entourage leave Voynitsky's house, crossing behind the sofa, without entering the main part of the room on their way through. Entrances and exits – and also the play's opening – are likely to be moments when the director will want to have some control over the actors' movements.

Nevertheless, it is not really the director's job to tell the actors where to stand or when to move. They are capable of this themselves, though they always want help and advice. The floor of the rehearsal space should be marked out with tape, or chalk, or paint, in the actual dimensions they will be in later performance, including making clear where there are doors or windows, steps (up or down) and so on. The actors are frequently anxious to fix the blocking – it gives them a feeling of security – and the deputy stage manager (DSM) noting the moves in her script is a reassurance to them (though they should make their own notes on their own scripts, too). Such notes, by the way, are best made in pencil, which can be rubbed out. Though the actors seek finality, the director should be more interested in provisional solutions. It is as well to note, too, that there are no rules for blocking. What it must aim for is clarity, so that the story is clear; and focus so that an audience has an idea of what is significant at any particular moment. Sometimes that is helped by breaking the old 'rules' – have actors standing in a straight line, let them turn their backs to the audience, don't worry about sightlines – at least in the early stages of blocking. Everything can be changed, modified, refined.

Blocking is not what makes a production live, though it may be regarded as a sort of skeleton upon which is hung what is really interesting about the show. But note – skeletons are not immobile within the living body, their joints are constantly altering. If movements are not prepared in advance, actors move as the impulse moves them (or as the director's impulse suggests), and this is likely to lead to the most dynamic and fascinating moves and groupings, because they will derive from the characters' intentions rather than some arbitrary pre-existing plan. Actors may be encouraged to try out ideas together in rehearsal: the director's best course is to watch and listen, and sometimes keep entirely out of the way – after all, the actor has to act the scene. Actors need to understand the reasons which prompted particular moves at particular moments, and they must always feel free to discard or change what they have done. Initially, blocking is worked on with books in the actors' hands, so that inevitably it cannot be much more than a sketch of the final performance. Embodiment can really only begin when the actors are not clutching their texts.

Trying to act with a book in hand is virtually impossible, and may even be a thoroughly disagreeable experience. But it may be necessary if the director does not want the actors to learn their lines too early. The best solution is to block through improvising, (see p. 114), but the truth is that given less than four weeks from first rehearsal to first performance, the time available for improvising is rarely adequate. Some actors would argue that one advantage of having a book in the hand during blocking is that the actor can then write the movements into the script at the appropriate place, and learn moves and lines at the same time. Some directors like to read a scene, then block it (or improvise it), and then read it again to check the meanings, motivations and so on, thus proceeding quite slowly. Some directors rush through the blocking, and only later go back and test it, one scene against another, as it were. Of course, as rehearsals continue, everyone learns more about the actions, characters and so forth: when to apply this increased knowledge, and how, is another conundrum for the director.

The best results from this phase of rehearsal may come through the use of improvisation, and it is often the case that time apparently wasted away from the actual script proves actually to be the most vital and the most useful in the whole process. After a reading of the play, an improvisation may be set up to explore the ordinary lives of the characters beyond the drama in a scene which the author did not write, such as the family's Sunday dinner, or a fashionable cocktail party. Sometimes it is worth improvising a parallel scene – a lovers' quarrel, awaiting a message – to explore not only the emotional content of the scene, but also physical relationships' tempo and rhythm: when do the characters come close to each other, for instance, or when are they still? Some actors benefit from solo improvisations – they are asked to tell their grandchild something, or sell an object to an imaginary crowd. It is also sometimes useful for actors to improvise a scene from the play they are working on, but with the restriction that they are not allowed to use any of the author's words. In this improvisation they must really listen and respond truthfully, opening vistas they might not otherwise have discovered. Stanislavsky's Method of Physical Actions involved the actors reading a scene, improvising it, reading it again, then improvising it again, and so on, until the improvisation and the text were virtually identical. Of course after each reading, and after each improvisation, the actors were expected to discuss with themselves and – importantly – with the director what they had done, how far their improvisation had coincided with the written scene, which rhythms and actions were 'true', and so on. This may in fact be the ideal, if it is virtually impossible to achieve in a workable timescale. It puts the emphasis to find a true staging on the actor, and the director's ability to create, in the present tense, here and now, and it enables the emotional and other demands, as well as the demands of the story, to grow through the actions of the actors, rather than being imposed on them as almost any system of blocking inevitably involves. Whatever method is chosen, however, it is vital that actors and director are prepared to experiment, change and try something different.

After the play is roughly blocked, and lines are learned, the director can begin to concentrate on the details of each scene and each action. Again, the best directors are those who are open and keen to investigate with the actor. The director needs to be prepared to entertain ideas she would never have thought of, to be flexible, accommodating and encouraging. These rehearsals are all stop and go, as the director intervenes seemingly endlessly. Sometimes, a director will let a problem slip past, but it is best to interrupt whenever necessary, because problems cannot always be solved later, and besides actors need to know their work is being properly and thoroughly considered. But the director must also remember how much time she has: if too much time is spent on the early part of the scene, the second half may suffer.

Often directors spend time in rehearsals helping an actor play specific actions. The director must insist that the actor never worry about the effect she is making on the putative audience, by signalling or indicating (listen for an actor's heavy breathing to indicate strong emotion). The actor needs only to play the action truthfully, in the present. The director will worry about the effect. This distinction between responsibilities is crucial.

Many directors try to help actors by demonstrating. It is almost impossible not to demonstrate on occasions, and some of the theatre's greatest directors have been inveterate demonstrators. The problem which this raises is actually not in the demonstrating as such, but in the way the actor copies the director's demonstration. There is a way of getting to the essence of an action without reproducing merely its externals which is very important for the actor, but which is often difficult to achieve. Where an actor cannot make this distinction, the director should consider carefully whether to demonstrate anything to her.

The director holds onto the key idea at all times. The final criterion for stopping and working on any part of a scene may be how best to further or express the key idea.

In terms of the rehearsal of details, one thing the director does well to remember is Stanislavsky's dictum, and look for the bad in the good, or the jolly in the depressing. As an exercise, a sad scene might be played lightly, a plotting scene 'publicly'. Scenes may be refreshed and improved if actors are asked to exchange roles and observe each other: an actor may learn much from watching someone imitate her. This phase explores the very basis of the work: how a character stands, sits or moves, for example. An actor may want to experiment with an accent, a stutter, a limp, or a slight disability, like myopia or hardness of hearing. Trying such possibilities out can be helpful, and of course can be dropped later. Games and exercises are always useful: play the 'in the manner of the word' charade, and find the best adverb for each character, and then let the actor walk, move, dance, hop in the manner of the word. If my character were a colour, what colour would she be? Why? What kind of food does she like? What would her pet be? What is her favourite music? What car would she drive for preference? If the character were an animal, what animal would she be? This last question may lead to extensive animal exercises in which the actor takes on the characteristics of the animal, characteristics which may later be transported into the action proper.

The director will also want to ask whether each character is 'consistent'. The question is more difficult than it may appear. Are real people consistent? And how far is real inconsistency applicable in this play? Vsevolod Meyerhold developed the idea of masks – each character plays a particular mask in each scene, but these masks may change from scene to scene. Other directors have followed Bertolt Brecht's idea of character as 'function', and asked what function the character fulfils in the play's overall scheme or in a specific scene.

Most actors' problems with particular details in their roles spring from faulty intentions. The sensitive director who notes a particular problem therefore asks first; 'What is the intention here? What does the character want?' But some problems are not so easily solved, and directors often ask actors to attend solo rehearsals to explore specific difficulties or challenges, for example, work on a long speech. Sometimes an actor is allowing herself to pre-empt the action, instead of playing absolutely in the present. The actor must do only what is true to the character and to the circumstances of the moment, not what is to come in a moment, or an hour. An actor's work may be improved if she is asked to paraphrase a speech, or mime it, to say it while rearranging the furniture or painting her fingernails. Finally, actors may be asked by the director to go away and think about the problem at home in the evening. Sometimes, the best solutions are brought about while the actor is cooking her dinner, or dropping off to sleep!

THE LAST LAP

A week or two in advance of the first performance, the whole play should be run through, no matter what state it is in. We need to concentrate now not just on the detail, but also on the flow, the through-line. Once again, the director checks that the key idea is clear. But she also needs to remember that the actors will be nervous at this point, and patience and forbearance should be her constant companions. There are likely to be several run-throughs, so that the actors can find and feel the rhythm, and also adjust the pace, or tempo of the whole. Gradually, everyone needs to feel even the pauses filling up with energy. The director will want to consult with the dramaturg here (as at most points through this process), and may invite one or two trusted outsiders in to watch an early run-through, and will talk to them frankly, in private, afterwards. After a run-through, the director will set aside time for detailed work on bits and pieces which have been exposed, and also for specific work with individual actors. And very near the first performance, she will probably ask for a speed run, or 'marking' rehearsal, in which the actors must run through the whole play at double speed – speaking and moving like a fast-wind film or video. There is no need to project their voices, or even articulate precisely: the aim is to 'mark' the performance, to see that it can be done virtually without thinking, and to expose what the actor is still unsure of. Moreover the speed run re-injects energy into the performance, as the actors feel they can fly with the play, and by giving them a significant confidence boost, it helps them to relax and feel able to change, adapt and improvise in performance.

Contact with the stage management team and the designer, which has been maintained throughout the rehearsal period, is now consolidated. The stage manager and her crew will certainly attend several run-throughs, and the designer, or scenographer, will also attend. Both will have attended other rehearsals, too, from time to time, but if the rehearsal period is no more than three and a half weeks, their scope for this may be limited. Members of the publicity team should also attend at least an early run-through.

Technical work is scheduled for the production week (or production period, since a week, though frequently all the time that is available, is really too short a time for the technical work to be completed properly). Once the set is complete and the lights hung and focused, the director must work with the scenographer, or scenography team, to plot the lighting, sound and other effects, setting the lights' brightness, the sound's volume and noting each time anything technical changes. The show may have many such cues, and each is noted punctiliously by the DSM (see Chapter 7, p. 175).

Then comes the technical rehearsal, when the whole play is run through on stage, with lights, sound and in addition now, with costumes and props. Everyone must be given time in this phase to adjust to the actual playing conditions, and again the director will notice that many of the company are nervous. She remains calm and serene throughout all the traumas of this phase in the production process. Before the actual run-through, the sensible director allows the cast time to 'walk' the stage, maybe before they receive their costumes, certainly in costume. Actors who need large wigs or outlandish make-up should be given an opportunity to work with these long before this point is reached, but they need to test these again now. They also need to test the furniture, assure themselves of the props, try opening or closing windows or doors, and so on. Actors are well advised to try speaking in the theatre in order to feel the acoustics there, though the director will remind them that the presence of an audience tends to deaden sound. The technical rehearsal, when it arrives, will be a full dress run-through, with all the technical elements added, and proper communication established between stage management, DSM and director. Technical rehearsals may be stopped so that problems can be attended to; dress rehearsals should never be stopped.

Some time close to the opening night a photo call will be arranged, and it is usual for the director to set up the scenes which should be photographed. The photographer decides whether the actors will pose for photographs, or whether the photos will be, as it were, action shots. The photographer also decides about how to light the shoot.

There should be two dress rehearsals at least. The first dress rehearsal is still likely to be slow, as actors continue to adjust to their new surroundings, and after it there are certain to be changes required, even if only to small details. An outsider who does not know the text may be useful at the first dress rehearsal, if only to check the actors' audibility. The dramaturg's attendance is certainly essential. After dress rehearsals, the stage manager and, probably, her team join the actors in the auditorium for notes. The good director's dress rehearsal notes are careful, constructive and positive; for actors they are more likely to suggest checking intentions than simply demanding changes to, say, particular moves. Certainly a director is not advised to start rejigging whole scenes at the dress rehearsal stage.

The professional theatre often has preview nights for the actors to accustom themselves to playing before an audience, and these provide opportunities to make adjustments, weigh up spectator responses and so on. On the first night, when everyone else's nerves are strung tight, but the director's job is all but done, the director should exude an air of quiet confidence. She will attend some performances (but not all if there are more than three or four), will keep contact with the company, and may give notes and even suggest changes and improvements. This is unlikely to transform into rehearsals after the opening, but the director, like the rest of the company, has a responsibility to ensure that standards are kept as high as possible all the time.

Summary

- The director, as we know the position, emerged in the late nineteenth century, probably in response to the rise of naturalism, though many of the great directors of the twentieth century rebelled against naturalism.
- The job of the director, assisted by the dramaturg, is to control the whole artistic side of the presentation; she is ultimately responsible for everything the audience sees or hears. This includes:

  - choosing the play;
  - working with the scenography team on preparation and design;
  - auditioning actors and casting the play;
  - researching the play, deciding the 'key idea', the style of the production, etc.;
  - preparing a 'book' to work from;
  - rehearsing the actors through discussion, blocking, run-throughs, etc.;
  - overseeing the production week, technical rehearsals and dress rehearsals.

FURTHER READING

Edward Gordon Craig's *The Art of Theatre* (London: Heinemann, 1911 and later editions) has been enormously influential over the last hundred years. *My Life in Art* by Constantin Stanislavsky (London: Bles, 1962) records his struggles to create truth on the stage.

Specifically on directing, Toby Cole and H. K. Chinoy, *Directors on Directing* (New York: Crown, 1970) is invaluable. Maria M. Delgado and Dan Rebellato (eds), *Contemporary European Theatre Directors* (London: Routledge, 2010) is an illuminating series of essays, each focusing on a particular director and concluding with a provocative chapter, 'The Director's New Tasks', by Patrice Pavis.

More or less practical advice is given in: Harold Clurman, *On Directing* (New York: Simon and Schuster, 1972 and later editions) and Frank Hauser and Russell Reich, *Notes on Directing* (London: Atlantic Books, 2006). Anne Bogart, *A Director Prepares* (London: Routledge, 2001) is more inspirational, and therefore idiosyncratic.

7

SCENOGRAPHY

THEATRE ARCHITECTURE

Theatres are places in which actors and spectators interact. Peter Brook has reduced this idea to its barest by suggesting that a person walking across an empty space watched by another person has performed an act of theatre, but throughout history the nature of this 'empty space' has been questioned, modified, developed and changed to serve different social and artistic imperatives. This has affected 'scenography', the technical side of theatre practice, and even the building in which the play is performed. This edifice itself may encourage reverence for the 'art of theatre', or it may be designed to facilitate social intercourse between those who attend.

The earliest theatres in Western Europe were those of ancient Greece, which were initially little more than natural amphitheatres found in the hills. Later buildings reproduced this shape, aiming to keep the naturally excellent visibility and audibility which the hillside provided. Over time, the Greeks refined their theatrical architecture, developing, for example, the *skena*, the building behind the performance area, the *proskenion*, a raised stage for individual actors, and an orchestra, a circular area in front of the *proskenion* and surrounded by audience for more than half its circumference. This configuration evolved further through the classical era, but with the collapse of the Roman Empire was largely lost.

Many medieval performances took place in churches or cathedrals, themselves designed for visibility and audibility, of course. But performers at this time also appeared in castles or great halls, on trestle stages in town squares or market places, in pubs and on village greens, and – in the case of mystery players – in 'mansions' or on pageant wagons. In many of these cases, actors and spectators were hardly separated, and there was an informality about even the most impressive performances which typified the time.

Something of this was lost when the Renaissance rediscovered and attempted to resurrect classical theatre architecture. But the Renaissance also discovered perspective, which scene designers wished to be incorporated into their stages, resulting in an 'end-on' configuration, with a proscenium arch dividing the 'scenic stage' from the auditorium with the actors on an apron stage in front of the proscenium arch. Significant developments in stage machinery and lighting also encouraged this design, which was at least partially vitiated, however, by social convention which demanded that spectators, especially upper class spectators, could sit on the stage. They came to the theatre to be seen as much as to see, and this desire had to be catered for, since aristocratic patrons paid high prices for what they wanted.

Meanwhile, in Britain something of the old informality was retained in the development of the first permanent playhouses in Elizabethan England. The builders of these theatres, including Shakespeare's Globe, echoed the shape of inn yards where plays had been staged, or of other entertainment venues such as bear-baiting rings. By 1600, therefore, in Britain the typical theatre building included a stage which thrust forward in among the standing spectators. Even though there were tiers of galleries around the central area, it was this yard where the major interaction between players and watchers took place. The thrust stage encourages a particular kind of spectator–actor interaction based on the fact that both occupy the same space. You can experience something of what this must have been like at a contemporary performance at Shakespeare's Globe on the south bank of the Thames today.

By the eighteenth and nineteenth centuries in Europe, theatre owners and managers were attempting to cram in as many spectators as possible — nearly 4,000 could be accommodated in Richard Sheridan's Drury Lane Theatre Royal which opened in the 1790s — and the thrust stage was nothing more than a memory. Now the actors performed behind the proscenium arch, totally separated from those who filled the auditorium. Such an arrangement encouraged pictorial illusion in presentation, and this search for scenic illusion was aided by developments in stage lighting and technology. The ideal was perhaps that of a room from which one wall had been removed; through this missing wall, marked by the proscenium arch, the audience peered at the evocation of 'real life' within.

This proscenium arch form was almost universal in the Western world by 1900. The stage had 'wings' at each side where actors waited to enter and lights might be posted; above the stage were the 'flies', where scenery (and occasionally 'flying' actors) might be suspended out of sight. At the back of the stage was the 'scene dock' where scenery was stored or set ready to be placed on stage, and besides dressing rooms, a costume store or wardrobe and similar working spaces, there was also the 'green room', where actors waited to be called on stage. The auditorium contained a 'pit', where benches set in rows immediately in front of the stage provided comparatively cheap seats, but which was gradually usurped by 'stalls', comfortable seats for better-off patrons. Behind the stalls and to the sides were boxes for the patrons who paid the highest prices (and who could be seen by their social inferiors in the more popular parts of the audience); the 'dress circle' for patrons in evening dress, above the stalls but below the galleries; further balconies, or galleries above them; and at the top, the 'gods', the cheapest seats where often rowdy lower-class patrons were accommodated.

In the twentieth century this architectural arrangement was gradually superseded by a wide variety of styles, which often attempted to provide more flexible spaces, intimate, imposing or unexpected. The 'black box' was conceived, a space in which an infinite number of configurations could be set, and each play or production could have its own arrangement. The end-on, proscenium or 'fourth wall' shape was not abandoned, but it existed alongside thrust stages, traverse stages (where an audience is divided into two blocks by the stage which runs between them) and theatres 'in the round' (with the audience completely surrounding the stage area).

In other words, there developed a new interest in how the scenic space may interact with the place of performance.

Box 7.1: Total theatres

Wagner and Bayreuth

Authors and directors have often imagined the perfect building for the staging of their works. As a young man in the 1840s, Richard Wagner dreamed of a special theatre where could be staged a national festival to unite his fragmented country, Germany. Over decades, this transformed in his imagination into a theatre for the staging of his own mighty operas. Though he did not know how it could be paid for, he nevertheless oversaw the laying of the foundation stone of this ideal theatre in the small town of Bayreuth in 1872.

The planned building was adapted by the architect, Otto Brückwald (1841–1904), from designs originally prepared with extreme care by Wagner for execution in Munich. Wagner wanted no ornamentation or ostentation, but a building to serve his artistic purpose, and on this he refused to compromise.

The auditorium was fan-shaped, instead of the usual rectangle, and steeply raked. There were no boxes or balconies, but Wagner insisted on perfect sightlines from every seat. There was a kind of double proscenium on either side of what Wagner called 'the mystic gulf' between audience and stage. In fact, below the mystic gulf and completely out of sight of the audience was the orchestra pit, screened by a huge curved wooden cowl. Orchestra and conductor were invisible. Behind the stage was a large area for the most up-to-date theatre technology. The whole building was completed in brick, plaster and wood, constructed for the best possible acoustics. And indeed this, together with the fan shape, afforded unequalled acoustic clarity for the time, richer and more resonant than anything experienced anywhere before.

In 1875 preliminary rehearsals were held here, but there was not enough money to complete the building. Wagner desperately set about raising it, giving concerts, holding receptions, selling subscriptions and making speeches. Finally, the lighting and machinery were installed, and on 13 August 1876, *Das Rheingold*, the first part of *The Ring of the Nibelungen*, was performed. Notably, the auditorium was plunged into darkness, perhaps for the first time in theatre history. Wagner's theatre was complete.

It was indeed his 'total theatre': not only was he responsible for the building, he also wrote the music and the lyrics of the opera, he coached the singers, he designed the scenery and he oversaw the staging.

Gropius, Piscator and modernist total theatre

Fifty years after the opening of the Bayreuth Theatre, the fiercely modernist director, Erwin Piscator, asked Walter Gropius (1883–1969) to design another 'total theatre'. Piscator's productions had involved revolving stages, multiple projections of both film and slides, and mechanised settings, but his Berlin theatre was simply incapable of responding to his desire to employ every technology the world could then supply. Gropius was an artist and architect who had founded the influential Bauhaus, which attempted to bring artistic concepts into everyday living largely through techniques of industrial technology.

The theatre he designed for Piscator was more or less oval-shaped, with an auditorium which echoed this shape and was extremely steeply raked, allowing office space beneath. The theatre was to seat 2,000 spectators in a single bank, with no balconies or boxes. Its chief feature was the use of revolving stages, one almost within the other, which enabled the theatre to change configurations from, first, a proscenium stage to a thrust stage, and then from a thrust stage to a stage in the round. Around the aisles were placed screens, each with its own projector for film or slides, and more projectors behind the stage area permitted back projection. Images could even be projected onto the domed roof. Unlike Wagner's Bayreuth theatre, Gropius' theatre, though its design was exhibited in 1928, was never built. It was, however, a strong influence on many theatres built later in the twentieth century.

DESIGN AND SCENOGRAPHY

'The art of stage production is the art of projecting into space what the original author was only able to project in time', according to Adolph Appia. He is one of a number of stage designers who made a significant impact on the way we understand theatre in the West by their investigations and presentations of the spatial elements of the production. Others whose work has been influential in British theatre include Inigo Jones (1573–1652), Philippe Jacques de Loutherbourg (1740–1812), Edward Gordon Craig (1872–1966) and John Bury (1925–2000).

Yet the modern scenographer does more than project the author's meanings into the stage space. Whereas the designer used to be concerned with creating a context (time, place, atmosphere) for the performance, the scenographer's job now is considered to be much more than this. The scenographer is responsible for the physical structures employed in the performance, the lighting and projected images, sound, costume and props in relation to each other, and crucially, in relation also to the bodies of the performers in action, the text, the space and of course the relationship with the audience. Scenography is an active agent in the creation of performance.

The old designer concentrated on the *mise-en-scène*, that is, the physical arrangements within which the performance was realised; now, the scenographer focuses on the performer within time and space. So gesture and movement as much as lighting effect and costume contribute to the scenography; and how the performers relate spatially and orally to one another is equally the business of scenography, as is the relation of the elements of the performance to the audience.

The following paragraphs of this chapter are intended to focus on the practical day-to-day problems and potential of design and scenography. But it should be remembered at all times that the crux of this area of theatre discourse concerns the relationship of a 'non-real' scene to a 'real' actor, or, more generally, the relationship between the world of the imagination and the 'real' world of wood and metal, light and dark, sweat and laughter.

STAGE DESIGN

Practically speaking, scenography covers the whole technical world of the theatre. Its component parts are very often covered by different specialists, such as the designer and the lighting designer. The scenography team, including wardrobe mistress, stage manager and others, works closely with, and is answerable to, the director.

For the scenographer, the first practical consideration is probably the visual impact. Some scenographers or designers do almost all their work before rehearsals commence, working everything out in advance, so that the director can be presented with a maquette (or scale model) at the start of rehearsals. Such a method of proceeding also involves the use of a stage ground plan, and most theatres have printed technical diagrams of their layout. Sometimes a designer will simply produce a series of sketches or rough paintings before rehearsals begin, in order to stimulate imaginations, and then work out the detail as rehearsals continue. Other designers, more daringly, work only during the rehearsal period, and the design is created in collaboration with what the director and the actors are doing.

The scenographer, or designer, must take account of the play itself, its dramatic form, the period in which it is set, its style (realism, poetic symbolism, whatever), and also try to respond to the director's ideas. This ought to produce a design which complements the work of the director. Moods or themes may be suggested in the design, an atmosphere or a general environment conjured up. The designer also concentrates on ways of making clear the stage metaphor.

A hundred years or more ago, the designer's work was largely pictorial, and then the scene painter was an important theatrical figure, but today design is closer to sculpture, or even architecture. Stages are less pictures to be decorated than spaces to be inhabited. It follows that designers must always ask whether they should use 'real' materials, or painted or other substitutes, surrogates or symbols. They must consider not just colour, shape and line, but also texture, and matters of perspective. The use of different levels on stage may also be worth considering sculpturally, as levels are not only interesting in themselves, they can also help to define acting areas, permit the use of simultaneous settings, allow actors in certain positions to dominate others, and enable the director to create interesting stage compositions. Different stage levels are also often useful for deploying a chorus or a crowd effectively.

These more or less aesthetic matters must also be informed by practical issues – not just where does each exit lead to (how is 'offstage' created?), but even more mundane matters: the relationship of the stage to the auditorium, the distance from the stage to the nearest spectators, and those furthest off, health and safety issues, fire precautions and the like.

The stage design must also work with the lighting design. This ensures that the actors are lit appropriately, and that effects such as sunrise, moonlight, even a flashing strobe light, are correctly knitted into the fabric of the production. The lighting is also crucial in the creation of atmosphere and mood, and in giving depth and authenticity to the action. The lighting designer therefore must know what areas are to be lit, from what angle (above, the side, etc.), how bright and what colour each light should be, and what shape of light beams are going to be most effective. The designer, and lighting designer, must collaborate in perhaps unique ways, involving both their aesthetic imagination and their practical know-how. The lighting must be seen as an active collaborator in the creative work of scenography.

ON STAGE

The world of the stage often seems like a magic cave, with its own extraordinary objects, and its own language to describe them. This and the next two sections seek to demystify this world, while pointing to sensible contemporary practice.

In a traditional end-on theatre, the proscenium arch divides the stage from the auditorium. Any part of the stage which extends into the auditorium is the apron or forestage. It is usually on the line of the proscenium arch that the front curtain or tabs are hung – on a rail, or tab track. Other pairs of curtains across the stage and meeting in the middle are known as runners. The safety curtain, to control the spread of any fire, is usually placed just in front or just behind the tabs.

The stage itself may be set on a slope, or raked, and may have trapdoors, usually known simply as traps, set in it for access to 'below stage' either for actors or stage hands. These open either by hinged flaps or by being slid apart. Above the stage, parallel with the proscenium arch, a series of short curtains, pelmets or borders, are hung to conceal lights, stage machinery, etc, from the audience (small borders are known as teasers), and long narrow curtains, usually black and known as legs, or tall narrow flats, known as wings, conceal the sides of the stage. Wings and borders are some-times designed to create a perspective effect. At the back of the stage, if there is no scenery, there is likely to be a cyclorama, a plain white or pale blue cloth, stretched tight across the whole of the back of the stage. Often curved, the cyclorama gives the effect of light and space to the stage. The right side of the stage as the audience looks at it is known as stage left; off stage on this side is the prompt side (or simply PS), since in former times the prompter sat here. In consequence, the other side of the stage is stage right, and the offstage area on that side is OP (opposite prompt side).

Above the stage, invisible to the audience, is the flies, or fly gallery, from where the flying system is worked. This usually consists of a series of ropes (known as 'hemps', though hemp is rarely used today), pulleys and counterweights for bringing in scenery (and sometimes actors) from above. The fly tower must be more than twice the height of the stage to enable scenery to be out of sight of the audience when not in use.

Traditionally in a proscenium theatre, productions alternate between set scenes and flat scenes. Flat scenes consist of either drops, that is, cloths with the scene painted on them, usually wound on rollers suspended above the stage and dropped down when they are wanted; or flats, usually canvas stretched on wooden frames, but occasionally hardboard, necessary if doors or windows are to be practicable. Originally, two flats were run onto the stage on grooves from opposite sides to meet in the middle and form a complete unit, but by 1900 there were many more sophisticated variations than this. Set scenes, in contrast to flat scenes, are designed to be three dimensional: originally they consisted of a drop or painted backcloth behind free-standing cut-outs, representing trees, boulders, tombs or whatever. These soon became increasingly sculptural and realistic. In some pantomimes even in the twenty-first century the alternation of set scene and flat scene continues.

The word 'set' describes what is set on stage, and flats and other pieces have become increasingly sophisticated. Two flats hinged together are known as a book flat and these may be self-supporting, though most flats are held upright and in place by various stage weights or braces, cleat lines, ropes and so on. Rostra may provide raised platforms, steps, pillars or ramps, and some flats or drops may be made of scrim or gauze or other open weave fabric which is opaque when lit from in front, but when lit from behind becomes transparent – useful for apparitions!

Box 7.2: The box set

In the mid-nineteenth century, the search for scenic realism in preference to the desire for theatrical splendour led to significant reforms of stage presentation. Perhaps they were only made possible by the development of theatrical lighting, first gas lighting, but later in the century, electric light. The longest-lasting, and perhaps most influential, example of nineteenth-century scenic realism – one which is still occasionally seen in theatres in the twenty-first century – was the so-called 'box set'.

The box set represented the interior of a building. It took the spectator into a room. Long-established stage representation of interiors consisted of a series of receding wings and borders, leading to a backcloth. On these were painted two-dimensional door handles, shelves, pots and pans, even doors and windows, for the actors entered, not through the painted doors, which could not open, but between the wings. The box set reconstructed this arrangement, substituting flats joined together to form continuous walls along the sides and across the back of the stage, and a horizontal cloth above to represent the ceiling. Into the walls were set practicable doors, windows and so on. Of course such a setting could only be successful once light could be projected into it, but once that was possible the stage could conjure up an apparently real domestic interior.

It is not clear when the first box set was seen on stage – perhaps as early as 1832 at the Olympic Theatre, London, perhaps at Covent Garden in 1841, both of which were controlled by Madame Lucy Vestris (1797–1856). But it was her later stage manager, Tom Robertson (1829–71), who was really responsible for the development of the box set, and his 'cup-and-saucer' dramas, exemplified in his best-known play, *Caste*, demand such a setting.

Significantly, a realistic setting like this cannot accommodate traditional histrionic acting: it demands a more realistic – or naturalistic – style.

LX – STAGE LIGHTING

Stage lighting is a world within a world – enormously complicated, alluring and riddled with its own obscure jargon.

Once drama was performed indoors (and all the earliest Western theatres existed outdoors), there was a need for artificial light, and candles were probably the earliest form of stage lighting. They gave way to gas in the early nineteenth century, but by the end of the nineteenth century most theatres were equipped with electricity, the use of which has developed extraordinarily. Now, the effects achievable – and often achieved – are truly astounding.

The basic element of LX (stage electrics) is the lamp or lantern, which is essentially a metal box open at one side and containing a bulb, with a reflector behind, so that the maximum amount of light is directed out. Lanterns must be 'rigged' – that is, hung, fixed and focused – for the performance. They are usually hung on a bar but may be fixed on a 'boom', a vertical metal pole. The commonest lights are 'floods' whose wide angle tends to spread light generally, and 'spots' or spotlights, which cast only a small circle of light, which can be precisely focused and controlled. A 'follow spot' is a moveable beam directed to follow a particular actor about the stage. There are also beam lights, which have parallel beams so that the size of the lit area is always the same, no matter whether the lamp is far or near, and footlights, now rare, which are set into the front of the stage at floor level.

Special lighting effects in the twenty-first century are too many to count. They include: gobos (cut-out shapes covering the lamp so as to project that shape onto the stage); black light or ultra violet effects; chasers; mirror balls; strobes (lights which snap on and off rapidly); other flicker effects; and ripple tubes. All these may be specials, a term referring to any light which is intended to create a particular effect.

Lanterns have frames at the front to enable coloured plastic sheets, known as 'gels', to be inserted to change the colour of the light projected; and fixed to the front of any lamp may be adjustable shutters, also known as 'barn doors', which alter the shape of the light beam. The whole obviously requires large amounts of cable, which may be plugged straight into the dimmer (the instrument which controls the way the light changes intensity), but may run to a patching panel which has many sockets connected to the dimmer. This allows for greater variety of possible uses and combinations of lights, because plugs from particular lanterns can be 'patched' to different sockets. Each electric circuit is known as a channel.

RUNNING THE SHOW

Having set the stage, and rigged the lights, there are still significant areas of preparation for the stage manager (SM), the deputy stage manager (DSM) and the assistant stage managers (ASMs). They must assemble the props, which may be made, hired, found or scrounged. They must create a CD or tape recording of the sound design for the required sound effects. If 'live' sound is also required, microphones (or 'mikes'), speakers (including perhaps woofers, tweeters and others), sound mixers, amplifiers, and so on must all be checked. And any special stage effects – smoke machines, dry ice, confetti canons, pyrotechnics or whatever – must be prepared.

Before the technical rehearsal, or 'tech', the lighting, sound and other effects must be plotted so that the tech will run as smoothly as possible, and this is always a time-consuming and trying experience. Essentially the tech is called to solve all the technical problems which any modern live theatre show presents. The tech will work out all scene changes, the timing and cueing of all lighting changes, the volume and cueing of all sound effects, actors' entries and exits, the use of props, as well as any problems with costumes, including quick changes, wigs, masks, make-up, etc.

At the tech, the stage manager (SM) or the deputy stage manager (DSM) will decide on setting props, on cueing any effects and on calls for the actors to come to the stage, including 'beginners' and 'places'. It is usual to 'call' actors from their dressing rooms or the green room formally: 'Call: Mr Smith and Miss Jones on stage, please.'

Variations on full tech rehearsals include cue-to-cue rehearsals ('Q2Q'), when technical effects and changes only are rehearsed, and walk-throughs, when actors simply go through their entrances, exits and other significant stage moves.

During the tech rehearsal, 'cans' or headsets connect the SM, the DSM and others with each other and with the director and the scenographer or designer. Immediately afterwards, the SM or the DSM makes up the 'book' or prompt copy which is an annotated play script, including every cue clearly marked. It is this which will be used by whoever 'calls' the performance (usually the DSM).

Every possible technical problem should be solved during the tech, so that the dress rehearsal(s) can be as like actual performances as possible. The dress rehearsals are for the benefit of the director and the actors, but may also be used to check anything which is unfinished or unconvincing technically, to ensure all the mechanics are in order, that light is not spilling anywhere, and so on. It is usual at the dress rehearsal to operate the 'half', the check that all actors are present thirty-five minutes before the performance is due to begin, and to work out the curtain call.

And from the first public performance on, the show is in the hands of the SM and the DSM.

Box 7.3: A rough guide to running a theatre performance

Stage manager

BEFORE THE PERFORMANCE:

1 Prepare a list to be posted (probably on the dressing room door (s)) of all actors and others who are involved in the performance. Thirty-five minutes before the performance is due to begin (the 'half'), check that it has been signed by all actors and other stage staff. Take whatever action is necessary if anyone has not signed in.

2 Prepare a 'running order' – a list of scenes, and who is involved in each scene – and post it prominently in the backstage area.

3 Sweep the stage and ensure the auditorium is clean and presentable.

4 Set the stage – furniture, props, etc.

5 Check any stage effects are in place and in working order.

6 Set up the props table, where any props to be used during the performance are laid out; and ensure the actors know where the table is. (Note: a list of all props on the props table should be clearly displayed on or near the table.)

7 Ensure backstage areas are lit by a dim light (perhaps a lantern covered with a dark blue gel) so actors can see to get to their places.

8 Check the first aid equipment is in position and in a properly usable state.

9 Check communication channels with the DSM and FoH (front of house, that is, the box office, ushers, etc.).

10 Check all safety features (e.g. safety curtain) are in proper working order.

DURING THE PERFORMANCE:

1 Communicate with the DSM (and FoH) as necessary. This must include signalling to the DSM when the stage is ready for the performance to begin, both at the start and after any intervals – that is, when the stage is set, and 'beginners' (actors) are in place and ready.

2 The SM is responsible for SILENCE backstage at all times.

3 Scene changes:

   (a) The SM must know what is to be set on stage (furniture and props) at each scene change, and where each is to be set. Also, what is to be struck. (N.B.: Wherever possible, the person(s) changing the set should bring on what needs to be brought on, set it correctly, and then remove what has to be removed: this means that in a scene change which does not use the tabs those who are executing it only appear once.)

   (b) The SM must nominate who is responsible for each part of any scene change (a named person – actor or assistant stage manager). A clear list of what each scene changer must do at each scene change should be pinned up in an obvious place backstage.

   (c) The SM must 'lead' the scene change – tell scene changers when to go, supervise what is being done, and check everything has been completed properly. When the scene change is complete, the SM communicates this to the DSM.

4 The SM is responsible for the operation of any stage effects (e.g. 'dry ice') or rail cues (e.g. curtains opened or closed, scenery dropped in, etc.) even if an ASM is the actual operator. Note: any stage effect must be cued by the DSM.

5 The SM may be responsible for 'calling' actors to stage before their entrances. This should be done about a page of text before their entrance, and the procedure agreed with the DSM.

6 Be prepared to deal with any emergency which may arise during a performance, either on stage or backstage.

AFTER THE PERFORMANCE

The SM must make sure the stage and backstage areas are ready for the next performance – e.g. check that all props have been returned to the props table.

Deputy stage manager

BEFORE THE PERFORMANCE:

1   Mark up the text, to create 'the book' from which the performance will be run:

(a)   Before 'plotting', make columns alongside the text (if possible on the facing page) for cues – LX, sound, FX (stage effects) and any other (e.g. band cues if there is a live band). Also actors' 'calls' where the DSM is responsible for these.

(b)   During 'plotting', agree with the director the exact point in the text for each LX, sound or other cue. Underline that word. You may wish to write 'LXQ6' (or whatever) in black ink in the script beside this cue word. Whether you do this or not, you must write the Q in the appropriate column as well, as follows: 'LXQ6 go', 'SQ4 go' or whatever. (N.B.: 'SQ' refers to a sound cue, and the cue is said: 'Sound cue four – go!')

(c)   After you have marked the cue 'go', mark the 'standby' by underlining a word about a page earlier in a similar way – in the text if you like, and without fail in the appropriate column – 'LXQ6 standby', 'SQ4 standby', or whatever.

2   Check communication channels with the SM, FoH, actors, LX and sound operators.
3   Check sound and LX systems (this may be delegated to LX and sound operators).
4   Check the LX preset, including that the house lights are on so that the auditorium is ready for the audience.

DURING THE PERFORMANCE:

The DSM effectively runs the performance.

1   When the SM has signalled the stage is ready, and the DSM is sure the LX, sound and other operators are ready, the DSM

signals to FoH that the show will begin in x minutes, or immediately, or whatever. The same procedure is followed after the
interval(s).

2   During the performance, the DSM 'cues' the performance. This
means she must follow the marked text very closely as it is performed, and give the cues as agreed with the director during the
plotting. This is done as follows:

(a)   about a page before the cue (where it has been marked)
warn the operator: 'LXQ6 standby', 'SQ4 standby', or whatever;

(b)   at the exact moment when the cue is to happen, order;
'LXQ6 go.' ('Go' should coincide precisely with the cue
word.) Or: 'SQ4 go'; and so on.

Note: At no time during the performance should these cues (or
anything else) be discussed with the operators. The operators must
execute the cues precisely as they are given by the DSM, and without
question – even when a cue seems to them to have been given
wrongly. The whole system hinges on this!

THEATRE BEYOND THEATRE

Particular technical considerations must attach to performances
which take place beyond the walls of conventional theatres. Such
performances have a very long and honourable history, which
begins indeed in the mists of unrecoverable time. But certainly in
medieval Europe (and beyond) troupes of itinerant players tramped
high roads and by-lanes in search of audiences, perhaps the most
famous to theatre historians being the Italian *commedia dell'arte*
companies of Renaissance Italy. Amateur groups – folk actors –
have also played alfresco from time immemorial, like the paper boys
of Marshfield, Gloucestershire, who present a play every Boxing
Day in the village square, or the mummers described by Thomas
Hardy (1840–1928) in his novel *The Return of the Native*.

Often, theatre beyond theatre, or street theatre, has had political
overtones or has attempted to agitate and propagandise their audiences of ordinary people. Thus, the revolutionary street performances – which often resembled, or even became, processions or

demonstrations – seen in France in the 1790s or Russia after 1917. In Britain, the workers theatre movement of the 1920s and 1930s performed short, sharp dramas from the backs of lorries to striking cotton workers or exploited tenants, and this agitprop urge reappeared in Britain in the politically volatile 1960s and 1970s. Such productions may be classed as 'guerrilla theatre', one-off performances which aim to make a political point before the performers depart to avoid police interference. Different politically-motivated performances have been provided by Augusto Boal's 'invisible' and 'forum' theatres which radically involved their audiences. (See the section 'Forum theatre' in Chapter 8, p. 188.)

Other street theatres have been more celebratory, perhaps associated with carnivals or festivals. In the Second World War leading ballet performers appeared in parks in the East End of London to raise the morale of bombing victims and others. For the last thirty years of the twentieth century, Welfare State International company delighted and amazed audiences at open air events all over Britain with their shows which often featured giant puppets and pyrotechnics, and in New York the Bread and Puppet Theater did much the same.

One of the most striking examples of the potential of theatre beyond theatre was provided by the National Theatre of Scotland's inaugural production in February 2006. Entitled *Home*, the show resulted from work by ten different directors, each charged with making a work round the word 'home', and each working with local people in a different part of the country. Perhaps the biggest, most far-flung 'opening night' in theatre history, *Home* ranged from, in the south, the recreation of 1940s Dumfries by residents of care homes, to, in the north, a trip on the ferry to Shetland, listening to poems and songs by Jackie Kay (b. 1961). In Edinburgh, schoolchildren provided a surrealistic version of the Scottish parliament's First Minister's Questions, while in nearby East Lothian there was a modernised version of an old fairy tale, as the audience was loaded onto a bus for a kind of magical mystery tour. In Glasgow, there was an outdoor spectacular, with actors abseiling down high-rise flats, and in Aberdeen a subtle and moving meditation contrasting local people's experiences with their hopes. Caithness' version was staged in a glass factory, Stornaway's in a doll's house, and Inverness' *Home* was a highly energetic performance inspired by a series of photographs of local families in their own homes.

Home illustrates perfectly how in this kind of theatre, the actor or performer goes out to seek the audience, where usually it is the spectator who seeks out the performer. In fact, this kind of theatre often specifically attempts to attract non-theatregoers. For this reason, performances may be designed for specific sites: an alternative name for this practice is 'environmental theatre', which may also overlap with 'performance art'. The presupposition is that the chosen site will add something singular to the work, that the space will offer new ways for spectators and performers to come together and, therefore, will question how we behave in specific places. The practice inherently challenges institutionalisation, not least the institution of theatre itself, for the new site has been chosen deliberately to illuminate or subvert the history or significance of the place – a building, a monument, a disused factory or an old canal bank. Moreover, street theatre has a here-and-now quality which undermines notions of the eternal in art. The performer has to grab the attention, and what is lost in subtlety may be more than made up for by gains in community-specific meaning.

For those who would engage in theatre beyond conventional theatre boundaries, there are important practical considerations. The most important of them concerns the chosen site itself, which may be in front of a building, out in the countryside (though natural amphitheatres are hard to find), or may be in some kind of ordinary room. Performers need to think how the site's natural or architectural features may be used so that the show can make the desired impact. Is noisy traffic (or aeroplanes overhead) going to interfere? The chosen performance area might need to be marked off by potted plants, or bollards, or delineated by something like a carpet, and exits and entrances need to be clear. Screens may be useful, and sometimes chairs for spectators are advisable. If the performance is to take place indoors, what sort of lighting is to be used? If outdoors, what effects will the weather have? If costume is to be used, where will the actors change?

Other matters to be worked out in advance include considerations of public access and car parking, how audiences are gathered and how they find their places. Will there be an interval? How will the spectators know the show is over? Will there be a collection of money? What toilet facilities will be available? What about sightlines and acoustics?

Street theatre, theatre under the sky, open air performance – these provide some of the most dynamic and exciting possibilities to the maker of theatre. After all, ancient Greece and Elizabethan London provided some of the greatest theatrical experiences in history, and theirs were open air theatres.

Summary

- Historically, theatre architecture has reflected the social concerns of theatregoers as well as the artistic concerns of theatre practitioners.
- Scenography complements the director's ideas of the play; it must be practicable and take account of other design elements, such as lighting and costume.
- The world of the stage is exciting, but has its own jargon which sometimes has to be 'translated' for its potential to be appreciated.
- Running a show depends on the stage manager and the deputy stage manager.
- Outdoor theatre and site-specific theatre has a long and honourable history, and still provides exciting opportunities.

FURTHER READING

The most significant books about scenography are probably: Joslin McKinney and Philip Butterworth, *The Cambridge Introduction to Scenography* (Cambridge: Cambridge University Press, 2009) and the more historically oriented *Theatre, Performance and Technology* by Christopher Baugh (Basingstoke: Palgrave Macmillan, 2005).

Of many excellent practical books about the technical and practical aspects of theatre, the following are among the most useful: Trevor R. Griffiths (ed.) *Stagecraft*, (London: Phaidon, 1982); Larry Fazio, *Stage Manager: The Professional Experience*, (Boston MA: Focal Press, 2000); and Francis Reid, *The Stage Lighting Handbook*, (London: A & C Black, 1996).

Recommended books about outdoor or site-specific theatre include: Jan Cohen-Cruz (ed.), *Radical Street Performance: An*

International Anthology (London: Routledge, 1998) which explores outdoor performance from Nazi Nuremburg rallies to the Greenham Common Peace Camp and the Bengali music-maker, Suman Chatterjee; Tony Coult and Baz Kershaw (eds) *Engineers of the Imagination*, (London: Methuen, 1983), centring on Welfare State International; and Stefan Brecht, *The Bread and Puppet Theater*, 2 vols, (London: Methuen, 1988), about the American Bread and Puppet company (see also Chapter 5, p. 127).

8

THE AUDIENCE

THE DRAMA'S PATRONS

In a Prologue written for David Garrick on the occasion of the reopening of the Theatre Royal, Drury Lane, in 1747, Dr Samuel Johnson (1709–84) wrote:

The Stage but echoes back the publick Voice.
The Drama's Laws the Drama's Patrons give,
For we that live to please, must please to live.

How far Johnson was correct about the power of the audience has been much debated. An Elizabethan pamphlet records how, one Shrovetide, one of the London companies was prevented from performing its announced play by Christopher Marlowe (1564–93) by the audience, who forced them to remove their 'tragic' costumes and perform a comedy instead. And this was not a single instance. When the actors refused, 'the benches, the tiles, the laths, the stones, oranges, apples, nuts flew about most liberally ... and dissolved (the) house in an instant, and made a ruin of the stately fabric' of the theatre.

On the other hand, campaigners against the theatre at that time based one of their most persistent arguments on the idea that the drama influenced the spectator, not the other way round. Another pamphlet asked its readers to

> mark the flocking and running to theatres and curtains, daily and hourly, night and day, time and tide, to see plays and interludes; where such wanton gestures, such bawdy speeches, such laughing and fleering, such kissing and bussing, such clipping and culling, such winking and glancing of wanton eyes, and the like, is used, as is wonderful to behold.
>
> (A. M. Nagler, *A Source Book in Theatrical History*, New York: Dover, 1952, p. 129)

The writer goes on to describe how the spectators find themselves a sexual partner at the theatre, and concludes that 'these be the fruits of plays and interludes'! As if, without the drama, the people would not dream of sex!

Though it is easy to scoff at such primitive outrage, it is still true that the traditional view of the part the audience plays in any dramatic performance is passive: the audience receives what the performers give. Increasingly, however, this view is seen as untenable. Audiences are no longer thought of as merely passive, and indeed few modern theatres would want that traditional passivity. If the audience are 'receivers', they are not like radio receivers, merely taking messages in; it is from what they receive that they produce meaning.

Box 8.1: Hiss the villain

Audiences in the Victorian theatre were notoriously noisy, and engaged with the action enthusiastically, as this description by John Hollingshead (1827–1904), a journalist and theatre manager, of a performance of *Oliver Twist*, illustrates:

The 'murder of Nancy' was the great scene. Nancy was always dragged round the stage by her hair, and after this effort Sikes always looked up defiantly at the gallery, as he was doubtless told to do in the marked prompt copy. He was always answered by one loud and fearful curse, yelled by the whole mass like a Handel Festival chorus. The curse was answered by Sikes dragging Nancy twice round the stage, and then, like Ajax, defying the lightning. The simultaneous yell then became louder and more blasphemous. Finally when Sikes, working up to a well rehearsed climax, smeared Nancy with red ochre, and taking her by the hair (a most powerful wig) seemed to dash her brains out on the stage, no explosion of dynamite invented by the modern anarchist, no language ever dreamt of in Bedlam, could equal the outburst. A thousand enraged voices, which sounded like ten thousand, with the roar of a dozen escaped menageries, filled the theatre and deafened the audience, and when the smiling ruffian came forward and bowed, their voices, in thorough plain English, expressed a fierce determination to tear his sanguinary entrails from his sanguinary body.

THE HORIZON OF EXPECTATION

By choosing to attend a theatre performance, the spectator voluntarily sets up the circumstances in which communication can take place. In other words, it is the spectator who initiates the theatrical event, not the performer. There are two problems which follow from this which need to be unravelled. First, what is it that the spectator sets out willingly to receive? And second, how does she deal with what is received?

To return to the concept of the linguist Ferdinand de Saussure (see Chapter 1, pp. 3–4), theatre may be seen as a system of 'signs' whose significance is tacitly accepted by a specific community. The theatre community (which may be very wide and consist of everyone involved with theatre whether maker or spectator, though it could also be taken as only the actors, technicians and audience at a particular performance) agrees tacitly at least for the duration of this performance to accept the coherence of certain signs with certain concepts. The signs may be sound images (received by an 'audience') or visual images (received by 'spectators'), but they will convey particular concepts implicitly agreed with the performers. The stage is a particularly potent means for according communicative power to bodies, things, sounds, shapes – a red nose signals a drunk, a patched jacket a servant and a top hat a boss, sounds such as twittering and croaks signify the countryside, three or four trees signify a forest, a pale yellow circular light projected onto a darker cyclorama signifies the moon. The unspoken contract between stage and auditorium is made by the shared acceptance of such signs.

In the performance, the signs may be categorised as of two sorts: the actors, and what they say and do; and the settings, lights, props, etc. The spectator reads these and tries to construct a world out of them. The problem for the spectator is that she receives many signs simultaneously, and must constantly adjust her understanding according to the new information which she is gleaning. How does the spectator process and decode the various different signs, especially because there are so many? She compares the signs she is receiving with similar real or fictitious signs previously received. The process is 'citational' and 'intertextual' (see Chapter 1).

In other words, no spectator ever comes to the theatre with absolutely no knowledge of how the performance will operate. She brings with her preconceptions which form what Hans Robert Jauss called the 'horizon of expectations'. (See the section 'Drama and Society' in Chapter 4, p. 90.) The production history of *The Seagull* by Anton Chekhov illustrates this. First produced as part of a popular evening of farces and light comedies at the Alexandrinsky Theatre in St Petersburg in 1896, it was thoroughly misunderstood and seemed likely to sink without trace. But in 1898 the Moscow Art Theatre gained permission to stage it as a piece of serious naturalism for their intellectual and educated audience – and it was now received as a highly original drama. And today *The Seagull* is acknowledged as a masterpiece, and approached as such. What is significant is just that – how the potential audience perceives the play. If the audience's horizon of expectation suggests that they are going to see a trivial farce, they do not know how to cope with a play like *The Seagull*. If they think it will be a serious (which does not mean not comic) drama, their expectations will be different. And if they know it is a masterpiece, their expectations are different again. It is the horizon of their expectations which gives the audience the first clues with which to decode what happens on stage.

There are, however, two kinds of horizons of expectation for the theatregoer. Plays are evaluated against productions of other plays, and perhaps against other productions of the same play; they are also evaluated against the spectator's own personal and social experience. If either of these horizons is exceeded, the spectator is delighted – so long as it is not exceeded by too much, at which point the play begins to become obscure, even indecipherable. *Waiting for Godot* by Samuel Beckett is a clear example of this:

when first produced, it aroused utter bafflement in most of its audience. Only later did it come to be seen as a masterpiece and 'ahead of its time'.

Jauss also pointed out that over time, expectations change. A history of Shakespearean production over 400 years shows that while audiences in the nineteenth century, for example, expected to revel in Shakespeare's 'characters', the early twentieth-century theatregoers concentrated their attention on the 'poetry', and later audiences expected insights from Shakespeare's understanding of political and social processes. Jacques Derrida pointed out tirelessly that there is no correct interpretation of any work, and indeed different audiences, and especially different kinds of audience (distinguished by, for instance, class or gender, a supportive or a resisting predisposition, etc.), with different kinds of horizons of expectation will respond differently. The power of the audience is seen in the fact that any author will be at least partly conditioned in her playmaking by her understanding of her probable audience's horizon of expectation.

From this it begins to be clear that any performance is completed, and validated, by the spectator. To adapt the provocative phrase of Roland Barthes, with the death of the playwright, the director and the actor, comes the liberation of the spectator.

THE THEATRICAL EVENT

When we go to the theatre, we make a special time out of time. We create a special world which we inhabit for two or three hours. This special world has its own coherence, logic and emotional adventures which do not impinge upon the coherence, logic and emotional adventures of our real lives, except by implication. This frees us from the bothers of the real world, though it is important that we do not forget the real world, for the play world will have some bearing on it.

As already implied, we go to the theatre with certain expectations. Is this a 'big theatre' production, or a fringe event? Do we know the company, or the star, or the director? The Royal Shakespeare Company will provide us with a different kind of experience than the 7:84 company. We know that 7:84 (in its heyday, anyway) performed almost exclusively for minority and isolated communities. And indeed there are different constituencies for different kinds of theatrical experience. Research has shown that theatre audiences are surprisingly homogeneous in terms of their social status, income, education and occupations. Consequently, it should be no surprise that there is drama which is suited to the middle class, drama suited to a lesbian audience, drama suited to members of a British-Caribbean or British-Asian community, and so on. An avant-garde lesbian play in the West End of London would be exceedingly unlikely to succeed, and similarly an Andrew Lloyd Webber (b. 1948) musical would be unlikely to succeed in many arts centres.

It is clear from this that 'going to the theatre' is a culturally controlled and structured event, and that it promises some kind of social event as well as a play performance. The spectator chooses to attend this theatre in preference to that theatre for a variety of significant reasons – social class and status, income, way of life, education, cultural level, aesthetic priorities, age, sex, race, knowledge. But it is worth noting that a series of decisions about the performance have already been made by others which have allowed the decision to attend this performance possible in the first place. For instance, the play has been chosen by someone, such as the theatre director, or by an institution, the management committee perhaps, that the prospective spectator presumably trusts. And the production has been made available to the public by some institution, too. If the performing company receives a subsidy, this may be significant – but if it does not, that, too, may be worth noting. The choice is also influenced by considerations such as critics' articles, publicity material, what other people say ('word of mouth'), and so on, so that a social relationship already exists between the theatre and the spectator before the spectator arrives at the theatre. Even the name of the play may be significant – *'Tis Pity She's a Whore* or *No Sex Please, We're British* obviously start with certain advantages!

In addition, theatregoing provides some sort of social occasion, which is influenced by other factors. What is the geographical location of the performance, and how will the spectator get there? Is it a traditional theatre, a community centre, a pub room, a park, a factory gate? What is the performance time – evening? midnight? lunchtime? workers' break time? How and when will the audience eat – before, after or perhaps during the performance? Are you a regular theatregoer, or is this some kind of special occasion? By buying a ticket, the would-be spectator buys a promise – of excitement, intellectual engagement, voyeurism. It is a promise she will enjoy herself, but there is no guarantee that the promise will be fulfilled.

Most theatre venues have some sort of foyer where patrons buy tickets or programmes or drinks or chocolates, hang up their coats and socialise. This is often a significant part of the experience – to see and be seen – and always has been. In the Jacobean theatre, 'crowds of people devoted to pleasure' attended the theatre, and 'for the most part (they) dress grandly and in colours', while the Restoration theatre was clearly a social gathering whose manners and attitudes were probably as important as the play itself. Samuel Pepys went to a performance of *Macbeth* on 21 December 1668, and the king and several courtiers were there, too, in company with his mistress, Lady Castlemaine. The royal party saw that Pepys was near a 'handsome woman', so they smiled at him, which obviously warmed him. Meanwhile, in the box above the king, Moll Davies, also one of his mistresses, exchanged meaningful looks with him, which when Lady Castlemaine saw, 'she looked fire'. Was Pepys as interested in the play as he was in the royal goings-on? Was the king more interested in the drama or the women in the audience whom he might seduce?

When the modern spectator enters the auditorium, she may not be entangled in any royal dalliances, but her experience is not as simple as might be supposed. The auditorium is still a social space, though interestingly each spectator in the contemporary theatre has her own private space within it, a specified seat, so that the experience is uniquely public and private. In older theatres, the audience may be divided into socially homogeneous groups – there are boxes for the wealthy, stalls for the well-off (or a pit in the Victorian theatre for less well-off aficionados), a dress circle, perhaps, and an upper gallery, the 'gods' for those once designated 'Olympians' – perhaps the servants of those in the stalls or boxes. Modern theatres tend not to have such divisions, though subtler distinctions are often made by price of ticket. Other factors which may affect the entrant to the auditorium include whether the curtain is down or up – and if up, what is presented to her on the stage – the shape of the playing space (conventionally end-on, in the round, traverse, whatever), whether the auditorium is large or small, how full or empty it is, and how light or dark the auditorium is. Also – is there a programme, and what sort of information does it provide? And as the lights dim, or the curtain goes up, the spectator is part of the audience, but also part of the performance.

This is because the theatrical performance, unlike, say a novel, or even a film, is not a finished product, it is alive in front of her now. And because the performance is being made in the presence of the spectator, the spectator must be contributing to the making and the meaning. It is worth wondering also what other extraneous happenings in the auditorium contribute to the process. Examples might be the noisy entrance of a latecomer, the rustling of sweet papers, or the persistent cough of some unfortunate member of the audience. Indeed, is the changing of the stage set by stage hands influential in the overall significance of the evening?

The final impression of the performance will also be influenced by the later part of the 'frame' round the performance – the end of the evening. There is, for example, the curtain call, when the actors bow and the audience clap. This, too, must be decoded. The way the performers respond to the audience's applause may underline the spectators' self-esteem. The centrality of the leading actor, the solo bow, eyes cast up to the 'gods', is one possible way. But how many calls there are, and the fervour of the applause are also finely nuanced parts of the total theatrical experience. Then – does the audience want to rush away, or do they stay chatting – and how animatedly? – in the foyer? Or on the pavement outside? Perhaps there is a post-show discussion with the actors. 7:84 Theatre Company often used to end their shows in the Highlands of Scotland with a ceilidh for actors and audience, with the intention of putting them on an equal footing. How the audience disperses is significant to the total experience. What sort of journey home will the spectator have? Will she have a drink or a meal? Will she chat about the performance? To whom? And what will be her attitude – or memory – next morning?

Box 8.2: Forum theatre

Forum theatre is an important strand in the Theatre of the Oppressed, created by the Brazilian theatre practitioner, Augusto Boal. (Other elements of the Theatre of the Oppressed are: Invisible

Theatre, Image Theatre, the Rainbow of Desire and Legislative Theatre.)

Forum theatre came about in the late 1960s during a production by Boal, which highlighted social oppression, and which included audience discussion and suggestion. One female member of the audience became so frustrated when one of the actors could not understand what she was saying that she took the actor's place on stage. This was the birth of the 'spect-actor', and signalled a new empowering of the ordinary audience member. Now change was not only imagined in discussion, it was practised, too.

Forum theatre begins with the acting company performing a play in which an injustice, or oppression, is played out. The play, usually quite short, does not allow the oppressed to escape from their oppression. After the play is over, there may be discussion with the audience, but soon the actors begin the play again, and this time any spect-actor may call out; 'Stop!' and replace the actor playing the oppressed individual. The replaced actor usually remains on stage, and may now make suggestions of her own to the spect-actor. Meanwhile, this new participant tries to alter the course of the play through improvised dialogue and action in order to overcome the oppression. She aims to use tactics not employed in the original play. But at the same time the remaining actors from the original play try to steer the action back to its original form and ending. If the audience thinks the spect-actor is going wrong or missing possible ways forward, they may intervene further, and indeed they may shout 'Stop!' and enter the scene themselves.

Thus forum theatre allows non-actors, often the exploited or down-trodden, to take the stage and explore their problems creatively in action. The event is in fact a sort of debate which proceeds dialectically: possibilities, ideas for change, and so on, are rehearsed and played out, or contradicted, and alternatives sought. The whole process creates solidarity, a sense of empowerment, and – perhaps – a better world.

Little wonder that this form of theatre has attracted practitioners from all over the world. Companies which overtly practise forum theatre for social ends include, in Britain, the Impact Factory, London, and, also in London, the Cardboard Citizens Company, probably the only homeless people's professional theatre. In North America, there are Headlines Theatre Company, Vancouver, founded in 1981 and directed by David Diamond (b. 1953), using its own version of forum theatre called 'theatre for living', about which Diamond has written extensively; the University of Northern Iowa's Students Against a Violent Environment (SAVE) Forum Actors founded in 1998 by Karen Mitchell (b. 1955); Pedagogy and Theatre of the Oppressed, based at the University of Nebraska, Omaha; and the Peace Troupe of North Carolina. This is only a selection of companies whose existence testifies to the power of Augusto Boal's simple, original and radical conception.

CONVENTIONS

The operation of the theatrical event depends on the acceptance of a series of conventions by performers and spectators. They are, in a sense, the terms and conditions of the agreement between the two parties, and are likely to include simple matters such as that the actor will pretend to be somebody she is not, and that one part of the space available will be for performers and a different part for spectators. More specifically, precise conventions applying to this performance will be established. One such might be that when an actor speaks 'aside', other characters in the playing area cannot hear her, though the audience can. Occasionally, conventions cause problems, as for example across cultures. The Chinese theatre's open use of stage hands during a performance, for example, is instantly understood and accepted by Chinese audiences, but met with bafflement and therefore without acceptance by Western audiences. Conventions change over time, too: fifty years ago in the British theatre audiences would clap when the curtain first rose if there was revealed an artistic or in some way beautiful set. Similarly, they used to clap the 'star's' first entry. I remember the original London production of *Rhinoceros* by Eugène Ionesco (1909–94) in 1960, in which Laurence Olivier played the insignificant protagonist, Berenger. Despite his inconspicuous shambling upstage entrance, the audience clapped Olivier's appearance enthusiastically – he was the star they had come to see. Such applause is unthinkable in the twenty-first century.

Convention also distinguishes the stage world from the real world. When we witness a real family argument, we feel awkward or embarrassed and may wish to intervene; but when something similar is played on the stage, we follow it with relish and interest, and never for a moment think to intervene. Playwrights and directors have also been able to make capital by deliberately breaking expected conventions. Thus, after the two tramps have managed to while away another few minutes in idle chatter, Estragon says in *Waiting for Godot*: 'That wasn't such a bad little canter'. He is commenting on his own performance as if he were a playgoer. But that is the spectator's role.

The theatrical 'signs', already referred to, operate within these conventions, and indeed conventionally the audience assumes that all signs are meaningful. It should be noticed, however, that some signs are denotative (this denotes that – a character wearing armour denotes a soldier going to battle), whereas some are connotative (this connotes something beyond that – the armour connotes courage). The interplay between denotative and connotative signs gives theatre some of its characteristic ambiguity. Moreover, the connotative nature of many signs takes theatre into the area of symbolic meanings, which is part of the explanation for our willing attendance at different productions of the same play (see Chapter 1).

A further convention concerns the curiously indirect nature of theatrical communication (also mentioned in Chapter 1). At its simplest level this may be seen in the fact that though Hamlet addresses Horatio, it is we the audience who listen and learn from what he says. Indeed the levels of relationship to which a spectator might pay attention are complicated and intertwined. There is the relationship between character and character (Hamlet and Horatio); character and spectator (who enters the fiction and 'believes' the story); the actor and her character and the other characters; the actor and the spectator (who may have come to see this particular actor play a favourite role, and who while responding to this 'star' may simultaneously accept the other actors wholly in their roles); the spectator and other spectators; and so on.

The spectator's consciousness is in fact many-layered. Most spectators are *equally* aware of the actor and the role. And the relationship is in a sense reciprocated: most actors are aware not only of what is happening on stage (at the various levels already suggested), but are also aware of the audience. It is common to hear actors make remarks such as: 'It's a good house tonight', implying that the spectators are responding to the actors' efforts; or, 'They're cold tonight' or 'Not much happening out there, is there?' which imply the opposite about the audience.

The audience may need this multi-layered responsiveness, because during the performance there is rarely much time to take stock and consider what is going on. There may be some seconds while the scene is changed, and many performances include intervals, but this is usually regarded primarily as social time, when spectators buy drinks, chat to friends, even go to the toilet.

Spectators' awareness of each other is also worth considering. Laughter and other audible reactions are often contagious: if you do not think the action funny when everyone else is laughing, you feel awkward, or even embarrassed, and wonder whether you have missed something. The contagion of laughter is a good illustration of the collective consciousness of the audience, and it acts to bind them together. It is also clear that your understanding and enjoyment is enhanced by your neighbour's understanding and enjoyment.

However, as has been noticed already, watching the play is also importantly a private pleasure. The situation licenses voyeurism: in the special circumstances of the theatre, in the privacy of the darkened auditorium, the individual may indulge in the 'gaze', which is impossible in most social situations. Here no guilt is attached – indeed, this is what the spectator has, in a sense, come for! So there is set up a dialectic between the response of the individual and that of the collective, which seems to be a significant feature of the working of live theatre. This too seems to be conventional.

Box 8.3: The gaze

According to Sigmund Freud, looking is a pleasure which is intrinsic to our sexuality. 'Scopophilia' means pleasure in looking, and is sometimes allied to 'voyeurism'. Freud showed how children take pleasure from a very early age in looking at adults' – especially their parents' – bodies, and particularly their genitalia. For some, this pleasure in looking remains extremely strong: for a peeping Tom, the most extreme pleasure is to be had in watching. Such voyeurism is also dangerous, however, for the 'gaze' inevitably objectifies what is gazed at. The pleasure of watching is at least partly the pleasure of controlling (objectifying) the other.

This power has in Western societies traditionally belonged to men. The male gazes at the female. The female displays herself for the male. The male is thus able to project his fantasy onto her, and her body is exhibited according to his desire. This fetishises the woman as a spectacle. Thus, the 'gaze' powerfully reinforces the stereotype of the male as active and dominant, and the female as passive and submissive. You can sell cars to men by draping languorous, scantily-clad women over their bonnets!

If the male gaze is a means to objectify the woman (and many paintings in the Western tradition, for instance, tend to demonstrate this), its object is to control her, to regulate her sexuality and to remove intrinsic value from her body, her sexuality and ultimately from herself. The Venus myth insists that the passive woman who is looked at is the embodiment of beauty and desirability; the woman who gazes back is the one-eyed hag, Medusa.

Where does this leave the theatre? In conventional naturalism, the audience gazes at the performers from the sanctuary of the darkened auditorium. Even the female spectator is encouraged to adopt the male-oriented viewpoint, and too often seems to succumb to a sort of narcissistic fascination with gazing at what is normally the preserve of the male 'looker'. How ironic then that naturalism was created in order to strengthen the stage's power over the auditorium! It turns out that on this level at least, it does just the opposite.

It has been argued that this situation degrades both the viewer and the performer. But it can probably to some extent be countered by a more open theatrical form than naturalism provides. Some twentieth-century forms, like expressionism, constructivism and epic theatre, as well as forms developed in the last decades of the century by feminist groups, groups struggling for racial and colonial freedom, and other 'fringe' theatres, all seem to offer something more honest in this regard than the pervasive naturalism. Perhaps a theatre which simply kept the house lights on (or maybe happened out of doors in daylight) would open up the closed state that naturalism seems to afford.

It may be noted, too, that women have obtained increasing power within some European and American theatres, as directors, playwrights, managers and so on. But this has surely not gone far enough. In 2012, neither the Artistic Director of the National Theatre, Nicholas Hytner, nor the Artistic Director of the Royal Shakespeare

Company, Gregory Doran (b. 1958), had ever directed a play by a woman playwright. This fact prompted Phyllida Lloyd (b. 1957), herself an opera and film director, as well as a theatre director, to suggest that half the members of these major companies should be women: 'It wouldn't be a stranglehold', she claimed, 'it would be liberating'. And the playwright Margaretta D'Arcy, whose plays explore the male-dominated society we live in, insists that all the male roles in her plays be taken by women.

AUDIENCE AND PERFORMANCE

Audiences are deeply involved in the theatrical event at all levels. Certainly they do more than simply follow the story. It has been suggested that drama, because of the way it happens, is able to relate at a deep level to our experiences and perceptions of love, hope, fear, despair and more. If we are to enter the drama's world, we need to suspend the moralising or inhibiting segment of our minds and imaginations so that we are free to be spontaneous. As in fantasy, we identify with the characters – different characters at different moments in the play, probably – as we are captivated by the vivid living images which the stage puts before us. These images – signs, perhaps – seem to be capable of exciting us below the level of the conscious mind. Thus, Oedipus may reveal our subconscious to us at a subconscious level – the response may remain buried, but it may still be active. It is often in ways that have yet to be properly explained that the spectator makes meanings out of the theatrical event: something enters our sense of identity, and enables us to explore it, to reassure ourselves or consolidate our ideas of self, or perhaps allows us to play with those ideas in ways which would be impossible in reality. It is like a child playing: understanding and fantasy merge, separate, contend, co-exist, and dreams penetrate fantasy which penetrates reality which penetrates dreams …

This is at any rate a possible solution to the puzzle of how a play works on us. It presents us with something which is like life, but which is not life, and which is made up of more or less decipherable signs and images. Audiences 'read' the work of the actor, and the director, the lighting, the stage set, the configuration of the building and so on and so on, simultaneously, and indeed the reading is itself part of the pleasure. But the decoding is feeding more than just the conscious mind: during the performance, each spectator is manufacturing her or his own kind of meaning from it, collaborating with the performers, with other members of the audience and with their own subconscious. As the play proceeds, so the decoding and the meaning-making also proceed. A play is what it does to us.

Summary

- Audiences have rarely been passive at any period of the theatre's history.
- The theatre's conventions are accepted by audiences in order for them to make meaning from what they see.
- The history of the reception of plays illustrates the audience's 'horizon of expectations'.
- Theatre is a special kind of social event, which partially determines the spectator's response to the play.
- Theatre can also offer the spectator private pleasure, associated with voyeurism and 'the gaze'.
- Exactly how the audience construes the theatrical experience is probably impossible wholly to pin down, but it may be in the reading of the work, rather than in just what is read, that at least part of the pleasure is to be found.

FURTHER READING

The standard work on theatre audiences is Susan Bennett, *Theatre Audiences*, (London: Routledge, 1997), and it is recommended.

Two books about practitioners mentioned here: Augusto Boal, *Theatre of the Oppressed*, (London: Pluto Press, 1979); and Margaretta D'Arcy, *Loose Theatre: Memoirs of a Guerrilla Theatre Activist*, (Crewe: Trafford Publishing, 2005).

GLOSSARY

Act Division of a more or less self-contained segment of a play: most Shakespeare plays are divided into five acts; or, to do; or, to perform on a stage.

Agitprop A drama, usually short and having a review-style structure, which seeks to propagate a particular (usually left-wing) politics and stir its audience into political action.

Alienation Method of presentation developed by Brecht, the aim of which is to demonstrate that what seems fixed and eternal is in fact subject to change.

Apron Area in front of the proscenium arch in an end-on theatre.

Audition Tryout by actors for the director before rehearsals begin; the director will choose a cast from those who have auditioned.

Auditorium The area of the theatre building reserved for spectators to watch the performance.

Biomechanics Actor training system developed by Meyerhold and centred in the actor's physicality.

Blocking The arranging of actors' moves on stage, including exits and entrances.

Carnival Disruptive, carnal, regenerative celebration, when the world is turned upside down and everyone has a good time; usually celebrated before Lent.

Character Any person in a play; or, the way a person behaves; behaviour defines character.

Climax The moment of maximum tension in a play.

Comedy Drama which attempts to correct the antisocial behaviour of one or more characters through laughter; or, which energetically celebrates life, love and sex.

Commedia dell'arte Form of improvisation-based performance by (usually) masked actors, developed in Italy, and flourishing c.1500–1800.

Denouement The moment in the play when all the complications of the plot are resolved.

Devising Creating a performance through research, group improvisation and text-making without the involvement of a playwright.

Dialogue Utterances made between two or more characters in a play, and addressed to each other.

Director Person who is ultimately responsible for everything the audience sees and hears during a performance.

Drama To do; or, the written text of a play.

Dramatis personae List of characters printed at the head of the play text.

Dress rehearsals Final rehearsals with costumes, scenery, lighting, etc.

Eight Basic Efforts Laban's categorisation of movement, based on the movement's direction in space, its speed and its weight.

Embodiment The actor's physical assumption of the dramatic character.

End-on A theatre in which all the auditorium seats face the same way towards the stage.

Ensemble Group or company of actors without hierarchical ranks between them.

Epic Poem or play which celebrates, justifies or examines community, and the individual's place in the community.

Exposition The imparting of necessary information to the audience early in the play.

Farce Fast-paced comedy without moral intent.

First night The first public showing of a rehearsed play; also known as the 'premiere'.

Foyer Area of theatre building between the street outside and the auditorium proper; may contain box office, cloakroom, bar, etc.

Harlequinade   Eighteenth- and nineteenth-century English farcical drama centring on Harlequin and Columbine's love, and their attempts to evade her father, Pantaloon.

Holy theatre   Theatre style usually characterised by intensity of feeling and involvement, which aims to purify the spectator.

House   The audience; so, a 'good house' means plenty of spectators.

House lights   Lights in the auditorium switched off or dimmed at the beginning of the play, and after the interval, so the audience can see the performance from the darkened auditorium.

Improvisation   Acting without the direct use of a written script; may be spontaneous, or more or less structured; may be worked up from a script.

Kathakali   Highly stylised theatre form from south India.

Katharsis   (Greek) A purging of pity and fear, felt by the spectator at the climax of a tragedy.

Key idea   The central thought, or main theme, in the production of a play.

Living newspaper   Dramatisation of contemporary events and concerns in revue-style structure.

Mask   Originally a face-covering; symbolically, any performed role.

Melodrama   Intense, sometimes tragic drama, lacking a philosophical dimension.

Method   American form of naturalistic acting developed from Stanislavsky's system.

Mise-en-scène   What is 'put on the stage', including scenery, furniture, props, lighting and actors.

Monologue   Long speech made by a character in a play.

Naturalism   Stage performance as close as possible to the appearance of real life.

Pantomime   British Christmas family entertainment, often based on a folk tale or nursery rhyme.

Performance   A section of human behaviour which is presented, highlighted or marked off in some way; especially as presented on the stage to an audience.

Performance art   Also known as 'live art', a presentation in which the performer appears as themselves and performs 'for real'.

Performative   A pronouncement which enacts something.

Performativity   Anything which is potentially a performative.

Physicality   The material presence of a body in space.

Play within a play A play presented by some on-stage characters to other on-stage characters, who form an on-stage audience.

Playwright Maker of plays.

Plot The arrangement of the incidents in a play; according to Aristotle, 'the imitation of action'.

Properties Moveable items other than furniture used on stage; also called 'props'.

Proscenium The stage, especially (in an end-on theatre) the front part of the stage in front of the 'proscenium arch'.

Read-through At the beginning of the rehearsal period, it is usual for actors and director to sit down and read through the complete play, each actor reading their own part.

Realism Naturalism; or, a performance which is able to evoke the reality below the surface of real life.

Rehearsal Meeting between director and actors to prepare for performance. Rehearsals take hours every day for several weeks before the 'first night'.

Run-through Rehearsal in which the complete play, or a whole act, is gone through without interruption; also known as a 'run'.

Scene Division of a more or less self-contained segment of an act in a play; most acts in Shakespeare plays have several scenes; or, where the action of a play is supposed to be located.

Scenographer Is ultimately responsible for all 'technical' areas of a production, including design.

Semiotics The interpretation of signs.

Sign The basic element in the making of meaning, comprising a signifier and a signified.

Soliloquy Speech by a character not addressed to another character.

Stage directions Indications included by the author in the written text of a play concerning ways to stage it.

Stage manager Is responsible for everything to do with the stage – settings, props, actors' entrances and exits, etc. – during the performance.

Subplot Secondary story which runs alongside the main story of the play.

Subtext The meaning behind spoken words. 'Goodbye' may mean 'good riddance' or may mean 'don't go'. These are possible subtexts.

Super-objective The overall aim of the play; or, of a character in a play (this meaning is also called the 'spine').

Symbol   One thing which stands for another, probably something abstract. Thus, a mountain may symbolise hope, or aspiration.

System   Stanislavsky's acting technique to create 'truth' in performance.

Technical rehearsal   Run-through of complete play on stage with all technical elements included, probably for the first time; also known as the 'tech'.

Text   The written script of a play; or, the whole performance.

Theatre   The place where plays are enacted; or, the artistic form which centres in the performance of plays.

Theatre-in-the-round   Arrangement whereby the audience surrounds the acting area.

Through-line   The line of inner action in a dramatic part.

Tragedy   Drama which tracks the protagonist's fall from good fortune to bad.

Traverse   Arrangement whereby the audience is in two blocks, facing one another on opposite sides of the acting area.

Unities   A now discredited idea that plays should be (1) set in a single location; (2) span not more than twenty-four hours; (3) concentrate on a single action.

Vice   Devilish character, often comic, energetic and unexpectedly charismatic, in medieval morality plays.

Warm-up   Before rehearsal or performance, actors limber up to get cold muscles working. A warm-up may also help the actors' concentration, and aim to start energy flowing through the body.

BIBLIOGRAPHY

The following list comprises books which have not been mentioned in connection with particular chapters in this book, but which will all be of interest and use to anyone wanting to know more about modern theatre and modern ideas about theatre.

Theatre practice

The following are reflections on their practice by leading professionals from the last seventy-five years: Bertolt Brecht, *The Messingkauf Dialogues* (London: Methuen, 1965); Peter Brook, *The Empty Space* (Harmondsworth: Penguin, 1969); John Arden, *To Present the Pretence* (London: Methuen, 1977); John McGrath, *A Good Night Out* (London: Methuen, 1981).

One more academic book (in three volumes), which covers much ground excellently: J. L. Styan, *Modern Drama in Theory and Practice*, 3 vols, (Cambridge: Cambridge University Press, 1981).

Anthologies

The following collections of writings, by practitioners and theorists, are always illuminating: Eric Bentley (ed.) *The Theory of the Modern Stage* (Harmondsworth: Penguin, 1968); Michael Huxley and Noel Witts (eds) *The Twentieth Century Performance Reader* (London: Routledge, 1996).

Two books which bring together more theoretical texts: Patrick Campbell (ed.) *Analysing Performance* (Manchester: Manchester University Press, 1996);

Colin Counsell and Laurie Wolf, *Performance Analysis* (London: Routledge, 2001).

Particularly recommended is Maggie B. Gale and John F. Deeney, *The Routledge Drama Anthology and Sourcebook* (London: Routledge, 2010), a huge anthology which includes both play texts and theoretical articles, and covers the whole historical period from Zola's naturalism to the present.

Theoretical books

Mark Fortier, *Theory/Theatre* (London: Routledge, 1997), is probably the most accessible general survey; Simon Shepherd and Mick Wallis, *Drama/Theatre/Performance* (London: Routledge, 2004), conducts the reader carefully through the arguments about theatre and theory in detail. See also the valuable Jane Milling and Graham Ley, *Modern Theories of Performance* (Basingstoke: Palgrave Macmillan, 2001).

And an older book, which is still as stimulating as any: Francis Fergusson, *The Idea of a Theater* (Garden City NY: Doubleday, 1949).

Reference books

Patrice Pavis, *Dictionary of the Theatre: Terms, Concepts and Analysis* (Buffalo NY: University of Toronto Press, 1998), is an indispensable work, more advanced than either of the following, which are, however, more accessible: Paul Allain and Jen Harvie, *The Routledge Companion to Theatre and Performance* (London: Routledge, 2006); Kenneth Pickering, *Key Concepts in Drama and Performance* (Basingstoke: Palgrave Macmillan, 2005).

INDEX